THE CIVIL WAR
IN
MISSOURI
DAY BY DAY
1861 - 1865

Our special thanks to Ge Ge Auger, who typed our new look.
Ge Ge is an avid Civil War history reader. She resides
in Denver, Colorado.

Our special thanks to Rocky Medley, artist, who designed
our new cover. Rocky is a self-taught artist and his
specialty is Civil War and Ozark subjects. Rocky resides in Fredericktown, Missouri.

Dealer inquiries welcome.
For additional copies contact;

TWO TRAILS PUBLISHING
7295 HOUSTON STREET
SHAWNEE MISSION, KANSAS 66227
(913) 441-3198

The beautiful state of Missouri ranks third among the states with the most battles and engagements in the War Between the States. She does not lay claim to the likes of a Gettysburg or a seige of Atlanta, but Missouri played host to both opposing sentiments almost on a daily basis.

For four long years the armies rode across Missouri, leaving behind the desolation and destruction of war. The cavalry horses' hooves ravaged the young crops. The dreaded flaming torch of the countless avenging bands; yes, these, and the sport of bushwhacking, would shape Missouri history.

This state, not unlike others, shared the scars of brother against brother and neighbor against neighbor for generations. The cruelties and injustices heaped high. After more than 100 years the scars upon the lands of Missouri have faded, but the sentiments are still strong.

Missouri at the onset of the Civil War was considered a Union state. Politicians shaped the rest. The majority of soldiers gathered from Missouri are listed as Union. These are from official records. However, the sentiments of the people, those who suffered, would be up for questioning. To have an accurate Confederate soldier count would be virtually impossible. One would have to consider the many hundreds that joined Price in his raids across Missouri. These numbers are guesses at best. Even though they joined for many reasons, some not so patriotic; nevertheless, they served the Cause. Frequently these men just rode along for the fight and didn't actually enlist in the regular Confederate forces.

Tragic as war in Missouri was, the humor of the situations arising from it come to the surface in the old records. One incident came in the form of an order from General Grant. It took place while Grant was on a campaign in Eastern Missouri. It seems a lieutenant in command of the advance guard inspired the mistress of a wayside house at which he stopped one day. He showed exceptional alacrity in supplying the wants of himself and his men by announcing himself to be Brigadier General Grant. Later that same day Grant himself stopped at this same house and was turned away. He was informed that General Grant and his staff had already been there that morning and had eaten everything in the house, with the exception of one pumpkin pie. Giving the kind lady a half dollar, General Grant told her to keep the pie until he sent for it. That evening while the army was in camp some few miles beyond the place, at the dress parade that was ordered, the following special order was published: "Lieutenant Wickfield of the --th Indiana Cavalry having on this day eaten everything in Mrs. Selvidge's house, at the crossing of the Ironton and Pocahontas and Black River and Cape Girardeau roads, except one pumpkin pie, Lieutenant Wickfield is hereby ordered to return with an escort of one hundred cavalry and eat that pie also." U.S. Grant.

The term "brother against brother" seems rather delicate in light of the "in-law against in-law" situation that existed in the family of Major General Philip St. George Cooke. The Cooke family, being for quite some time residents of Missouri during General Cooke's early army life, was stationed at Jefferson Barracks in St. Louis. When the Civil War loomed, although a Virginian by birth, Cooke remained loyal to the Union and became a most conspicuous cavalry general of the highest esteem. His son, John D. Cooke, born in Missouri, joined the Confederate Army and was made a general. Another son, T. Easton Cooke, went with his brother. A daughter of General Cooke became the wife of General Jeb Stuart, the Confederal Cavalry leader. Many times General Cooke narrowly missed being captured by General Stuart, much to the amusement of the latter. Of his children who took up the Southern Cause, General Cooke became estranged, and that remained the state of affairs until long after the war was over. The General's family was only one of many who suffered the same fate.

Many Missourians were rather taken aback by the sudden shift of politics in the State and changed sides during the early stages of the war. Some more than once. Hostility on the homefront was just as severe as on the battlefield. As one reads the letters and accounts, often it was safer in battle.

During the four long, dark years of the war, the citizens of Missouri were hard pressed to survive. With first one army in the morning crossing their yards, and the opposing one in pursuit in the afternoon, they suffered constantly. The location of the State made it very advantageous for either army to occupy. It was this struggle for possession that heaped daily hardship on the innocent citizen.

In the year 1991, the Civil War seems so very long ago. It lives on for our generation in books, parks and massive, cold stone monuments to its heroes. These tell our generation of the past. However, as we walk across the lush green mowed grasses of the parks or the lonely, deserted, old battlefields, a person cannot help but be transported back in time. Somewhere in your mind, very far back, you can almost hear the shouts, the cannon bursts, the clanking of swords. You can almost smell the sweat of the lathered horses and feel the suffocating dust churned up by the pawing hooves. The sharp odor of gunpowder and smoke is ever present. You can almost feel the pent-up emotions of those who lay in hiding, awaiting the enemy or trembling in fear and anticipation of what is bound to come...and then it's over. Time stands still. It is of this we are reminded as we walk across the land. Lands where at one time, for some, time stood still. For many it stops forever and for many the rich, brown soil of Missouri became their eternal resting place.

Missouri suffered many indignities during the Civil War. Not the least of these was Order No. 11, which laid waste to the Kansas border counties. This cruel order forced hundreds of families to abandon their homes, farms and their labors of a lifetime. Many fled just ahead of the flaming torch.

The southern counties bordering Arkansas, from the East to the West, can lay claim to the same treatment without the benefit of the official military order. In these counties at times entire families were hunted down, and the Spectre of Death rode the land.

Colonel M. Jeff Thompson's farewell speech to his men at the war's end says it all:

"To the Missourians who are present, I would speak plainly, and advise them not to think of returning to Missouri unless they have a clean record. There are many who have been fair, honest and chivalrous soldiers, who can have no charges against them, except the one of being true to the South; there are many others who have forgotten the laws of God, the laws of man, and, the laws of war, and they of course cannot expect to live in Missouri in peace...Then there are the others, who, though they have been honest soldiers had determined in their hearts to have private revenge at the end of the war, had we succeeded and some who have said that the Union man must leave if they won...Each of you know to which of these classes you belong, and you must, 'do as you would be done by.' And, act accordingly."

MAP OF
OPERATIONS IN
MISSOURI, 1861.

SCALE OF MILES

Governor Claiborn Jackson

"Your first allegiance is due to your own State, and you are under no obligation whatever to obey the unconstitutional edicts of the military despotism which has introduced itself at Washington, nor submit to the infamous and degrading sway of its minions in this State. No bravehearted Missourian will obey the one and submit to the other. Rise, then, and drive out ignominiously the invaders who have dared to desecrate the soil which your labors have made fruitful and which is consecrated by your homes." Governor Claiborne Jackson.

March...The Home Guards are being organized and drilled in the mechanics of warfare. Francis B. Blair, Jr. knows these men need arms to be effective. The State of Missouri holds a large arsenal at St. Louis, but at present these arms are unattainable for Blair. The Southern faction is rising under Governor Claiborne Jackson, and he most certainly has other ideas for these arms which do not include arming the Home Guards. His idea is to overthrow the arsenal through a network of politicians and plots, thus arming the men of Missouri for the now evident separation of the government. Governor Jackson went so far as to enlist the help of General D.M. Frost, who commanded a small group of Militia, to overthrow the arsenal in the name of the State. Thus, the arsenal would be under Governor Jackson's control and not the U.S. Government. General Frost went along with the plan. Frost, being a military man, knew this could not be done without resistance, and the necessity of siege guns and mortar weapons was a requirement to execute this plan. With the assistance and blessing of Jeff Davis, who ordered the weapons to be turned over to Captains Colton Greene and Basil W. Duke. Governor Jackson accomplished his feat. This little subterfuge took place in Montgomery, Alabama.

The plan was now in place. However, the best plans, especially one on such a grand scale, needs secrecy. Needless to say, the secret leaked out.

April 20th...At 10:00 in the morning a body of armed men from Clay and surrounding counties took control of the Liberty arsenal. The yards and depot were full of men rapidly removing the ordnance, as Nathaniel Grant wrote in his dispatch to Colonel H.K. Craig, Chief of Ordnance at Washington City. Mr. Grant had no men or means to protect himself. A few cannon and some 1,500 arms were distributed to some of the citizens of Clay County. Note is made that the Missouri River at Independence is now blockaded.

May 4th...An affair in Kansas City resulted in the confiscation of much property.

May 10th...Camp Jackson came under the command of General Daniel Frost, who was now considered to be a disloyal Union man. Arriving upon the scene in St. Louis, disguised as an elderly, hard-of-hearing woman sporting two heavy pistols, was the young Captain Nathaniel Lyon of the U.S. Army. The plan to overthrow the arsenal was foiled. Captain Lyon quickly swore in 3,486 men and 70 officers for the protection of the arms and U.S. Government property. The takeover got out of hand and spilled out into the streets. The commotion by now drew considerable crowds of both sentiments. When the smoke cleared that day, over 20 citizens and seven officers lay dead in the streets of St. Louis. The arsenal was still under the control of the United States. Among those who witnessed the rioting were William T. Sherman and his small son. They were forced to take cover in a gully to escape the barrage.

Different accounts describe the taking of the arsenal and the events that transpired shortly thereafter. One such account has General Frost and his men being marched off to prison, singing and proudly displaying the Stars and Stripes. In all, some 50 officers and 639 enlisted men were taken prisoner. Most were given the oath of allegiance not to bear arms again against the U.S. Government and released. One, Captain Emmett McDonald, declined to accept the offer and was made a prisoner of war, as was General Frost. These men were quickly exchanged and went on to serve the Southern Cause in Missouri and elsewhere.

The Confederate sympathizers became frenzied with the possession of the arsenal and the feeling of violation of the state's right being unable to command such a facility within its borders. The state sprang to life. Hundreds crowded the streets of Jefferson City, some to hear the latest news, but for the most part to enlist and exercise their God-given rights of enlisting and protesting.

It was evident from the start that Captain Lyon was a fighting man. If he and Blair would have remained in control of the situation, the rush to enlist and war fever would have been dealt with by force. However, General William S. Harney, who was the head of command of the Military District of the West in which St. Louis was a part, was a conceding man, and he struck a deal with General Sterling Price. This pact lasted just long enough to allow Blair to have Harney relieved of his command at St. Louis.

May 31st...Captain Nathaniel Lyon replaces General William S. Harney. Upon this little bit of news Governor Jackson and General Sterling Price ordered the Militia to be made "field ready."

Some gentlemen of a quieter nature felt that some sort of agreement could possibly be reached between the newly-promoted Nathaniel Lyon, Sterling Price and the Governor. A meeting was arranged at Planter's Hotel in St. Louis. Governor Jackson, Sterling Price and Nathaniel Lyon, along with some aides, attended. After some dialogue, Lyon terminated the meeting in no uncertain terms. No agreement would be forthcoming in the future. Governor Jackson was escorted out of the military lines.

This action and the handling of the protection of the arsenal, plus the slaughter of innocent citizens in the process, caused Sterling Price, who had been a staunch Union man and against any form of secession, to lend his aid to the Governor. Price felt, as President of the State Convention, that it was nothing less than his duty to right these affronts.

Thus, the actions of a "mere captain of infantry, a little rough-visage, red-bearded, a weather beaten Connecticut captain," had disrupted a great master plan, disarmed the Southern element arising under Governor Jackson, turned the politics of the very well-respected Sterling Price, disposed the Governor, made prisoners of war of the State Militia, and in taking the arsenal, created nothing less than street riots. All of this took place within a few days.

It is reported that almost as soon as Jackson had been escorted out of St. Louis, Nathaniel Lyon started giving orders. One of his first was to order Colonels Sweeney and Sigel southward to intercept the army of men Governor Jackson was raising. Rumor reached back to Lyon that General Benjamin McCulloch was gathering an army in Arkansas. The purpose was to unite with Price and Jackson to win Missouri, one way or another, for the Confederacy.

What a sight it must have been watching Lyon get down from his carriage, wearing clothing borrowed from Blair's mother-in-law, Mrs. Alexander. (We wonder how much veiling he had to don to cover the ever-present red beard!)

May 15th...Expedition from St. Louis to Potosi.

May 16th...Union citizens of Potosi complain to the State government of being driven from their homes for their loyalty. They request the presence of an army for protection. This call was answered by Captain Nathan Cole who, with a small command of 176 men, arrived at Potosi at 3:00 in the morning. Upon arrival they surrounded the town with a line of sentinels. Sentinels were also posted at each house of those identified as being opposed to the government and who had been active in the death threats to the loyal residents. These houses were soon emptied of their occupants and a diligent search was made of the premises for weapons. The men arrested, 56 in all, were then herded to the courthouse which had been readied earlier for this purpose. Of those arrested 47 took the oath, and the rest were confined to the jail as prisoners of war in St. Louis. A local smelter and the railroad depot were visited next, and some 425 pigs of iron and some uniforms that were being made were confiscated. Upon leaving Potosi the troops rode to DeSoto where a large secession meeting had been held. They succeeded in rousting the disloyal members and capturing 15 of their horses. Upon retiring from the area, they lowered the Secession flag and proudly raised the Stars and Stripes in its place.

June 12th...Governor Claiborne Jackson issued a proclamation pleading for 50,000 men to take up arms against the United States.

June 13th-17th...There is an expedition from St. Louis to Boonville and General Lyon is calling for men. He is still in pursuit of Governor Jackson. Rumor has it that Jackson has gathered about 4,000 men. Colonels Sigel, Salmons and Brown are dispatched from St. Louis. They established camps at Sarcoxie and Neosho, Missouri.

June 14th...General Lyon captures Jefferson City and raises the United States flag again over the courthouse. Governor Jackson again escapes, heading south, and with him went the State seal.

June 17th...Boonville is taken, but Jackson still eludes capture. Also today in the skirmishing at Independence, the troops gathered at Blue Mills to impede the movement of Union soliders from Leavenworth and Kansas City. General Nathaniel Lyon landed in Boonville in pursuit of Jackson. He arrived on the morning of this day about six miles below the town or about two miles below the enemy camp. While moving toward the town, the enemy opened fire upon Lyon in earnest. He was successful in routing them. They now apparently have headed for Lexington. Lyon left part of his men posted within the city and sent the rest back to the boats positioned opposite the fairgrounds at the lower side of the town. The fairground buildings were taken for an arsenal in which many old rusty muskets were found. Lyon lost two men killed, one missing and nine wounded on this day. Two of the wounded later died. It was reported that General Sterling Price was in Lexington today. It was also reported that several thousand men had answered the call of the Confederacy there.

June 18th...Cole Camp was the site of a skirmish.

June 20th...General Lyon suggests to General George B. McClellan that he place a whole regiment at Boonville with an advance post at Warsaw. The whole area was reported as being full of rebels. They have reportedly massacred Union men at Cole Camp.

June 22nd-23rd...There is a large deployment of Illinois troops to Missouri. Also, an expedition started today at Cairo, Illinois and Little River.

June 28th...Colonel Sigel received information that General Price and a command of some 700 or 800 strong were encamped near Pools Prairie. Upon hearing this information, Colonel Sigel decides to attack Price and then swing around and get Governor Jackson and Rains. The armies were about one day's march apart. Before leaving camp on the morning of the 29th, Sigel is advised that General Price has moved his camp and is headed toward Elk Mills, some 30 miles southwest of Neosho. Captain Conrad of Company B

Rifle Battalion, 3rd Regiment, is left behind at Sarcoxie to guard
the Union citizens against depredations by the oncoming Confederate
Army. Conrad has orders to retreat if necessary but not to engage
in combat with them.

July 1861...A state force of about 3,000 men were encamped at
Robion Springs, a short distance from Marshall in Saline County,
commonly called Camp Marshall. This camp was finally broken up on
September 2nd when the men marched to join up with General Price
near Nevada. They were just in time for the battle of Dry
Woods in Vernon County.

July 1st...Colonels Sigel and Salmons are encamped in Sarcoxie and
Neosho. They start to move their commands toward the town of
Carthage.

July 4th...The Union soldiers made camp this evening southeast of
Carthage behind the Spring River. They had marched some 20 miles
this day. Intelligence comes in with the report that Jackson is
now some 4,000 strong. Also, Farmington, Missouri was the site of
skirmishing today.

July 5th...Battle of Carthage (sometimes listed as Dry Fork).
After crossing Dry Fork Creek and advancing a total of some nine
miles from Carthage, the armies met in heated combat. The
Confederates numbered, "by sight," about 3,500 men. Colonel Sigel
took his time and placed his men with their seven big guns in
strategic positions. The Confederates already were hotly
contesting the rear lines of his army. Sigel, using his artillery
strength to the maximum, ordered, "commence firing." The big guns
burst forth in unison with an earth-trembling shudder, seeming to
shatter the very air, spewing death without mercy. Again and again
the smoking cannons thundered, sending shell after shell at the
entrenched Confederates. Colonel Sigel needed to gouge a break in
the lines and afford himself a weak spot. For two long hours this
battle raged under a relentless July sun. Twice the Confederate
flag went down, twice it was again taken up, and the fighting
became more intense. Jackson's army finally managed to completely
flank Sigel. This caused Sigel to move his army, for the safety
of his baggage and ammunition trains, back toward Carthage.
However, to manage this Sigel had to cross Buck's Branch, and it
was here the enemy had taken cover. Sigel swung his great guns
around and met the challenge with all he had. After one heavy
round, he gained some ground toward the Springfield Road. Had the
Confederates been able to hold him and tighten the noose, he would
have been cut off from all retreat. Taking advantage of his gain,
Sigel ordered his troops to fall back and to pass Carthage and the
eastern heights of the Sarcoxie Road. The Confederate cavalry took
to the woods, crossing Spring River at any point they could,
fighting relentlessly against the rear flank of Sigel's army. They
pushed from all sides. Sigel finally took position on the heights
behind Carthage and in the woods two miles northwest of Carthage.

As the army passed through Carthage, the houses and fences afforded shelter from the rifles. This caused much property damage to the structures of the town. Many of the citizens left their homes in front of the armies and made for safety from the big artillery guns.

Two good stories have emerged from this battle. It seems that Jackson had amassed about 4,000 men who were armed and 2,000 who were not at the time of the clash at Carthage. The armed men were sent to man the front, the unarmed men were sent to the woods to flank Sigel's rear guard. Sigel saw these men but had no possible way of knowing that these men were unarmed. Assuming they were, he retreated. Credit was given in history as "a battle won by 2,00 unarmed men."

The other story was told by Confederate Captain McCown who watched while Sigel placed his artillery guns. Into the camp rode General Rains. He dismounted and, taking his glass, peered at the guns of Sigel. Captain McCown remarked to the General, "We are going to catch it." The General replied, "Oh, no, we are out of range." The big guns of Sigel belched forth and a solid shot from his battery crashed through a section of horses killing one man and wounding three others, besides killing four horses. Then, almost instantly, an unexploded shell detonated and exploded amid the green troops which fled in all directions. General Rains hurriedly mounted his horse in a "very unmilitary style" and rode out of range. He was later quoted as saying, "They were damned sight better gunners than we gave them credit for!"

In this action Colonel Franz Sigel was outnumbered at least four to one. He finally made it to safety at Sarcoxie at 3:00 in the morning, being pursued by heavy fighting until darkness took over. Of the estimated 2,300 he started with, 13 were listed as killed and 31 wounded. He lost 10 horses and part of his baggage train. All of the 94 men left at Sarcoxie under Captain Conrad were taken prisoner without a shot being fired. These men were later released on their oath never to bear arms against the Confederate Government.

July 5th...Brigadier General Ben McCulloch camped on Buffalo Creek near Neosho with his prisoners, the captured Union command of Captain Joseph Conrad and his 80 men. In determining how to manage this capture, General McCulloch split his army, approaching Neosho from two directions. One of the detachments belonging to Captain James McIntosh, arriving ahead of the rest, took the honors of the capture. Within 10 minutes of his arrival, the command of Conrad had surrendered itself and all its weapons. They were marched off to the courthouse. This became their home until the morning of the 8th, at which time all were given the oath and released. Leaving Neosho about 5:00 in the afternoon, they were escorted to about four miles from town by a detail of about 30 Confederates for their own safety. The residents of the town threatened to shoot them.

The tired, haggard men arrived at Springfield very trail worn from walking 85 miles in 50 hours. They had no food, no water and no shelter. Captain James McIntosh camped this day at Barlin's Mill.

July 9th-11th...Monroe Station skirmish. Troops were deployed from Palmyra to stop the advance. Captain Robert F. Smith met resistance at the hands of one Harris, a Confederate, and his men about 12 miles south of Monroe Station. Captain Smith succeeded in driving the rebels from their timber cover. The next morning he was advised of trouble at Monroe Station and removed his command to that point. Upon arrival he found the station outhouses, other railroad buildings and 17 passenger and freight cars in flames. After a few well-placed rounds, he was victorious in routing the Confederates. He then took possession of a building known as "the Seminary," it being a solid, sturdily-build brick building which he believed would withstand any attack. Here he rested and regrouped his command. The next day this building was almost his downfall. By noon on the 11th he was surrounded by 1,500 to 2,000 men and by 1:00 in the afternoon they opened fire with great gusto. Their artillery, however, was ill placed and the shots feel short. Smith's command, virtually out of ammunition, took out one of the deadly pieces and Harris moved the other a safe distance away. He commenced firing but with the same short-fall results. About 4:30 in the afternoon, after a day of hard skirmishing, a train carrying reinforcements appeared on the tracks, and Smith held the day. By dark the rebels were keeping up a skulking operation in the woods around the station.

July 10th...Brigadier General Monroe M. Parsons encamped on Cowskin Prairie as did Colonel B.A. Rives, CSA.

July 15th...Mexico was the site of heavy skirmishing.

July 15-17th...There was minor skirmishing at Wentzville today.

July 16th...There was a minor skirmish at Millsville. The Union loss was reported at seven men killed.

July 17th...There was a skirmish at Fulton in Callaway County. Skirmishing at Parkersville lasted two days.

July 18th...There was skirmishing at Martinsburg, as well as at Harrisonville (Cass County). Major R.T. Van Horn met opposition from the citizens of Harrisonville. On his first night out he traveled about 20 miles and camped at the Little Blue about 20 miles from Camp Union (Kansas City) on his route to Austin to relieve Major Dean. His command consisted of a little band of about 150 men without tents or proper clothing, and 10 citizens who were all mounted and armed. Trailing along behind was a hospital wagon and 10 days' rations. By Thursday about midday he halted at a spring about five miles north of Harrisonville. Benjamin F. Hays approached the camp and identified himself as the local sheriff.

After explaining that no citizens would be harmed, etc., the sheriff left and promised to return. He did not. However, the good Major was warned they were not welcome.

About 2:00 in the afternoon the soldiers were approached by about 350 to 400 horsemen on the prairie, who proceeded to surround their little camp. Although most were mounted, among them was one company of foot soldiers. The firing then commenced. The command of Van Horn took cover in the log cabins around the spring and in a cornfield. Finally, at sundown, after a heated skirmish, the house of Mr. James Smith became the stopping place. Van Horn had the corn surrounding the small cabin cut to deter any sneak attack through it. The enemy about this time was reinforced by about 100 more men, all armed. It was decided to fell some trees and make a stand, thinking they had about 2,000 rounds of ammunition. This proved very incorrect. Van Horn found the ammunition turned out to be for muskets, not rifles. Then very heavy rains started. About 2:00 in the morning the command broke camp and headed back for the State line. The rain, not cooperating, began falling in sheets and forced a dead halt. With no shelter and no fires, the men stood in the rain until it was light enough to proceed. Upon reaching Grand River, they found it swollen and in crossing lost the wagons and all the clothing and supplies. The march continued all day through flooded bottom lands until they reached Camp Prince about 18 miles southwest of Harrisonville. There they halted for three days.

July 19th...A letter dated 19 July 1861 from Hudson City states that Harris is moving about in timbered lands in Callaway County with from 800 to 1,200 horsemen. U.S. troops were reported in pursuit on foot. The trains containing U.S. troops on the North Missouri Railroad were fired into four times en route to Mexico, resulting in one soldier being buried at Montgomery City and several wounded put on trains at Mexico. Two State Guards (MSG) were caught and shot. No prisoners were taken. The newspaper has been seized at Mexico and the sheet put out by U.S. troops. The oath has been administered to many citizens. Doctor Bass, member of the State Convention, was taken prisoner in his own house. He, his horses and mules were taken to Montgomery City. The doctor was released the next day on parole. In addition to the stated on the morning of the 18th, 40 U.S. Cavalry of Hammer's Command left Montgomery City for Mexico. Ten miles west of Wellsville they were attacked by State troops (MSG) and driven back to Wellsville with the loss of some horses.

July 19th...Lieutenant Colonel Richard A. Vaughn is encamped at Camp Lee, Missouri.

July 20th-25th...A large expedition of Iowa, Kansas and Federal troops is reported moving from Springfield to Forsyth.

July 22nd...On the road from Forsyth to Springfield: Brigadier General T.W. Sweeney marched through Forsyth, a town reported to be full of Confederate rebels, and took control after much fighting. The entire affair lasted only one hour, but was hotly contested from the brush and timber. Upon taking the town of Forsyth, Sweeney gained a quantity of badly needed goods, such as sugar, syrup, clothing, etc. They found the courthouse had been used as a barracks for the departed Confederates. In all, Sweeney marched his men 45 miles in the rain and captured a town in only 50 hours. He left Forsyth on July 23rd, thence turned his command toward Springfield. Also today saw skirmishing at Etna.

July 24th...Action took place at Blue Mills, Jackson County.

July 25th...Skirmishing today at Dug Springs and Harrisonville.

July 26th...At Lane's Prairie, near the town of Rolla, a skirmish took place with the Home Guards and local guerillas. Also today there was a skirmish at McCulla's Store. (McCulla's farm is located 24 miles from Springfield on the Fayetteville Road.)

July 27th...Skirmishing continued today at Harrisonville.

July 28th...New Madrid is now occupied by the Confederacy.

July 29th...Major General John C. Fremont assumes command of all forces in North Missouri. Brigadier General S.A. Hurlburt is assigned to command the forces along the line of the Hannibal and St. Joseph Railroad from Quincy and Hannibal to St. Joseph. His headquarters are in Macon City. Colonel Ross of the 17th Illinois Volunteers will occupy Warrenton. Colonel Palmer will post his regiment at Renick and Sturgeon, fixing his headquarters at Renick. Colonel U.S. Grant of the 21st Illinois is assigned to Mexico (Audrain County). Military headquarters will be at Mexico, Missouri.

August 1st...There was skirmishing today at Edina in Knox County. Around Bird's Point the Federal forces are very busy cutting all the timber and throwing up defences. This is in preparation for an attack planned by General Pillow and others, coming into the area from various directions. The game plan is to meet at Jackson. Hardee is to advance directly upon Greenville, which is on the direct route from Ironton. This leaves Pillow to handle all the Federals on the river. He either has to face them or go through a mountain, starting first with Cape Girardeau. He will then have to contend with the forces at Bird's Point, which are certain to come to the fight just as soon as his route is discovered. There is no way of retreat. Reports from Hardee also state that he is only advancing with about 3,000 men, leaving behind the balance of less than 5,000 for want of transportation.

August 2nd...A large scouting party, consisting of the 24th Illinois Infantry, is reported to be on the road from Ironton to Centerville. Today also saw a small action at Dug Springs. General Nathaniel Lyon was informed that Confederate forces under the command of Brigadier General James S. Rains were advancing upon Springfield. On the second day he moved only about six more miles and found an advance party about one mile beyond Hayden's farm. General Lyon's men were suffering horribly with diarrhea from their steady diet of beef, making most of his command unfit for duty or the march. They could not possibly march and meet the enemy, then make it to the campsite where water was available to them, approximately four or five miles ahead. That night he encamped at Hayden's farm. The Confederate advance, mostly mounted, became bolder and threatened from various points. About 1,000 of their infantry advanced with the cavalry. General Lyon's men fired into them. His cavalry, rather spontaneously, charged without orders and drove the Confederates back. The Confederate cavalry again advanced with a great thrust only to meet the fire from Lyon's artillery. During the night Brigadier General Rains moved his command out without resistance. With the sickness that ravaged his command and the shortage of supplies, General Lyon moved back to Springfield. His next problem will be the end of the three month term of enlistment for the larger portion of his force. With these gone, his army will be reduced to about 3,500 men, badly clothed and without a prospect of supplies, and still he must defend Springfield.

August 3rd...McCulla's Store was the site of renewed skirmishing.

August 5th...There was fighting at Athens, Gentry County.

August 7th...Upon arrival at Price's Landing, which is located on the Mississippi about 25 miles from Cape Girardeau, Major John McDonald marched through cornfields, through deep, dense woods and arrived at the Landing about 2:00 in the morning. He promptly surrounded the premises, and at daylight he entered the house. Price had not returned from his camp, which was located about 14 miles south of his residence. A force of about 1,100 Confederates is reported as being stationed at the camp. McDonald then took as prisoner Price's son, William Price, who is said to hold a captaincy under his father, and his son-in-law. Also found in the warehouse at the Landing was a quantity of stores marked, "General Price, Charleston, Missouri." The loot consisted of 20 barrels containing, in the center, firkins of butter on top of which were potatoes and oats. After setting the torch to the bounty, Major McDonald proceeded on to Commerce. He halted at the house of one of Price's officers, but at his home he was told the officer was in camp. Upon arriving at Commerce, he apprehended two notorious rascals known as "the Rebel Post Office." From there he proceeded to Benton, about eight miles west of Commerce. There, supposedly encamped, was Colonel Jeff Thompson with his large Confederate M.S.G. command. At the approach of the Major's forces, Thompson moved out and up the river to General Pillow's camp, about 48 miles from Benton. Major McDonald, not quite finished, was detailed to Hamburg about five miles northwest of Benton. There he found the town deserted of male inhabitants. In his report of the affairs of the past few days, Major McDonald makes official complaint against Captain T. Q. Hilderbrant for permitting his men to loot and break into a locked house and stray beyond the sentinel lines without permission.

August 8th...Brigadier General John Pope (Union) wants to know who fired on the passenger train near Palmyra. He gave orders for anyone connected with this to be shot. The Confederate commander, W. J. Hardee, is now in Greenville just 18 or 20 miles from Ironton. He is gainfully employed tearing up the railroad, burning bridges and interrupting all the communication lines, at which endeavor he has been unsuccessful.

August 9th...Brigadier General John Pope sent a clear-cut message to the commanding officer at Boonville. This instructed him to appoint a committee of five from among the wealthiest families, of which three will be Secessionists, for a committee of public safety. He is also instructed not to accept any exceptions from service on this committee. Copies of the order will be made and distributed to all those within Cooper County and adjoining counties, informing them that any disturbance of the peace or any assembling of armed forces hostile to the Federal Government will be promptly followed by occupation of the houses of the people by strong bodies of U.S. troops, who will be fed and transported by the residents for the entire period necessary to restore peace and to insure its being kept.

August 10th...Battle of Wilson's Creek. It was during this battle that General Nathaniel Lyon was killed while at the head of his command. It was this battle, also, that was a culmination of the movements of both General Lyon's forces and those under Brigadier General Rains, General Ben McCulloch and many others. Each was laying a trap, hoping to maneuver the other into a favorable position and location upon which to do battle. In this battle, which has been well documented in history books, the position of the forces in opposition was the key. The terrain afforded a great advantage. Mistakes were made, and these are brought out in reports, such as Colonel A. Sigel riding clear around to flank the Confederates and becoming cut off from lending assistance. Three serious conflicts took place in this battle. A vast number of casualties was suffered by both armies. The forces under General Lyon charged time and time again only to be repulsed. Lyon's command, being outnumbered, gave ground but regained it. Finally, the green troops under Generals Sterling Price and Ben McCulloch carried the day. The Federal retreat was greatly hampered by the great mounds of the dead, making escape difficult. Many more lost their lives or were wounded from this circumstance alone. It was during one of the charges when Lyon was rallying his men that he became the victim of death's bullet. His body was entrusted to Mary Phelps (wife of Governor Phelps) for burial. This was accomplished after many problems. Ten days after his burial, his remains were removed by his brother-in-law and taken to St. Louis for reburial. The beaten army removed and marched to Springfield, and although they could virtually have been decimated by the forces under General Price should he have taken the pursuit, they marched without molestation. This infamous day in history also saw action being confronted at Potosi in Southeast Missouri. The attack was made upon the Home Guards, resulting in the wounding of five of their number. It was estimated they were attacked by about 120 men commanded by Captain White (MSG) of Fredericktown. Also, marauders were reported to be active in Bellville Valley, northwest of Ironton.

August 11th...Hamburg was the site of a heavy affair, and U.S. Grant sent one company of troops to Caledonia. Two companies were to report to Colonel Kallmann for the protection of the railroad and four companies to Potosi from Ironton. The Home Guard was to be deployed as spies to ascertain the location of the Confederates.

August 12th...General McCulloch called for Missourians to choose their own destiny. He declared the Union people would be protected, but, in short, "choose a side." The Confederacy now controlled the southern-most part of the State. It is around this date that some Home Guards began to organize in earnest. The people of Missouri were splitting over the question of sympathies and allegiance. News was made today by General Hurlburt. He removed Speaker McAfee of the House of Representatives from Macon to Palmyra. He also gave orders to have him tied to the top of the cab of the train engine but was finally dissuaded. General Hurlburt in a report chastised Colonel R.F. Smith of the 16th Illinois Regiment for not punishing people of Marion County for their connivance in the various outrages committed within their limits. Colonel Smith is also guilty of not enforcing contributions. The object of the Colonel's duties were to compel the people to ferret out, seize and deliver to the command the men who had fired on the trains, and those who have committed outrages on the bridge tenders and other peaceable citizens. If the Colonel has supplies, then he may remain where he is; if not, he is ordered to move in and occupy the houses of the most prominent persons in town and live at free quarters (Palmyra).

August 13th...Dr. H. Caldwell was taken prisoner at LeGrange, Lewis County, today. He was reported to have commanded the MSG artillery at the Battle of Athens, and was reported as having marched at the head of the Confederate forces on Edina, driving the Union men from their homes. Today also finds a letter written by J. T. K. Hayward

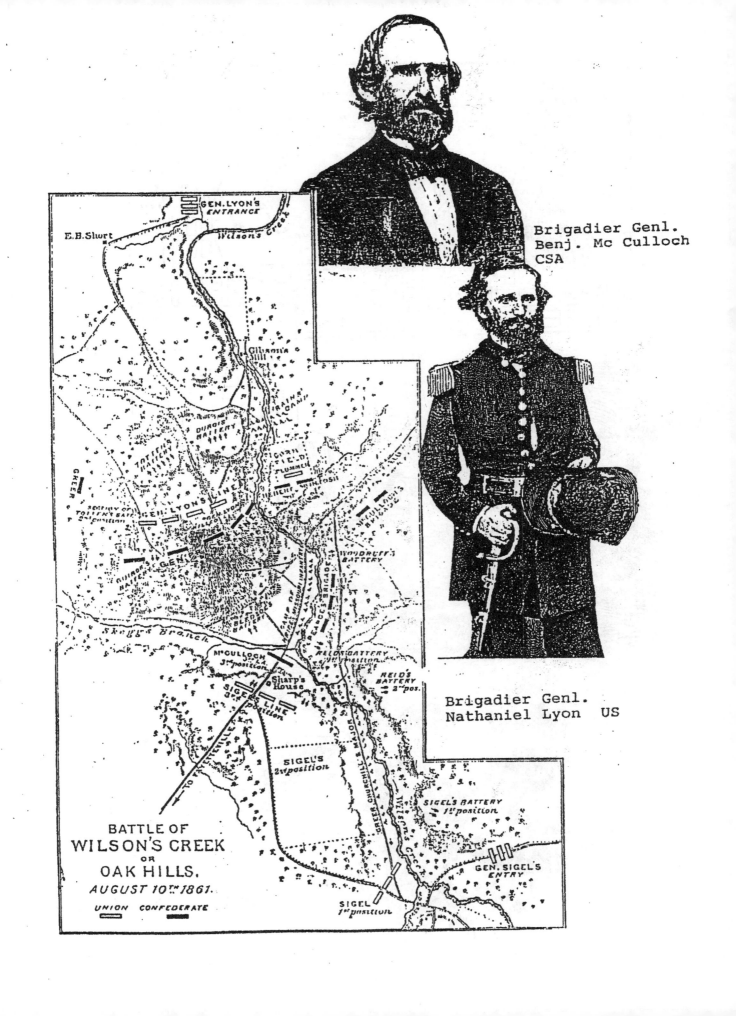

Brigadier Genl.
Benj. Mc Culloch
CSA

Brigadier Genl.
Nathaniel Lyon   US

BATTLE OF
WILSON'S CREEK
OR
OAK HILLS.
AUGUST 10TH 1861.
UNION   CONFEDERATE

SIEGE OF
LEXINGTON. MO.
SEPT 18,19,20,1861.

Colonel Jas. A. Mulligan

to one J.W. Brooks. Extracted information from this let's us have an inside look at the treatment that McAfee, former Speaker of the House, was forced to endure as a prisoner under General Hurlburt: "Then as a sample of what is done by some officers last week a man named McAfee was arrested. General Hurlburt ordered him to be set to digging trenches and pits for necessaries at which he was kept all one day when the mercury ranged about 100 degrees in the shade. A few days after he was taken from Macon to Palmyra and the general ordered him to be tied to the top of the cab on the engine. It was prevented by our men, who, when persuasion failed, the engineer swore he would not run the engine, if it was done, and, as he was being marched to the engine to mount it, the signal was given and the train started giving them barely time to get on the cars. When there is added to this the irregularities of the soldiery, such as taking poultry, pigs, milk, butter, preserves, potatoes, horses, and in fact everything they want; the entering and searching houses and stealing in many cases; committing rapes on the negroes and such like things..."

August 14th...Martial law is declared in St. Louis.

August 15th...A large Federal expedition is sent to St. Genevieve. Assistance is requested for reinforcements to hold back further invasion of Price's army. Major John McDonald arrived in St. Genevieve and surrounded the town. He remained in hiding until daylight. Finding no Confederates closer than Pilot Knob, he then occasioned the Merchants Bank of St. Louis to be opened and removed from it a strong box said to contain $28,633.30 in coins and $29,680.00 in currency and took the same on board the steamer Hannibal. Before leaving, Major McDonald made an open threat to return and take his vengeance upon those doing harm to local Union sympathizers.

August 16th...There was an expedition to Fredericktown (Madison County). Gunboats were reported at Cairo on the river.

August 16th-21st...Fighting all around Kirksville.

August 17th...Skirmishing at Brunswick. Hunnewell and Palmyra were the scenes of small battles. (Brunswick in Chariton County, Hunnewell in Shelby County and Palmyra in Marion County)

August 19th...MISSOURI WAS ADMITTED TO THE CONFEDERATE STATES OF AMERICA. A skirmish was reported at Klepsford. (We take this to be near Charleston, Missouri, as Dyer's book mentions actions there the same day.) A Confederate force had gathered in the vicinity of Charleston, and Colonel Dougherty of the 22nd Illinois Regiment set out to capture this little camp of Confederates. He arrived at Camp Lyon with 300 men and remarked, "We will take Charleston tonight." Captain Abbott was detailed to amuse the enemy until the Colonel could return, so off to the town they marched. Upon nearing the town somehow the companies became separated, leaving

two companies well in the advance and the others well behind. As
they encountered the rebels, the leading companies succeeded in
driving in the enemy pickets and charged into the town. This
accomplished, Colonel Dougherty ordered the courthouse to be taken,
and at once the building was attacked. The Confederates returned
the fire from the courthouse windows. Finally, the lines broke and
as the courthouse was stormed, the Confederates left. Many were
captured, but some escaped through the windows. Later in the day
another company of Illinois cavalry overtook one detail and
captured 40 prisoners.

August 20th...There was action at Charleston and Bird's Point
(Charleston, Mississippi County). According to Colonel Lawler's
report, Dougherty's command arrived at Charleston by cars as far
as the burned out trestle bridge about two and one-half miles from
Charleston, and thence marched into Charleston. There a welcoming
committee awaited. The Confederates, about 500 strong, were given
notice of the advance of his army and formed in the streets, in
business windows, corners of the streets and from houses on the
town square. The city was brightly illuminated by the firing of
the blaze of the firearms. The battle lasted only about 10 minutes
by Colonel Lawler's report and the Confederates left. A prisoner
was taken from the Confederates who "showed" the way to their camp,
where 33 prisoners were taken and all ammunition left, etc. Also
August 20th there was an attack on a railroad train near Lookout
Station, Missouri. It seems the Pacific Railroad train left
California, Missouri on the 20th densely filled with Home Guards,
160 belonging to the command of Lieutenant Colonel B. W. Grover,
70 from Tipton and 60 from California. When the train neared
Lookout Station it was ambushed by a concealed body of men. The
Home Guards, many riding on top of the cars, returned the brisk
fire. Three were killed and three were wounded.

August 20th-22nd...Fighting around Jonesboro.

August 21st...Kirksville and the area surrounding were sites of
much activity. It was supposed that about 2,000 rebels were
encamped at a place called Bee Branch, about eight miles northeast
of Kirksville, and they were threatening to attack Kirksville. The
hospital stores and the sick were sent ahead to Brookfield by Union
commander Brigadier General S.A. Hurlburt. He left Macon City on
a Tuesday evening with wagons for transportation and marched the
command to Atlanta where heavy rains overtook them. The march
continued through La Plata and finally into Kirksville. Upon
arrival they took position at Felb's Bridge in the southwest corner
of Knox County on the Salt River. The Confederates steadily passed
them heading toward Ralls and Monroe Counties, probably planning
to cross the railroad at Clarence. Just prior to his arrival in
Kirksville, the command of Corporal Dix met with a heavy fight, and
the Corporal was killed. The Confederates laid out his body in a
most decent manner and sent word to the Union camp. The body of
the Corporal was recovered and buried with full military honors.

Being now outnumbered, the Confederates left Kirksville. Hurlburt learned that Corporal Dix's ammunition, etc. was at the farm of a man named Jackson. The rebels had camped on his farm at Bee Branch. General Hurlburt proceeded to this farm. Sending a detachment after the weapons, a fight ensued at Jackson's house. One man was killed and Jackson was wounded. Fourteen Confederate soldiers were found, some of whom had been wounded in the fight with Dix. All those able to do so had departed the scene. Also today, Colonel Jeff Thompson put Colonel J.H. Hunter under arrest for bungling the Charleston ambush. He is to be charged with cowardice.

August 23rd...Medoc was the site of skirmishing (Jasper County).

August 28th...There was a skirmish at Lexington involving Home Guards. There was also a skirmish at Ball's Mills. An expedition starts to Jackson (this is probably in Cape Girardeau County). General Ulysses S. Grant is informed of 4,000 Confederates at Benton and 1,500 more are encamped behind the hills two miles below Commerce.

August 29th...Fighting at Morse's Mills again.

August 30th...Northeastern Missouri is the site of continual actions through September 7th. General Jeff Thompson received word today that 4,000 men have landed at Commerce, marching from Cape Girardeau with 150 wagons. A large force under General Prentiss (Union) left Ironton today with the sole purpose of capturing General Hardee. General Thompson also received reports of at least 1,000 Yankees at Dallas, and he reports that he has only 1,200 men at Lakeville and no ammunition.

September 1st...There was a skirmish at Bennight's Mills. The Missouri 10th Infantry started an expedition through Jefferson County. It lasts until the 3rd. Ebenezer Magoffin of Pettis County is charged with wantonly killing George W. Glasgow, a sergeant in Company C, 1st Illinois Cavalry by shooting him with a ball from a gun or pistol. This allegedly took place at Georgetown in Pettis County on or about the 1st of September. The other charge against Colonel Magoffin is violation of parole. He was paroled on his honor not to abet the Confederacy, he already being an officer of the same. He also was given a safe conduct pass into Pettis County for the purpose of seeing his dying wife for the last time. Mrs. Magoffin died while in his arms. Magoffin was sentenced to be hanged and confined to a prison at Alton. He later received a presidential pardon.

Also on the 1st of September an expedition was sent to Iberia.

September 2nd...Skirmish at Dallas (probably in Harrison County). Actions at Dry Wood Creek and Fort Scott in Kansas. The 12th Illinois Infantry starts an expedition around Belmont and Charleston. The Federal troops removed $700,000 from the bank at Cape Girardeau today. Colonel Nelson Williams is marching toward Shelbina, and quartering his men in the courthouse in Paris on this day. Also on the 2nd Colonel Kallmann left guards at St. John Boeuf Creek, Big and Little Berger Bridges and some at Miller's Landing (all in the vicinity of Washington in Franklin County). More troops were deployed on the line between Franklin and Gasconade Counties on the Bourbeuse River. The Confederates are heaping depredation upon the good Union men in that area.

September 3rd...Colonel Jefferson C. Davis (Union) started an expedition across the river at Jefferson City in the direction of Columbia, Boone County. General Thompson (CSA) is moving his camp to White or Little River at Wagner's or Carpenter's Ford in order to intercept those after Hardee. Supposedly, there being some 7,000 men now at Jackson awaiting General Thompson, he felt it prudent to move. These men are moving from Jackson toward Bloomfield.

September 4th...Action at Shelbina (Shelby County). The gunboats Tyler and Lexington arrived on a reconnaisance in the river around Belmont and New Cairo. General Hurlburt arrived in Shelbina on the 4th. He had left Kirksville on August 30th with 500 men and 150 Home Guards. On the first day they marched to Wilson's, a distance of about 16 miles. On the second day they marched a distance of about 15 miles to Lakeland, and on the 1st of September from Lakeland to Bethel which is another 15 miles. At Bethel he was joined by Colonel Moore's command of about 850 men with one piece of artillery. Part of the command was sent by Philadelphia to Palmyra. Colonel Moore was ordered to follow Greene's force, and Colonel Smith was to hold Palmyra. Information was that General Greene (CSA) was at Philadelphia. With the sick in tow, he then moved through Shelbyville to Shelbina. Upon arrival at Shelbina, he was advised that the command had been send to Brookfield (Linn County). The command was Colonel Williams'. Then Colonel Williams wires that he is under heavy fire and needs assistance. Greene starts to assist then is notified that Colonel Williams has left Shelbina and taken up a position at Clarence about 12 miles east of Macon. There, as it was approaching darkness, he waited for Colonel Williams. Upon his arrival he was questioned about the withdrawal. It seems that most of the men he had with him, their terms of enlistment being up, had only been induced to accompany the Colonel with the promise of payment from the monies that were to be secured from a bank there. These men also carried a statement from General Fremont instructing them to return home and reorganize.

September 5th...Fighting at Papinsville (Bates County). The Confederates molesting Belmont have now taken up a position at New Madrid.

September 6th...Action at Monticello Bridge.

September 7th...The 24th Indiana Infantry is moving across Missouri on an expedition to Big Springs in Carter County in search of a rumored Confederate camp. The rumor proved false. Also today Colonel A. P. Hovey encamped his troops, the 24th Indiana, at Sulpher Springs.

September 8th-9th...Pursuit of Greene's Confederate command started today.

September 8th-19th...Reconnaissance of Columbus (Johnson County). There was an engagement of forces at Lucas' Bend (near Belmont and Cairo). A reconnaissance was also made toward Norfolk by the 8th Illinois Infantry.

September 10th...Brigadier General John Pope clashed with the Confederate Commander Colton Greene at dark on the previous Sunday. Greene escaped but left much camp equipage behind, such as provisions, forage and much of the public property that was taken at Shelbina. The bulk of Greene's force now has crossed the North Missouri Road at Renick and making for the woods of Chariton. Today also found Colonel Wagner starting from Norfolk toward Belmont, supported by the gunboats Conestoga and the Lexington. They ventured as far as Beckwith's farm about 5 miles below Norfolk (Norfolk is in the vicinity of Cairo and Bird's Point.)

September 11th...Lexington is defended by Colonel James A. Mulligan of the 23rd Illinois Infantry, which is better known as "The Little Irish Brigade," and the 13th Missouri Regiment. Mulligan and the Missouri Regiment had about 2,800 men and an estimated 40 rounds of ammunition, seven field guns and a very small amount of provisions. They took possession of the hill east of town upon which stood the Masonic College. His lines encompassed about 18 acres which he attempted to fortify. With only about a half day's work on these, on the evening of the 11th the Confederates made their appearance. The fighting began in earnest on the morning of the 12th. This valiant little group made a gallant stand for days. They were without water and food, were reduced to catching rain water and casting some shot for the guns. They endured until the 20th. The battle fought was against tremendous odds. The privates of Mulligan's command and that of the 13th and 14th Missouri were paroled. The officers were held as prisoners. This is known in history as the Battle of Lexington or the Battle of the Hemp Bales, since the Confederates ingeniously rolled these ahead of them as cover in their attack. In Mulligan's valiant attempt to salvage his ground, he desperately needed the cover of a large house that stood on the property. In the ensuing taking of the house,

Mulligan's men shot the Confederates that remained in the house in "cold blood." (Much was made of this murder in official reports.) Union losses were listed at 1,624 captured and 108 missing and wounded. Confederate losses vary with the story teller. Brigadier General J. S. Rains (CSA) saw the American flag flying high above the southeast corner of the battlements, and he offered a large gold coin to the artillerist who could take it down. The battery was set up near Mr. Tott's house. It was quite a distance to where the flag floated innocently in the soft breeze. Finally, Captain Churchill Clark won the gold coin.

September 12th...Actions at Blackwater River (Wayne County). Major General Fremont met resistance with his reconnaissance under Major Gavitt toward Hardee's position at Greenville. He drove in the Confederate pickets and then attacked Talbott's camp, killing two and taking three prisoner. Intelligence has reached General John Fremont of Colonel Colton Greene's attempt to cross the river in three columns, one each from Hudson, Brookfield and Sturgeon. Phinneas P. Johnson, William Shiftell, Jerome Nall, John Q. Williams, James R. Arnold, Charles Lewis, John Deane, Doctor Steinhoner, W.W. Lynch, T.J. Sappington, James Thompson, Thomas Grigsby, John Crow, David E. Perryman, John W. Graves, Alfred Jones, William Durnham, C.H. Hodges, James Marr and G.S. Yertes were released from St. Louis prison today. Many were found with no charges against them and other had trivial charges. Being unable to procure witnesses against them, the Commission rendered the oath and set them free.

September 13th...St. Joseph is captured. Help does not reach Mulligan at Lexington. Colonel Eads from Syracuse reports that about 3,000 men under General Sterling Price's column are advancing to Boonville. The Home Guards are called out and by daylight they are holding their own with Price's men. Colonel Jefferson C. Davis (Union) informs General Fremont that he will send a regiment on the steamboat War Eagle with some cannon to Arrow Rock and Glasgow. He hoped to prevent Colonel Greene from crossing the river for Boonville. Later communication states that Greene has already crossed. Davis will now send troops to Syracuse to flank Greene.

September 14th...Skirmish at Old Randolph. At Boonville Major Epstein has held his position against the Confederates and for now they are waiting for Greene to join them with reenforcements. A detachment reported that a few days ago Greene had crossed the river at Glasgow and captured the steamer Clara Bell. So far at Boonville the Confederate loss is about 12 killed and 40 wounded. The Federal loss is one man killed and four wounded. Brigadier General Sturgis (Union) is at Mexico and is now sent to Jefferson City with his entire force and all artillery.

September 15th...Brigadier General Jefferson C. Davis (Union) makes plans that after crossing of the La Mine Bridge by Greene, he will burn the bridge behind him, thus preventing Greene's retreat.

September 16th...Boonville is quiet. Colonel Greene is amassing forces on the opposite side of the river. In St. Louis today Joseph Aubuchon, a former Confederate lieutenant from Ironton, Iron County, is charged with open rebellion. He was ordered to take the oath and then paroled to his home.

September 17th...Liberty was the site of slight skirmishing, as was Morristown. Help does not come. Leaving Cameron in a heavy rainstorm and with bad roads, only seven miles was made the first day by Lieutenant Colonel John Scott's command as they headed toward Liberty. The next day he fared somewhat better and made it to Centerville, some 10 miles north of Liberty. By sunset that day cannon fire could be heard in the direction of Platte City. On the next day, Lieutenant Colonel Scott left Centerville for Liberty and later in the day, the advance guard fell in with the enemy pickets, which they drove in, following closely. Lieutenant Colonel Scott bivouacked on the hill north of and overlooking the town, dispatching scouts to ascertain the position of the Confederates. They numbered 1,400 and had passed through Liberty two days previously, heading for Blue Mills Landing. They were reported to have four pieces of artillery. By 11:00 firing was heard in the direction of the landing, reported to be a battle with the Confederates and some Union forces contesting their passage over the river. Lieutenant Colonel Scott moved his command of 300 of the 3rd Iowa, a squad of German artillerists and 70 Home Guards. Four of his scouts had already fallen victim of the Confederate guns. The scouts found the Confederates concealed on both sides of the road and occupying the dry bed of a slough. Scott's left rested on the river and on the right out of observation. The Confederates opened a murderous fire and made repeated attacks on the frontal position of the Union forces. In the thrust of the Confederates, all the artillery was taken out with the exception of one brass six-pounder. This was left without sufficient force to man it because some of the gunners had abandoned their positions, running off with the matches and primer, and could not be rallied. The artillery useless, and with many officers wounded, the Union made its retreat. In the departure the ammunition wagon became wedged between a tree and a log and could not be rescued. It was left for the Confederates. The 3rd Iowa lost four men killed and 20 wounded as it received the heaviest fire. This number accounted for one-fourth of the total lost this day. General D. R. Atchison (CSA) was under a disadvantage. He had to deal with over 100 wagons in his train during this action. General Price is forcing the hand of the hapless Union troops holed up at Lexington.

September 16th...Major General John C. Fremont orders Colonel Jefferson C. Davis (Union) to Jefferson City to move forward and attack Georgetown (Pettis County).

September 17th...General J.H. Lane (Union) sent out two mountain howitzers, two companies of infantry and cavalry, in all about 600 men against a guerilla encampment near Morristown in Cass County about five miles from the border. Seven were killed in the rout from their camp. Horses, horse equipment, tents, wagons, etc. were captured. Lane lost two men killed and six wounded.

September 18th...Two Union regiments were sent to Arrow Rock.

September 19th...Skirmish at Glasgow. Colonel Colton Greene (CSA) is attempting to cross the river again.

September 20th...An action at Osceola is described as minor (St. Clair). Lexington falls to the Confederates. "To the victor go the spoils." General Jefferson C. Davis cannot help in the defense. He has no teams or wagons at hand. He feels Warsaw should be occupied. Meanwhile, on the other side of the river, fighting was brisk at Blue Mills Landing when the Secessionists were driven across the river. The Federal loss, reported by telegraph, was 50 killed and 25 wounded. General Price took at the fall of Lexington 3,500 prisoners, among whom were Generals Mulligan, Marshall, Peabody, White and Glover, Major Van Horn and 118 other commissioned officers, five pieces of artillery and two mortars, over 3,000 stands of infantry arms, a large number of sabers, about 750 horses, many sets of cavalry equipment, wagons, teams and ammunition. He also took more than $100,000 worth of commissary stores and a large amount of other property. In addition, he recaptured the great seal of the State and the public records which had been stolen from their proper custodian and about $900,000 in money that had been taken from the bank.

September 21st...The steamer War Eagle just returned. The Indiana scouts fired on their own killing three men and severely wounding Major Tanner and several others. General Sterling Price fought with a regiment of Home Guards and a small troop of soldiers headed from Lexington to Warrensburg who were bent on the intent of arresting some Johnson County citizens and taking the cash from the bank. Price had camped about a mile or two west of Rose Hill. Upon reaching Warrensburg, Price found the Home Guard had done their work and burned the bridges into town.

September 22nd...Fighting resumed at Osceola. There were actions at Elliott's Mills and Camp Crittenden.

September 24th...The Confederates proceeded to hole up in the buildings within the little town of Osceola. General J. H. Lane, contesting this, promptly shelled them out. This caused utter destruction of the town, reducing it to smoking rubble and ashes. Meanwhile in St. Louis William Perry is being charged with crimes. His belongings, etc. will be seized by the Provost Marshall at Potosi. The prisoner will be kept at work on the fort at Ironton and under guard when not working.

September 26th...Belmont, Hunter's farm and Lucas' Bend were the sites of skirmishes. General U. S. Grant took several prisoners in retaliation for those taken for their loyalty throughout the neighborhood.

September 27th...There was a skirmish near Norfolk and fighting at Beckwith's farm about five miles below Norfolk. The Federals rode into an ambush. Upon the first firing, the Federals under Captain McAdams succeeded in a full rout of the rebels. Although the Confederate steamer Jeff Davis is lying at the bank of the river, being anchored only about two miles downstream, it did not molest the raiders. The Federals are scouting in the vicinity of Hunter's farm near the same area.

September 29th...William Hildebrand was tried for treason before a military court held at Ironton. He was sentenced to hard labor for the duration of the war. Thomas Cooper was tried for treason, and he is also confined to hard labor for the duration of the war. George Higgenbotham was released from confinement, and the court orders no further arrests of citizens without proof of their crimes. Cooper and Hildebrand will be sentenced to work on the fort at Pilot Knob.

Major General Sterling Price C.S.A.

November 22nd...Brigadier General Thomas L. Price (Union) in a message to Major General Henry W. Halleck informs him that his little command stationed at Jefferson City numbers only about 1,000 effective men. These are furnishing the city with a police force and guarding the Osage and Moreau Bridges on the Pacific Railroad and the five bridges over Gray's Creek on the same railroad. Colonel G.M. Dodge reports on this date that the rebel forces between Springfield and Lebanon are large. Their pickets extend 10 miles this side of Lebanon (toward Rolla). They are foraging throughout the countryside.

November 23rd...Captain George F. Kenedy (Militia) arrived in Sedalia, meeting up with the balance of the wagons which were feared to have been captured.

November 24th...Fighting at Lancaster (Schuyler County) and Johnston.

November 25th...General Sterling Price is rumored to be moving toward Jefferson City with the intention of attacking it. This little town is in a bad way with only 900 effective men able to do combat. Two batteries and one cavalry company are totally unarmed. The fortification is incomplete.

November 26th...There is skirmishing at Independence on the Little Blue River.

November 27th...Steen's Division (CSA) is now located at Wilson's Ferry, 10 miles from Clinton Prairie, at Osceola. The countryside is full of returned Secessionists who are driving out the loyal Union men. To countermand this, Brigadier General William T. Sherman has ordered all remaining forces at Lexington to advance upon this place. Sherman is encamped at Sedalia. Major General Halleck stops this order. There are five divisions in the field, two at Rolla and three near Sedalia. Generals Price and McCulloch are said to be crossing the Osage near Osceola and intend to attack either Lexington or Jefferson City. There is skirmishing all along their advance. Price's forces are estimated at 15,000 men. All is not well in St. Louis. The Federal troops there are unpaid and without arms or clothing. Many were never properly mustered into the service. Hospitals are overflowing with the sick. Of one division of 7,500 men, over 2,000 are on the sick list. Local rebels have armed themselves in Ray County and are amassed at Albany. General Prentiss is moving on them from his position at Chillicothe.

November 29th...Fighting at Sedalia and Black Walnut Creek (Pettis County).

November 30th...Skirmishing at Grand River.

December...General Samuel R. Curtis (Union) takes command of 12,000 national troops at Rolla and advances on General Sterling Price. Price removed his army to just across the border into Arkansas. Here he was again joined by the Confederate command of Ben McCulloch. They set up camp in the Boston Mountains.

December 1st...Shanghai was the site of a skirmish.

December 3rd...Skirmishing at Salem (Dent County)...The action at Salem was fierce. Colonel Dodge with a command of about 40 men went out to bring in some witnesses to testify in the case of a prisoner being held at the fort. The illustrious Freeman was in the vicinity with a reported 80 to 100 men. Colonel Wyman increased his little band to 120 to assist. All were now under the command of Major Bowen, 1st Battalion of Missouri Cavalry. He left on Friday and reached Salem, a distance of 25 miles. Freeman was not to be seen. Finally on Monday morning about 4:00, Freeman, with over 300 men, crept up on the camp. When they were within about a mile of the camp, they sneaked through the brush and managed to get inside the picket lines. A surprise attack followed. Freeman was defeated and by 6:00 in the evening Wyman and Bowen were in possession of the small town. Intelligence received that day reported that Freeman and Turner's commands were going to winter in Dent County. Heavy forage and supplies were being brought in. In the fighting of the day, two men were killed, two mortally wounded, one of whom died. The rebels counted six dead, 10 mortally wounded and 20 slightly wounded.

December 3rd-12th...Scout through Saline County. Major George C. Marshall's command was composed of 300 men of a regiment of Merrill's Horse and three companies of regular cavalry. The party set out on December 3rd and marched northeast through Richard Gentry's farm and encamped at Union Church on Dr. Cartwright's farm. They took several prisoners on the way.

December 4th...Fighting broke out among the citizens of Dunksburg. The scouting party, making its way through Saline County, marched 15 more miles northeasterly. Their advance guard was fired upon by a portion of a company of about 60 Confederates. This occurred in front of Belwood's farm, their rendezvous point. Upon searching Belwood's house, two kegs of powder and a quantity of cavalry equipment were found. The scouts encamped this night on Mrs. Wingfield's farm.

December 5th-9th...Bowen's 1st Battalion of Cavalry was on expedition through Current Hills (Current River runs through Dent, Shannon and Texas Counties). The long pursuit lasted two days and two nights in the saddle. They were pursued from Jack's Forks to Spring Valley. They managed to elude in fine form through the rough timbered country. On the 5th the scouting party through Saline marched another 15 miles. The Union scouting party took more prisoners, some horses and mules and encamped on the farm of the "notorious" Claiborne F. Jackson (Missouri ex-Governor). They raised the Stars and Stripes over his house while there.

December 6th...The expedition through Saline County marched north about 18 miles through Arrow Rock, where they found several kegs of powder concealed in warehouses. They destroyed a ferryboat and, whole doing so, were fired upon. Leaving Arrow Fork they marched north through Saline City, where more arms and ammunition were captured. They encamped this night on the farm of Judge Robert Fields.

December 7th...The Saline expedition marched another 18 miles north and captured Captains Weed and Simmons (CSA) of General Clark's staff. The command halted about two miles from Glasgow. Here the command was left in charge of Major Hunt while Major Marshall, with a detachment of 25 men, proceeded to Roper's Mills opposite Glasgow. Thought to be camped there was the command of Captain Robert Swinney (CSA). Captain Swinney's pickets were taken prisoner in a surprise attack. The rest of his command was caught cooking breakfast, and some were playing cards. The alarm was given by one of the pickets who managed to give them a real good chase before being joined by the others. Part of the command had been mounted and was caught crossing the river. The number of prisoners totaled 28. The little group moved north through Cambridge and encamped on the farm of William T. Gillham.

Colonel W.J. Judson commanding at Fort Scott, Kansas, was willing to trade some prisoners for B.F. Potter, Charles Harding, James N. Bittle and John C. Allsup. They had been taken prisoner by a Montevallo company under the command of Captain Gatewood while attending B.F. Potter who was a very sick man.

December 8th...The Saline expedition camped on the property of Mr. Softly.

December 9th...There was skirmishing at Union Mills, and the Saline scouts marched 15 miles west. They found government wagons and they destroyed three and brought in five. They encamped on the farm of Mr. McReynolds, two miles from Waverly. Joseph Shelby (CSA) brought his command out and fired night shots at the scouts. He bombarded them with a 10-inch mortar cannon packed with mud.

December 10th...The Saline scouts marched through Waverly without meeting any resistance. Learning there was some powder stored there, they proceeded to search buildings and found nine kegs concealed under a platform in Joseph Shelby's store. The celebrated mortar was also found and captured. Shelby deployed his men upon a high ridge and they amused themselves by firing at the scouts. Lieutenant Kelly was again called upon to disperse the force. In the chase and confusion one of the regulars broke his leg when his saddle turned and one Samuel Jones shot himself accidently. Leaving Waverly and marching back five miles, they camped on Mrs. Murphy's farm.

December 11th...The Saline scouts marched east through Marshall, about 27 miles, and encamped on Mrs. Wingfield's farm. There was fighting also today at Bertrand.

December 12th...The scouting party marching through Saline County reached its end this day. They marched to Sedalia through Georgetown, about 23 miles.

December 13th...Skirmishing at Charleston.

December 14th...Brigadier General Jonathan Pope (Union) informs Major General Halleck that a large number of utterly destitute immigrants driven from Southwest Missouri are arriving at Syracuse and at Otterville. Unless something is done for them, they will perish of starvation or exposure. There are no means to shelter them nor provide for them. Rations have been issued, but no shelter can be obtained. The government must provide something for these people, at least through the winter. The countryside is sparsely populated and supplies are already nearly exhausted.

December 15th...After being replaced by troops from La Mine, Union Brigadier General Pope's command, numbering about 4,000 men, has set out to stop Sterling Price and his command moving south from the Missouri River. This force is reported to be 4,000 to 6,000 strong with a large train of supplies. Pope's command encamped on the 15th 11 miles southwest of Sedalia. Hoping the Confederates would be misled as to their intentions, word is sent out that this expedition's move is upon Warsaw. On the 16th of December this force marched 27 miles and by sunset occupied the position between the direct road from Warrensburg to Clinton and the road by Chilowee. This route is commonly used for returning soldiers and recruits. The Confederate pickets were captured at Chilowee and from them it was learned that there was a camp of about 2,200 six miles north of Chilhowee. The companies were repositioned upon the Warrensburg and Rose Hill Road as protection to the 10 companies of cavalry that were now advancing upon the Confederate camp. Merrill's Horse was then ordered to push forward as far as possible toward Osceola, stemming any retreat in that direction. He succeeded in capturing the pickets and one entire company. The pursuit of the rebels continued throughout the 16th and all day the 17th. Merrill finally occupied Johnstown that evening. As the Federals moved closer, the rebels went in all directions. Wagons were abandoned in farmyards, and being ordinary farm wagons, it was not possible to identify individual ones. One band of Confederates moved toward Butler and another toward Papinsville. On the 18th the scouts returned and reported a large Confederate contingent marching from Waverly and Arrow Rock and were expected to encamp that night at the mouth of Clear Creek just south of Milford. Part of Pope's command was posted at Warrensburg and Knob Noster and the balance sent to march upon the town of Milford. The rebels were encountered near the mouth of the creek. Clear Creek is deep, mirey and impassable except by a narrow bridge that was occupied in force, supposedly by Colonel Ebenezer Magoffin. The pickets were driven back across this bridge. The Confederate force was finally taken but not without loss of life. On December 18th part of General Pope's command under Colonel J.C. Davis and Major Marshall, surprised a camp of Confederates at Milford a little north of Warrensburg. A skirmish ensued and 1,300 prisoners were taken, including three colonels (Magoffin, Robinson and Alexander), a Lieutenant Colonel Robinson, a Major Harris, 51 commissioned company officers, 17 captains, 1,000 stands of arms, 1,000 horses, 65 wagons and a large quantity of tents, baggage and supplies. Union losses were two men killed and eight wounded. The prisoners were sent to St. Louis. Also on this day it was rumored that two tons of kegged powder was found on Governor Jackson's farm. A scouting party returned from Rolla. It pursued an unidentified troop of Confederate soldiers to the south of Houston. Also, about 100 of Price's men were taken and released on oath.

December 20th...Ambrose R. Tompkins, a citizen of Boone County, is accused of burning and destroying certain railroad bridges, rail ties and timbers which are necessary for the use of the North Missouri Railroad Company. This took place at or near Sturgeon, Boone County, on or about the 20th day of December. In a court hearing, Tompkins pleads not guilty. He is 42 years old and a carpenter by trade. He states he was at the bridge on the 20th of December and was taken prisoner by the rebel troops. "The men who took me burned down the Sturgeon Bridge and then proceeded on to Long Branch Bridge and burned that one also. There were 300 to 500 men." Adam Gosling was a witness for the accused. He states the actions were done by a Captain Watson. Other witnesses, including Jacob Crosswhite and W.R. Schooler, were also called. Captain Absalom Hicks was called to testify. He is a captain of the Sturgeon Invincibles of the 3rd Military District of the Missouri State Guard. He states under oath that as Tompkins' commanding officer, he gave the order for him to burn the bridge.

December 22nd...Major General Halleck ordered those who are caught damaging the telegraph in Missouri to be shot.

December 23rd...Expedition to Lexington. General Pope's men destroyed the foundry and the ferryboats. A party of bridge burners was also taken prisoner. There was also fighting at Dayton today. Under orders Brigadier General Benjamin M. Prentiss proceeded from Palmyra for Sturgeon.

December 24th...Skirmishing at Wadesburg.

December 25th...Colonel George R. Todd crossed the river with a command of Ohio Volunteers and a part of his own regiment, leaving the balance of his command at Hermann. His only practicable route to Danville was High Hill, about 10 miles east of Danville. Possession of the town was taken peaceably.

December 26th...Brigadier General Prentiss (Union) arrived at Sturgeon.

December 27th and 28th...There was a skirmish near Hallsville and an action at Mount Zion Church. Five were killed and 63 wounded. General Prentiss, hearing of a large Confederate camp near Hallsville in Boone County, sent one company of cavalry forward to reconnoiter in that vicinity. No enemy was found. About two miles beyond Hallsville Colonel Dalsey of Prentiss' advance encountered the Confederates. Captain Howland, endeavoring to draw off his company, was overpowered. Being wounded, he was taken prisoner along with one private. The rest of his men managed to escape and arrived at Sturgeon about 6:00 in the evening. On the morning of the 28th, after marching 16 miles, one company was engaged by Captain Johnson (Union) in a position to the left of the road leading from Hallsville to Mount Zion. The forces of both armies met at Mount Zion Church (Boone County). The Confederate wounded were placed in the church and locals called to tend to them. The Union total losses consisted of three killed, 17 severely wounded and 46 slightly wounded. Confederate losses totaled 25 killed and 150 wounded.

December 29th...Brigadier General Jeff Thompson and his main body was readying for descent upon Commerce to join others of his force who were operating there. Also today there was an unsuccessful attempt to take the steamer City of Alton. All the men of the town of Commerce were made prisoners and taken into the forest. The Confederates hid behind the long rows of woodpiles on the docks awaiting the arrival of the City of Alton with her precious stores and mails. The steamer usually put into the dock at Commerce and took on fuel. To prevent any warning, the women and children were gathered into little groups and were forbidden to give any warning of the ambush upon the threat of death. As the City of Alton swung into the landing, the Confederates smiled, clutched their weapons and held their breath for the signal. Suddenly Mrs. Sarah L. Everson sprang out of the midst of the other women and ran to the edge of the river screaming at the top of her voice and waving her arms. There was a clanging of bells. The steamboat's paddlewheel reversed with all power to the engines. The Confederates rose to their feet and sent a volley after the escaping prize, and with many curses, departed. After the war Congress voted to pay Mrs. Everson $15,000 in recognition of her bravery.

December 31st...Confederate Captains Fulkerson, Scott and Brity, with from 150 to 300 men, were at Dayton making preparations, recruiting and outfitting for General Price's army. Lieutenant Colonel D.R. Anthony (Union) went after them. Two Confederate companies under Colonel Newgent camped on the evening of the 31st at Austin. The main body had returned to a place about six miles distant at the junction of Walnut Creek and Grand River. About 15 Union families had moved into Kansas. Dayton had been used voluntarily by the inhabitants as a depot for recruiting and supplying the Confederacy. There was only one Union house in the town, so all the Union men desired the town's destruction. Dayton was burned with the exception of the house belonging to the Union man. Although there were 46 buildings in the town, only two men were found to represent the whole male population.

By the close of 1861, the available reports gave the Union losses at 568 killed on Missouri soil. In the listed engagements, in which only Missouri Union troops were listed, available records show 106 perished.

Dyer's records list over 1,700 as wounded. One can surmise many died of their wounds. In the first 10 months of the war Missouri played host to soldiers belonging to the following: the Union Army, Illinois, Iowa, Kansas, Indiana, Wisconsin, Ohio, Texas, Arkansas, the Cherokee Nation, Louisiana, Tennessee, Mississippi, Home Guards and the Missouri State Guards.

1862

January 1st...Crowded prisoner conditions at McDowell's College in St. Louis has prompted a letter to alleviate the same. They request that a room be prepared to handle the sick who are now compelled to lie and listen to all the bustle and noise of the others. Measles is a major concern as it is spreading rapidly through the inmates, and many have never had this disease. Deaths are already reported from the spread of various diseases and an alarming mortality rate will be forthcoming unless something is done. At Martinsburg Brigadier General Schofield makes his report on scouring the countryside. He has captured 50 prisoners, among whom is Captain Owen, the leader of the bridge burners around High Hill, and one Colonel Jeff. Jones. Colonels Todd and Morton are now moving with their Confederate commands toward Danville and Wellsville.

January 1st-3rd...Expedition from Morristown to Dayton and Rose Hill. This resulted in the destruction of Dayton. The Kansas 1st Cavalry was involved.

January 3rd...Skirmishes at Hunnewell (Shelby County).

January 5th-12th...There are countless skirmishes in Johnson and Lafayette Counties. There is movement by the 1st Kansas Cavalry. On the 5th, a party of 12 armed and mounted Union citizens of Johnson County came into the Federal camp and informed Lieutenant D.R. Anthony of the 1st Kansas Cavalry that a party of some 300 Confederates, commanded by Colonel Elliott, was committing depredations upon the loyal Union men, and they requested assistance in stopping this outrage. Major Herrick with 200 men proceeded to Holden in Johnson County to capture Colonel Elliott and his men. No enemy was found.

January 6th...Part of General Joseph Shelby's command has been arrested and released at Sedalia. Joe H. Nichols and Frank Thomas are described as being notorious in nature. Nichols is reported to have been part of the band that robbed the steamer Sunshine. While on his way by stage, it is reported that Nichols pulled a Secession flag from his pocket and displayed it at every place through which he passed.

January 7th...From Bird's Point Colonel Nicholas Perczel placed his command on the cars and upon arrival, joined the cavalry and proceeded to the house of one Swank, where supposedly there was a body of about 1,000 Tennessee cavalry encamped. The night being cloudy and rainy the guide lost his way several times. Finally by morning the command had passed the supposed place of encampment in the foggy darkness. From the faint sound of a bugle about 4:00 in the morning, they knew they were close to camp. Finally locating a house, directions were obtained. About 5:00 in the morning they finally reached the back track into Charleston.

January 8th...There was skirmishing again at Charleston, and Colonel Poindexter with 1,000 Confederates took up a strong position at Roan's Tanyard on Silver Creek located seven miles south of Huntsville in Randolph County. Here they were attacked by about 500 men under Confederate Majors Torrence and Hubbard. After about a half-hour of fierce fighting, the troops under Poindexter were routed. The victors promptly set about burning the camp. Federal losses were four killed. Confederates left seven dead on the field and carried many off. A Federal encampment is now on the La Mine near Otterville.

January 9th...Skirmish at Columbus (Johnson County). No enemy was found on the 5th by Major Herrick in Johnson County, but today Captain Merriman was sent with a detail of 50 men to the town of Columbus. The citizens of the town informed him that there was no enemy in the vicinity; however, on his return, about a half mile south of the town, he was fired upon from ambush by Colonel Elliott's men. Captain Merriman made a hasty retreat, losing five killed. He was soon joined by Captain Utt of Company A with 50 additional men. Upon scouring the countryside, they found that Elliott had escaped their capture. The camp, although deserted, was located in a rocky ravine. Captain Merriman, feeling the citizens' betrayal had decoyed him into an ambush, burned the town of Columbus. The town was well known as a rendezvous place for Elliott's men. Fifty or 60 Union families were removed from Holden under the protection of Major Herrick. The Major also brought in 60 head of livestock belonging to the men who rode with Colonel Elliott.

January 10th...Fighting at Bird's Point. Also, Lewis Merrill of Merrill's Horse received a message that a party of about 300 to 400 Confederates had camped near Renick and were to move the next morning to Roanoke some 12 to 15 miles, crossing the river at Arrow Rock or Brunswick. Later communication stated that the rebels were camped on Smith's farm about five miles from Roanoke.

January 13th...Major Hubbard's command is on the north side of the river at Boonville. He captured 160 horses, 60 wagons, 105 tents, 80 kegs of powder, 200 rifles and shotguns, a large quantity of bed quilts and 28 prisoners. Confederate General Poindexter is recruiting in Howard County. In St. Louis, William Hearst is on trial. He is described as a citizen of Jefferson County, a peaceable farmer. There appeared to be some De Soto men in the Home Guards that just didn't like Hearst, according to witnesses, and would report that Hearst had been drilling for the purpose of whipping some Home Guards, and through their actions he became satisfied that his life would be endangered if he remained at home. Thus he left, and much to his later regret, he joined General Jeff Thompson's command. He has often expressed that if the Home Guard would not pester him or bother him, he would just go home and stay there. William Hearst was found guilty of treason and sentenced to be shot. This harsh sentence was appealed by Brigadier General S. D. Sturgis, Colonel Richard D. Cutts, Lieutenant John Scott and Major E. W. Chamberlain, all of the U.S. Army. "The members of the Commission engaged in the trial have reason to believe that the prisoner, William Hearst, is an unusually stupid and ignorant man, and not capable of discriminating between the lawful commands of a superior officer and those that are criminal; that he enlisted in the rebel ranks more from unfounded fear of his neighbors than from any deep-seated feeling of disloyalty; that he voluntarily delivered himself up as prisoner when he could have escaped arrest." (It is mentioned earlier that he was captured on his way to giving himself up as a prisoner of war at the insistence of his friends.) He left the Confederate Army when the order was given to burn bridges. Feeling this wasn't right, he did not take any part. However, he was present when Big River Bridge was burned and possibly at Blackwell Station on or about the 16th of October in 1861.

January 14th...Doc Jennison's Kansans have burned 42 houses in the vicinity of Rose Hill.

January 15th-17th...An expedition of a detachment of the Illinois 7th Cavalry, a detachment of the 17th Illinois, a portion of Campbell's Battery and a detachment of the Missouri State Militia moved to Benton, Bloomfield and Dallas. Citizens from Stoddard, Scott and Bollinger were aroused and joined Jeff Thompson's forces at New Madrid. Confederates at Bloomfield were attending a gay ball preparatory to their reenlisting and were taken by total surprise by the expeditionary force.

January 22nd...Wright's Battalion of Cavalry occupied Lebanon and there was skirmishing at Knob Noster involving Missouri's 2nd Cavalry. Lebanon is now occupied by Lieutenant Colonel Clark Wright who took possession this day at 1:30 in the afternoon. The Confederate Rains has now moved to Granby to run the lead furnaces with only 400 men. The rest have gone home for the winter. Another squadron of 200 Confederates passed Miller's place on the head of Spring River going south. Captain Tom Craig of Lebanon was killed in a running fight. He was considered "Yankee-proof" by his sesesh lady friend. Captain Craig's wife has requested his body for burial.

January 27th...L. V. Nicholas, who delivered a duplicate letter of correspondence, admits being a member of General Sterling Price's command. When questioned, he said he had passed through the Union military lines dressed as a civilian traveling from Springfield to St. Louis, avoiding all military posts. He produced from his pocket a stick with a dirty handkerchief tied on the end as a flag of truce. He will be returned with the warning of the penalty for spies that are caught.

January 29th...February 3rd...Missouri 7th Infantry moved to Blue
Springs in Jackson County. There is a search in the area for
Quantrill and his men. Witnesses have visually seen him rob
coaches, steal the horses and rob the mails. Being mounted on the
very best horse flesh in the country, he is uncatchable. He now
is camped near the bottom of the ____ and the Blue River, working
a circuit over 30 miles. After a two-day chase, only six of his
band had been killed. Discovered in a cache belonging to him were
six or seven wagons loaded with fresh pork and a large quantity of
tobacco. Also recovered was a very valuable stagecoach and team.
The Union men are coming into town and requesting military escorts
so they may return to their farms and retrieve their belongings.
They had been driven from their homes. A detail marched from
Morristown to Independence. They had no boots or shoes. The
suffering men have filled the hospitals with frostbite, plus there
is no sugar available and has been none for over two weeks.

February 3rd...Captain Edward Harding (Union) will superintend the
building of blockhouses at the Peruque and Salt River Bridges on
the North Missouri Railroad. In Columbia, the leading citizens are
requesting the penalty of death be dropped or changed for Stephen
Stott and John Patton of Boone County. These illiterate men are
charged with bridge burning and are to be shot. Men of the area
feel this will incite hostilities toward the locality. Nothing but
two more dead will be accomplished by the punishment.

February 6th...The Illinois 7th Cavalry arrived at Bloomfield.

February 8th...Affair at Bolivar. A small party under Lieutenant
Colonel F. W. Lewis of the 1st Missouri Cavalry struck out on a
rampage, riding down into the town of Bolivar and spreading terror
all over. On the return to camp, 125 head of cattle came with him,
being collected from the rebel army. Doniphan is now occupied by
armed forces.

February 9th...Skirmish at Marshfield (Webster County).

February 12th...Fighting at Springfield lasted throughout two days
and took the life of two Confederates. As the Union flag now waves
over the courthouse again, the Confederates are moving southward.

February 14th...There was skirmishing at Crane Creek, and today in
St. Louis, Captain Jeff Jones, a Confederate bridge burner,
complains over the loss of his livestock and teams. The seizure
now is quite legal when the accused is found guilty of breaking the
laws that govern bridge burning. These laws were recently enacted
by the present Federal military courts.

February 15th...Skirmishing at Flat Creek.

February 17th...Skirmishing at Keytesville (Chariton County).

February 18th-19th...The 3rd Iowa Cavalry started a reconnaissance toward Norfolk. This move also resulted in a skirmish at West Plains (Howell County). There was also skirmishing at Independence and Mount Vernon today.

February 19th...Capture of Bentonville by Bowen's Battalion of Cavalry and the 10th Cavalry.

February 20th..."In consideration of the recent victories won by the Federal forces and of the rapidly increasing loyalty of citizens of Missouri who for a time forgot their duty to the flag and country the sentences of John C. Tompkins, William J. Forshey, John Patton, Thomas M. Smith, Stephen Stott, George H. Cunningham, Richard B. Crowder and George M. Pulliam, heretofore condemned to death are provisionally mitigated to close confinement in the military prison at Alton. If rebel spies again destroy railroads and telegraph lines and thus render it necessary for us to make severe examples the original sentences against these men will be carried into execution..no further assessments will be levied or collected from any one who will now take the prescribed oath of allegiance, etc." signed; N. H. McLean Asst. Adj. Genera, St. Louis.

William J. Forshey, George M. Pulliam, John C. Thompkins, Richard B. Crowder and John Patton were found guilty of burning the Sturgeon Bridge, Long Branch Bridge and others on the Northern Missouri Railroad, 20 December 1861. Dr. Thomas S. Foster was charged with burning the railroad bridge known as the Salt River Bridge, the same being on the regular route between Hannibal and St. Joseph Railway, 10th July 1861. Among the witnesses called was Ann Evans of Shrinkietown. She was taken prisoner by Dr. Foster. Dr. Foster was sentenced to be shot. James H. Benedict was also charged with open rebellion toward the government in the rebel army, as was Thomas Benedict, James W. Rumans, Ransom Batterton, James P. Tuggle and George F. Jones. They were charged with burning the bridge and giving aid and assistance to those involved with the Long Branch and the Sturgeon Bridges, as were Thomas M. Smith, Stephen Stott and George Cunningham. James H. Benedict, Thomas Benedict, James W. Rumans, Ransom Batterton, James P. Tuggle, George H. F. Jones, James R. J. Jones, John S. Mitchell, Austin Chrisman and John Powell were also charged, but will be remanded to prison. The others may prepare for execution. Sterling Coulter, Albert Pulliam, Robert M. Hannah, Samuel Groff, Barzillai Powell and Lafayette Wright were released after taking the oath.

February 21st...William C. Berry from Hickory Place, Carroll County, makes an oath that he was discharged as a prisoner of war on the 18th instant by taking an oath of allegiance to the General Government of the United States. He complains that he has never been anything but a Union man and if it had not been for the outrages of those who are called the Home Guards and who never

belonged to any regular army, many men would have remained loyal
to the Union. The night upon his return home, while in bed very
sick, 10 Jayhawkers broke into his house and abused him very much.
Upon leaving Berry's home, they went to the home of an old, blind
man, whose helpless family was totally dependent on him, and took
almost half of what he possessed on eath. He also was a man who
had never taken either side in any way whatever. These actions are
driving men by the droves into Price's Confederate Army. Mr. Berry
is quite satisfied that if these outrages were stopped, General
Price could not raise 10 men in the whole county. Otherwise,
hundreds will be driven there by desperation. The Home Guards go
around at night stealing every good horse, saddle, bridle, whiskey
and goods of every description. The regular troops do not allow
such things where they are stationed. If there could be stationed
a dozen regular troops at Dewitt, a town within a few miles of Mr.
Berry's residence, he feels all of this will cease.

February 22nd...Jefferson Davis took the oath as President of the
Confederate States of America in Richmond, Virginia. In St. Louis,
orders are given to recall Confederate Captain Sweeney's parole.
Supposedly he is not a commissioned officer in Price's army and has
committed more outrages in the northern district of Missouri than
any other man of the whole secessionist group. He is to be
returned to prison. All officers under parole now at Alton will
also be withdrawn, and they will be sent under escort to prison at
Columbus, Ohio.

February 23rd-24th...Troops are moving toward Pea Ridge Prairie.
Also on the 23rd John Pope received the command of the Army of
Mississippi at Commerce.

February 24th-25th...Troops are moving from Greenville to St.
Francisville (Greenville is in Wayne County. St. Francisville is
in Clark County.) There was skirmishing at Mingo Creek near St.
Francisville and New Madrid. Skirmishes also took place in Henry
and St. Clair Counties.

February 25th...Actions at Keytesville, Chariton County.

February 26th...Affair at Humansville, Polk County. About 2:00 in
the afternoon a lady came into town and informed Captain Gravely
("he being a lady's man") that a large force of Confederates was
marching upon the camp. The alarm was given, and a few minutes
later the enemy was seen passing town from west to east, to the
south of the camp. On the east side of town is a thicket of
underbrush coming up to within 50 paces and extending south and
east about a mile. Feeling this is where they would take cover and
attack, a company was covering this. The other various companies
were located around the town site. The heavy firing commenced,
finally driving the Confederates into a retreat. They numbered by
various accounts from 250 to 400. Captain Stockton (Union) had his
leg broken. Captain Cosgrove (Union) was severely wounded in the

arm. Confederate Colonel Frazier and Captain McMinn were killed
and four were left on the field. Twenty more wounded were treated
by the Union surgeon. In Cape Girardeau Confederal General N. W.
Watkins complains that his property, to a very large amount
negroes, horses, mules, wagons, etc., were taken from his
plantations and used or destroyed by the Union Army at Cape
Girardeau.

February 28th-April 8th...The operations to protect the government
holdings began around New Madrid and the very strategic Island No.
10 area. This was one of the more concentrated troop movements and
among the largest. The Confederate batteries were set up to
protect the Mississippi from both sides. Some described the
artillery fire as "spectacular."

March 1st...Skirmish near Sykestown in Scott County. The project
of dismantling the fort put up by the Confederates around New
Madrid has begun.

March 2nd...Skirmishing continues at New Madrid.

March 3rd-4th...Severe two days of fighting at New Madrid.

March 4th-11th...There are scouting parties throughout LaClede,
Wright and Douglass Counties.

March 7th...Point Pleasant was the site of a skirmish.

March 7th-10th...Operations around Saline County lasted four days.

March 8th-9th...There are troops gathering for operations around
Rolla.

March 9th...Actions at Big Creek and Mountain Grove Seminary,
Wright County.

March 10th...Lexington, Lafayette County, was the site of
skirmishes.

March 11th-14th...In daily fighting and skirmishing, the capture
of New Madrid finally took place on the 14th of March, producing
many casualties and wounded. This was a very important point for
the Union to hold. General Leonidas Polk spent 20 years prior to
the Civil War as Bishop of the Protestant Episcopal Diocese of
Louisiana. At the onset of the war he decided to give the
Confederacy the benefit of his West Point education. This was the
man who was instrumental in setting up the fortifications around
New Madrid. The Federal forces led by General John Pope moved down
the west bank of the Mississippi against the position of New
Madrid. By the second day this battle virtually raged. Many lives
were lost during this torturous rout. The digging of a channel
through the swamps was only a small part. The sheer physical

labors continued into the battle. Leonidas Polk was caught between impassable swamps and the Union army at the end of the bloody contest. General John Pope captured virtually the entire command, about three generals, 273 officers and 6,700 soldiers. He also carried away, or turned around for their own use and protection, 158 guns, muskets and rifles, a gunboat, a floating battery, six steamboats and all the little plunders of victory. Those Confederates not captured escaped across the river or farther down river to safety.

March 15th...Two days' skirmishing at Marshall, Saline County.

March 17th...Action at Riddell's Point. Work on cutting the canal channel across Island No. 10 was commenced. The work was completed on the 4th of April. The canal was 12 miles long and six miles of it were through heavy timber. The trees had been cut off several feet under the water.

March 18th...It is stated that Quantrill is now severely wounded, perhaps even mortally. There were two recruits in the State Militia at Liberty. One was shot in cold blood after being taken prisoner. Eight others were taken prisoner. The flag raised by General Prentiss was torn down and a secession one raised. Colonel Catherwood, finding this, tore down the flag of secession and raised the Stars and Stripes again. Taken prisoner by Colonel Catherwood was President Thompson of the Baptist College at Liberty. In St. Louis Robert W. Donnell, President of the Branch Bank of St. Joseph, and citizens, Israel Landis and William K. Richardson, were also taken prisoner. They were all charged with failure to post the prescribed bond.

March 22nd...A detachment of the 6th Kansas overtook Quantrill's Raiders today near Independence. They killed seven of his men and the rest headed southeast.

March 25th...A Baptist preacher named Caples, a prisoner on parole in the area of Glasgow, is now unable to preach the gospel. It has been understood that his teachings have been most productive in making trouble in Chariton, Saline and Howard Counties. He is appointed to preach in Glasgow on the 29th and 30th of March. He may no longer function as a public speaker or as a minister of the Word in these counties by order of Federal authority. Also on the 25th Robert Donnell, Israel Landis and William K. Richardson of St. Joseph, Henry L. Routt and President Thompson of Liberty, were taken to St. Louis under guard to be imprisoned. Matthew Houx, rebel guerilla leader, has written asking under what terms he and others would be allowed to return to their homes, if at all. He represents some 300 willing to submit under some sort of terms. If they are to be treated as outlaws, they vow to ruin the country, burning houses and murdering loyal men.

March 26th...Quantrill's 200 guerillas met up with Major Emery Foster's command of 60 men. Warrensburg became the battleground. Major Emery found protective shelter behind a heavy plank fence. From there his little command kept up a heavy fire. They succeeded in causing the guerillas to retire, but not before leaving behind nine dead and 17 wounded. The Major lost 13, including himself, as one of the wounded. This same night a band of an estimated 500 Confederates or guerillas attacked the sleepy town of Humansville. They were put down by four companies of Militia. The attackers again were driven off, leaving 15 killed and a large number wounded. Also on the 26th a skirmish took place just before daybreak. Captain Ostermeyer (Union), with 25 men, was fired upon from the woods 15 miles east of Boonville and three miles east of Gouge's Mill. The Confederates left one dead in the woods. They were thought to be the same ones that were dispersed in Jefferson City, numbering about 40 to 50 men.

March 30th...Skirmish on the Blackwater near Warrensburg. Captain James D. Thompson and his new command of about 130 men marched from Sedalia and by forced march reached Warrensburg on the morning of the 28th. Scouts sent out that day located a Confederate camp of about 300 to 400 some 15 miles distant. They were camped on the Blackwater near a place known as Murray's Ford. The command was then divided and proceeded to surround the enemy camp. After this was accomplished, the camp was found to be abandoned. Finally, on the afternoon of the 29th while emerging from a stand of woods, Captain Thompson met up with the notorious Confederate leader, Colonel Parker and about 60 or 70 of his men. A running battle ensued, crashing through over four miles of heavy almost unpenetrable underbrush. The Confederates were finally taken. Among the prisoners captured was Colonel Parker. The Colonel had long been the terror of the northern counties of Missouri. A few nights prior to Captain Thompson's arrival in Warrensburg, the Confederates set fire to Colonel McCowan's residence in Warrensburg, entirely destroying the house, furniture, etc., leaving the family, consisting of his wife and some four or five children without anything to support or protect them. About this same time they, or another band of them, proceeded to the household of Mr. Burgess and shot him and his brother and burned the house over the heads of his family. Again on this black Sunday, Captain Thomas W. Houts, while out with about 50 men, killed one Mr. Piper and burned five buildings, turning the families out of doors and destroying everything in the houses. This last incident was reported by one of the men with him at the time who refused to take part in this outrage committed by the good Federal Captain.

March 31st...Quantrill, with his collection, is now at Pink Hill about 19 miles southeast of Independence. Captain Peabody from Independence has started in pursuit of them, joined by the command of Lieutenant White. After arriving at the area of Pink Hill, they searched the area. Upon passing a double log house in an elevated position, they located Quantrill's men only from a perfect volley of shots that were shot through home-structured loopholes developed by knocking the chinking away. This afforded Quantrill a fort-like structure. Peabody and White finally, after a desperate charge, managed to rout the troops from the house by storming under heavy fire. Six of the men inside the house were instantly killed and many wounded. Quantrill fled for the protection of the timber close by. The houses, four structures in all, were promptly fired and destroyed. Again pursuit of Quantrill resumed.

April 1st...Skirmishing on the Little Sni, Jackson County. This was part of the expedition sent to Pink Hill. They succeeded in capturing 10 kegs of powder, each containing 25 pounds, said to belong to one Parker who rides with Quantrill. Captain Peabody now has Quantrill and Parker located. The outlaws were found about nine miles from Pink Hill upon a high bluff over the waters of the Little Sni. The rocks on the ridge offered them protection. The ridge was impassable for horses. After commencing firing, the time it took the Federals to secure the horses and scale the bluff afforded Quantrill enough time to remove his force. In the short fight Quantrill lost five men killed and six wounded and one prisoner was taken. Parker's and Quantrill's men now numbered over 200. (You will note that supposedly Colonel Parker was previously reported as captured.) Within the area it is reported no Union citizen is safe. Another man named Grigsby is marauding also in the vicinity with about 200 men under him. It seems Grigsby had acquired the assistance of some of the locals to go with him to the aid of Parker and Quantrill at Little Sni. Today saw fighting at Doniphan also. Colonel Carlin ran into a Confederate camp with his advance guard while fording the river at this place. One Confederate lieutenant was killed. The remainder got away and the skirmishers continued in pursuit.

On the 1st a complaint was filed concerning the arrest and maltreatment of Dr. Sidney Robinson and others at the hands of Lieutenant Walldorf, Company I, 6th Missouri Militia. The particulars of the arrest were supplied by the doctor's daughter now in Jefferson City, and to her by John Morris, James Morris, William McCloud and Mr. Slocum, Union men living near Versailles. Dr. Robinson was arrested in Versailles where he had gone to attend a sick grandchild. His hands were bound, a rope adjusted to his neck and other preparations for hanging him were made. Finally, it was proposed to let him off if he took the oath. He refused and then it was announced that he would be sent to Cairo. Among others arrested were Mick Jetter, Mick Robinson and ____ Johnson. An identified man was twice suspended by the hangman's rope until senseless.

Dr. Robinson had been known to give shelter in his home to wounded Union soldiers, one dying under the doctor's roof and the doctor, at his own expense, tended to the burial. The doctor was also known to believe in the right of secession by politics, not taking any oath nor taking part. He also had enemies in his neighborhood of 15 years, and these were all now professed Union men. There is no doubt that they instigated this whole affair. Dr. Robinson is being held at Tipton, Morgan County. A later correspondence by Lieutenant Walldorf suggests that the hanging of Dr. Robinson was under the suggestion of Captain Rice, and not finding anyone among those assembled to speak in his behalf, he was considered to be a rebel sympathizer and one of bad character. Only one man spoke up in the doctor's behalf, and he had been arrested by Captain Rice as a spy on the same evening. News has just arrived at Jefferson City of the capture of some of the gang at Warsaw. John McCloud, referred to as being among them, rode a horse stolen from Mr. Parks. It seems that many night rides were being made through Morgan County and many Union citizens molested. The trail of these men was assumed by a large group of horse tracks leading from Dr. Robinson's house. These tracks were followed. Many robberies, murders and general terror have been the rule of Morgan County for some time. The men are always in disguise, such as false whiskers, clothing, etc., and they sneak through the darkness. The man who was hung the most in this outrage was one Chittenden, and he confessed his complicity with the gang, told five names connected with it and said there were 10 to 12 others; he also described the horses they had stolen and said the gang left that morning and would camp that night on Buffalo Creek, some 20 miles distant.

April 2nd-4th...There is a large reconnaissance from Cape Girardeau to Jackson, Whitewater and Dallas, Missouri. Mr. James Noel, County and Circuit Court Clerk of Bollinger County, was taken prisoner and held four days. The court records and other valuable deed records were carried off by Confederate Major Kitchen and 120 Secessionists. They took horses and citizens as prisoners. Among the prisoners were two men, Miller and McIntee. McIntee was killed by a miscreant named Bowles, and Miller was killed by Bowles' orders. Mr. Noel was taken below Bloomfield where he was released by the interference of his friends.

April 4th...The Carondolet and the Pittsburg, two gunboats, were taken under cover of darkness through the canal across Island No. 10.

April 6th...Colonel W. L. Jeffers (noted Confederate officer) attacked a company of Missouri Militia under Captain William Flentze and scattered them.

April 7th...The Confederates abandon Island No. 10.

April 8th...A scouting party is led by Colonel Clark Wright through Gadfly, Newtonia, Granby, Neosho and the valley of Indian Creek. There was skirmishing all along the route. On the 9th, Wright is in camp at Cassville. Colonel Wright and Captain Banning had a very large train of supplies and subsistence and 65 head of cattle. The train was routed through the towns above listed. There were many skirmishes with rebel commands and guerillas. Killed was

Lieutenant Cole, Dr. Adams, Dr. Cummons and severely, if not mortally, wounded were Yancey Richardson and Dr. Wills Allison. Some 125 prisoners were taken. All but 24 were released. All bands were driven down to Stand Waites' command, a point on the line of the Indian Territory some 15 miles below Neosho. About 600 are encamped there. They were camped between Cowskin and Buffalo Creek and also some 10 miles below. Also on the 8th Colonel King, the commander at Chillicothe, and the guard stationed at Medicine Creek were fired upon by a small band of guerillas. They returned the same. The two bands operating in that vicinity are under the commands of Keisengro and Small.

April 9th...Skirmish at Jackson. A command under Sergeant Randall, Lieutenant Wolfers and Lieutenant G.W. Hummel was led into an ambush successfully commanded by Confederate Captains William Jeffries and Kitchen. Seeing a band of retreating Confederates near the road running by Benton and Jackson, they followed. The Union suffered loss and retreated. Captain William Flentze (Militia) reports that the arms they used were of such a variance of bore that the ammunition wouldn't stay in the chamber, thus leading to the decision of a hasty retreat. Reuben McDonald (MSM) was killed. William M. Browner, who was wounded, has since died and W. W. Praffer is missing. Lieutenant Hummel was severely wounded and taken prisoner but later released on his oath and exchanged. John A. Taylor and James Tergin (MSM) were also wounded. Also on the 9th, a scouting party was on its way to Shiloh Camp on Hoyle's Run, near Quincy, and skirmishes developed. A scout was sent to Little Niangua, in Hickory County and another expedition sent from Humansville to Montevallo in Vernon County.

President Lincoln has again intervened in the case of Colonel Ebenezer Magoffin. "If prison conditions are such that they are materially endangering the Colonel's health, President Lincoln wishes it mitigated so far as it can be consistently with his safe detention."

April 26th...Confederate General John S. Marmaduke attacked the town of Cape Girardeau. He met with fierce opposition from General John McNeill and was driven away with large losses.

April 27th...Marmaduke's advance guard covering his retreat was surprised and attacked near Jackson by the 1st Iowa Cavalry and other troops. Two howitzers loaded with musket balls were fired at them when they were not more than 30 yards away, and instantly the Iowans charged down upon the luckless command in a spirited charge. Not one Confederate escaped.

May 11th...A skirmish at Bloomfield killed one man and 11 were captured.

June 11th...Fighting at Deep Water. The command of Captain William E. Leffingwell of the 1st Iowa had a run-in and hand-to-hand combat with a force under Confederate Colonel Upton Hayes. Colonel Hayes was taken prisoner and is now at Butler. The fighting ensued as a command of Hayes was crossing the Osage at Taberville. The fighting and skirmishing continued for two days, finally dispersing the band of Confederates. Losses to Confederates, besides Colonel Hayes whose shoulder was broken, were Captain Ballare and three privates taken prisoner, three men killed and four wounded. The Union loss was a broken hand suffered in the hand-to-hand combat and two dead horses. On this day at Pink Hill fighting broke out again when the Federal mail train was fired into about 15 miles from Independence. Two men of the mail escort were killed and two wounded. Colonel Buel, who was instructed to keep the route open and keep the mails safe, is now stating that he will no longer deliver the mail and will leave it up to the Secessionists to carry for a while. They seem to be able to travel safely.

June 17th...Lieutenant Sandy Howe with the 7th Missouri State Militia today was surprised by riding upon a band of Bushwhackers at the house of Mrs. Davenport nine miles west of Warrensburg. They fired upon the Militia and then took to the brush. The Militia following suddenly found themselves chasing the band through heavy underbrush for over a mile. Finally the Lieutenant reached an impasse and was surrounded by the Bushwhackers. Sending for assistance, he made a stand. The nearest help was about three miles away. Making a valiant effort, he succeeded in driving off the enemy but left three of his men lying on the battlefield wounded. The summoned assistance, Major Emory S. Foster, went to the field to bring in the wounded and dead. Upon finding them, he discovered the bodies stripped of all clothing and the corpses badly mutilated. One had been coldly inflicted with a dozen revolver balls after his death. The trail of the guerillas was followed, but heavy rain interrupted the search. Upon returning to Mrs. Davenport's house, Lieutenant Howe found it deserted and a large amount of provisions cooked and packed in baskets. The long table was set for dinner for a number of men. He ordered the house burned, and the order was complied with. Upon leaving the burning house and starting across the prairie, he found one of the wounded, Corporal Holstein, who had crawled six miles through the underbrush.

Depredations in the area are being committed each day. A man named White was shot down while plowing his field. Two Bushwhackers that now reside in the jail at Warrensburg will be shot today in partial payment for his life. Houses are being burned on a daily basis, the hordes of citizens are moving to towns with what little they have left. The guerillas in this area have been joined by Confederate Commander Upton Hayes, thus making his command and those of Snelling and Brinker now estimated at over 200 strong. Miss Mattie Brinker, a sister of the notorious John Brinker, and her younger brother were discovered near the area of the battle of the previous day. They are now in confinement. Miss Mattie has long been suspected as relaying information to her brother.

June 18th...The hunt for guerillas, Park Randolph and D. Gresham culminated in a skirmish at Hambright's Station not far from Independence. The household of Mr. Allen was visited and he obliged by giving directions to the residence of one Mr. Renick. Thus Mr. Renick and Mr. Relfe were arrested. A negro at the residence advised First Lieutenant James M. Vance of the 7th Missouri Cavalry that two of the guerillas were hidden in the haystack, and the firing commenced. Two of the hidden enemy were wounded and a third member was killed. Park Randolph and D. Gresham were killed. Kit Chiles is reported as operating in that neighborhood. He was trailed up the river to the home of his mother. No more intelligence could be gained as to his whereabouts. The detail returned to the house of Mr. Matthews and made arrangements for the burial of Randolph and Gresham.

Following orders, the grocery of one Mr. Barnes was burned and he was arrested.

June 23rd...Major Miller of the 2nd Wisconsin routed the Confederates under Major Russell at Pineville taking horses, mules and several prisoners. A special court was held today in St. Louis over which Colonel Lewis Merrill presided. Confederate Captain Absalom Hicks was arraigned and tried. He is charged with violation of the laws of war and the act of burning the Sturgeon Bridge on or about the 15th of June 1861. He was sentenced to be held now as a prisoner of war at Columbus, Ohio. Also on the 23rd skirmishing took place on the farm of J. R. Lowe near Raytown. Operations began in earnest today around Sibley and Pink Hill. Major Eliphat Bredette marched on the road to Sibley with 48 men of Company K, Captain Loring of Company F, Lieutenant McQuary with 60 men, and all arrived at Wellington. There prisoners were made of 54 men, all charged with aiding and abetting the rebellion. They were sent under a guard of 12 men to Camp Powell at Lexington. On this same mission the command took 25 more men prisoner at Napoleon, three of whom had just returned from the Confederate Army. Others were implicated in the capture and plundering of the steamer Little Blue. It was reported that many outrages were committed against the 40 sick soldiers on board. In a general search of the town, contraband was found in the haystacks, outhouses and secreted in cellars.

June 24th...Lieutenant Wightman, in command of one of the divisions of the above detail, reported with seven prisoners taken in the bottoms below Sibley. One, Burns, was found with a safeguard in his pocket along with some stolen government property. A stolen carriage and a pistol, which bore the name of a most notorious rebel guerilla, were found. The safeguard had been issued at Independence. Burns was returned to that post for trial. The scouting party continued to about eight miles below Sibley, from which the enemy was approaching. Preparations were made to welcome them by morning light.

June 25th...The scouting party around Sibley met with firing on this day. Through a misunderstanding, Lieutenant Vance and his command closed his files to the river at Cogswell's Landing while Major Bredette's skirmishers moved from Sibley. They were a considerable distance apart. Not being on this line, the Bushwhackers made an easy escape. Skirmishing down a chain of vedettes on the mainland followed for nearly two miles down an island.

June 26th...Quantrill, with 800 men, was reported as being sighted on the evening of the 25th at St. Clair, about 10 miles south. Major Bredette marched to intercept him. Again, Quantrill was sighted about four miles out, and now being about two miles distant, was heading for Pink Hill. Major Bredette sent eight men disguised as Bushwhackers to the neighborhood to learn from the secesh citizens what Quantrill's plans might be. Finally, Lieutenant Wightman brought back the news that Quantrill had passed through Pink Hill, departing an hour previously. It was thought he had headed toward the Mapa Settlement about 12 miles distant from Pink Hill.

June 27th...The search and pursuit of Quantrill continued today in the Mapa Settlement area. Again, Lieutenant Wightman, with a small detail of about 50 men, went into the area and found that he had indeed been through the Settlement and had again departed. The pursuit was now abandoned. The prisoner count has increased now to 24. The scouting continued with Lieutenant Vance heading toward Independence. Major Bredette headed toward Lexington, halting about five miles from Pink Hill for the night. Patrols scouted the country throughout the night hours hoping to find the camp of one Ducates who is operating in that neighborhood.

June 28th-30th...Operations are taking place in Johnson County under Captain Kehoe and 100 men and Second Lieutenant A. Gourney. They scouted west and northwest of Warrensburg with instructions to divide the command into three parties. They were all to proceed to Blackwater and scout the surrounding country, searching out Bushwhackers. The country was reportedly full of them. They also had orders to shoot "on the spot" each and every one of them they met under arms. It was reported that this morning a brother of a Union man was killed by a certain Thomas Colburn. He is a rather notorious horse thief and jayhawker. As the message was being sent to Captain Kehoe, he was attacked by Colburn but with little success. It appears that Colburn was in cahoots with a man named Houx (probably Matthew Houx) and one unidentified man. On the morning of the 29th Captain Kehoe had another run-in with them, and this time Kehoe succeeded in killing two, Oxford and Greenwood.

July 1st...Major Bredette arrived in Napoleon today and arrested four men and destroyed two barrels of contraband whiskey. Today also saw skirmishing at Cherry Grove in Schuyler County as the Confederates Joe Porter and Bill Dunn were being chased. The pursuit ended finally some six miles from the Iowa line in a "shoot out." The Confederates lost about 12 killed and 25 wounded. The Militia lost one man thought to be mortally wounded and six horses. Porter and Dunn were reported to be 130 strong. Pursuit was continued at first light on July 2nd. The horses, some 435 of them, are being returned to the post at Hudson, all having succumbed to the forced marches and hard riding.

July 4th...Confederate Colonel Clarkson moved his large command from Cowskin Prairie to Cabin Creek in the Indian Territory of Oklahoma about 20 miles distant.

July 6th-8th...A large scouting party was on its way from Waynesville to the Big Piney. Headquarters having received special orders dated July 6th at Waynesville, Lieutenant Colonel Joseph A.

Eppstein (Militia) started with 30 men of Companies B and F under Lieutenants Ellington and Brown to Wayman's Mill on Spring Creek, 12 miles distant. A company of Coleman's Confederates was supposedly camped about 20 miles from the mill on the Big Piney. While advancing upon this place messages were received that Coleman had taken the town of Houston, Texas County, on the 5th and was now moving toward the Springfield Road. Not knowing what to believe, the detail proceeded to Johnson's Mill about 30 miles from Waynesville, there arresting one of Coleman's men. The prisoner told them he had left camp at least an hour before and was only headed home. His father, also a member of this rebel band, resided about 10 miles beyond Johnson's Mill. After some persuasion the prisoner was convinced to show the Militia the way to the camp. The detail left about sundown on the evening of the 7th for the campsite. After about an hour and a half, another mill was reached. From there the rest of the journey was on foot. About a quarter of a mile up the road they followed a dry creek bed for about 300 yards. Finally, by a deep and stagnant creek, the command was ordered by an unidentified voice to "halt." Ignoring this order, but being unable to cross, precious time was lost in finding another fording place. Upon climbing the rocky bank, the party encountered the armed rebels in position about 12 yards in front of them. The rebels opened fire. It was returned promptly. The Militia's ammunition being low, the order to "fix bayonets" was given. A bloody skirmish ensued. The rebels made for the safety of the nearby timber, leaving behind coats, blankets, camp equipage, boots, hats, etc. Pursuit was useless as darkness was upon them. Leaving the campsite a wounded man belonging to the rebel command was found and four bodies. The young prisoner and guide, Bradford, tried to escape during the bayonet charge and was run through. He was left wounded on the field, but a neighbor was hastened to his relief. Prisoners are William Hamilton, George Logan and James Ormsby, all from Company A, Coleman's Battalion. Coleman had recruited about 300 men prior to his return to Missouri from Arkansas. The force now numbers close to 900 men.

July 7th...Major H.A. Gallup of the 3rd Missouri (Union/Militia?) took command of a detachment of 205 men and moved to Crow's Station. The next day a wagon was sent directly to Salem, and the other companies proceeded to Stevenson's Mill on the Current River. A small detachment of 15 men was left at Spring Creek to scout the area. Taking the balance of the command, and hearing that three commands of Confederates were camped at the head of Inman Hollow down the river from Salem, the Militia headed in that direction. Three Confederates were encountered gathering corn from a barn near the road. Chasing them back to their camp at the house, 11 were killed and one wounded. No further pursuit was made due to the lack of horseshoes. Meanwhile, today at Newark every horse was used, and all contraband mounts rushed to the rescue of Captain Lewis, who was supposed to be trapped by very superior forces under the command of Confederate Commander Joseph Porter. After a fast, hard ride of some six hours, Captain Lewis was found holed up in

a brick house near the border of the woods. It was the same house
in which Porter and his command had encamped the previous night.
Porter took his leave during the night and traveled northward.
Captain Lewis encountered Porter's command about three miles from
Newark and in the fight that followed, the Captain was cut off from
his horses and forced to retreat and do battle. Porter offered
under a flag of truce an unconditional surrender which was refused.
Lewis lost two of his men to the battle. As Porter was making his
way northward, he is reported by a lady to have "203 or 204" men.
The Confederates had stopped at her residence and taken everything
movable. This Newark expedition was sent out originally from Camp
Scott.

July 8th-9th...An expedition from Blackwater to Chapel Hill reports
the deaths of John Smith, Peter Berry and a third unidentified man.
They were killed by Lieutenant White of Company C, 1st Missouri
Cavalry.

July 9th-11th...In the sweltering July heat, this period of time
consisted of fighting with Quantrill's men at Lotspeich's farm on
Sugar Creek near Wadesburg, at Sear's house near Pleasant Hill and
at Big Creek Bluffs near Pleasant Hill. Quantrill was very
successful in picking advantageous places of protection, thus he
slipped away after losing only some of his men, making camp within
one mile of the home of Lotspeich. The farm was a place of
rendezvous for assistance of companies from Warrensburg and Butler
which joined in the chase. The trail of the sly Quantrill was lost
and finally located by Captain Kehoe. It followed along a dry
creek bed at Lincoln Ford. Captain Kehoe once again took up the
chase. The other commands followed passing east of Rose Hill,
Johnson County, and passing up Big Creek bottoms in a northeasterly
direction. They finally overtook Captain Kehoe at the home of Mr.
Hornsby, at whose house Quantrill and his men had taken dinner.
After a long march of about 50 miles, the Militia companies went
into camp throughout the neighborhood. Captain Kehoe took off
after his quarry early the next morning. A confrontation took
place three miles west of Pleasant Hill. Captain Kehoe and his
command rode up as Quantrill was preparing to burn another Union
man's barn. This was the property of Mr. Sears. Captain Kehoe
took a terrible licking from Quantrill. The Captain, finding
himself surrounded on all sides and all of his advance guard
killed, fought his way back to the timber, it being his only avenue
of escape. He lost three horses shot from under him. The Captain
was wounded in the shoulder. The fighting continued over a two
square mile area. Every man for himself was the order. After the
battle, besides the six advance guard that were killed, nine more
appeared wounded. The deceased from Kehoe's command were taken to
Pleasant Hill for burial. Meanwhile the large command that had
assembled struck Quantrill's trail again, it appearing now that
some of his men had gone down a wooded road into the Big Creek
timber, and the pursuit was once again taken up. Quantrill, ready
for them, had taken a very protective position in the rocky cliffs

49

of a ravine at Big Creek Bluffs. He was finally routed, but not before Captain William A. Martin had charged him seven times. The losses were larger now to both sides of the conflicting armies. The Militia had three more killed and 10 men wounded. Quantrill left behind 14 dead and many wounded. It was reported that Quantrill had suffered a thigh wound. Observers stated that Quantrill's command was enlarged by the additional commands of Matthew Houx and Colonel Upton Hayes. Among the plunder left by Quantrill's men was his spy glass, the company roll and a mailbag and lock.

July 18th...A most desperate fight took place today at Memphis between a Confederate command numbering about 600 under Joseph Porter and Dunn and Militia. Porter and Dunn chose a strong position for their camp, which was partially concealed by heavy brush and timber. Major John Y. Clopper and his forces of Militia and cavalry attacked when he first learned of their location by their firing upon his advance guard. The valiant command of the Major made five desperate charges across the open prairie in full face of the Confederates. Each time he was driven back. On the sixth attempt, having located the hiding place, they charged again. This time it ended in hand-to-hand combat. This resulted in the Confederates leaving behind their dead and wounded on the Missouri earth as they retreated to safety. The Militia lost 83 men. Major Clopper moved his command near Pierce's Mill to rest and bury the dead.

July 19th-23rd...Starting on the 19th a large scouting party proceeded into the southern parts of Dallas and Polk Counties. This concerned a detachment from three companies of the 14th Regiment of Missouri Militia. The detail started in the direction of Buffalo, stopping the first night at Pomme De Terre 17 miles north of Springfield. There the command was divided into three smaller commands of about 15 men each. One detail was sent to the Highland neighborhood, one to the Mayfield neighborhood and the third went on to Pleasant Hope in Polk County. The return meeting place was the home of Moses Bennett, eight miles south of Buffalo. The object of this little mission was to arrest "thought to be Bushwhackers." This resulted in 25 men being sent to the prison in Springfield. The others were released upon taking the oath. At the home of Benjamin Botter, they had the misfortune to run into Confederate Captain Tom Lofton. The commander of the Militia called all of his men back in. On the return trip, they had another brush with Lofton. Two of Lofton's men, Arnold and Greene, were killed.

July 20th...The virtually unguarded Union camp was caught asleep by the Confederates. A perfect rout was accomplished. This resulted in much investigation into the reason for such a perfect execution. The men of the camp were reported to be drunk the previous night and this night also. Insufficient guards had been posted and those posted were called in, leaving one whole side of the camp unguarded and totally open. The camp was virtually destroyed, all rifles but 35 were taken, 77 horses and mules and commissary stores. It was finally proven that six men were on guard that night, but none patrolled the wooded side of the camp. The hardest hit company was camped in an orchard about a half mile north of the village of Greenville near the Fredericktown Road, which runs past the orchard under the bluff between it and the St. Francis River. Other companies were encamped in close quarters upon the bluff. The Confederates helped themselves to a camp ambulance to carry away their wounded.

July 22nd...Confederate Commander Joseph Porter and 300 men rode into Florida today from the north and encountered a small force of 50 Militia stationed there. Killed, wounded and missing Militia totaled 26 after a very hasty retreat. Major H.C. Caldwell of the 3rd Iowa makes a plea for more men. As it stands, he doesn't have a chance against the likes of Porter.

July 23rd...A force of 162 men are occupied with the pursuit of guerilla bands in Johnson County. They struck again at Columbus. Fighting and pursuit followed a skirmish on the Blackwater. Four of the guerillas were killed.

July 25th-26th...Fighting today at Mountain Store. A detachment was sent out from Houston of two companies and some artillery in the pursuit of Coleman (CSA) meeting in a spirited skirmish on the right hand branch of the Big Piney. Eight of Coleman's command were killed and many taken prisoner after two sharp skirmishes. Of the 17 prisoners taken, four carried passes for safety by oath from a Provost-Marshal. They threw down their arms when arrested. A camp was made about 4 1/2 miles upstream from the home of a Mrs. Forrester. Coleman was encamped about four miles farther on near the home of Mr. Harrison. This man also owned Harrison's store in the area.

July 26th...The scouting party left Greenville with 50 men, marched about 30 miles and encamped on the Castor River. The river was followed downstream to the home of Daniel Bollinger's Mill. Reinforcements joined the party there. They then moved to William Cat's and encamped again. More reinforcements joined the command at this place. Finally the trail of the command was picked up by the Confederates, and as they were preparing to leave camp on the morning of the 28th, they were attacked heavily for some 30 minutes. On the return near Fredericktown, the Confederates again were met in force. Sharp skirmishing broke out.

July 28th-31st...Scouting parties roamed over Pettis County. One man named Givens, a supposed Confederate, was shot.

July 29th...The area of Saline County from Blackwater at Marshall Bridge to Arrow Rock was scoured by the 6th Missouri Cavalry (Militia) today. This driving of the lawless bands lasted three

days. Many of the Confederates and guerillas are attempting to
reach Poindexter just across the Missouri River.

July 30th...General Sterling Price is reported in Chariton County
on this date and taking on the U.S. Army and local Militia. He put
out the word he would attack Major Mullin at Brunswick. Lieutenant
Colonel Alexander M. Woolfolk went to his rescue. Upon arriving
at the camp, all was quiet. Scouts brought in information that a
small camp was sighted east of Chariton River about three miles
from "Keetsville" (Keytesville?) The chase was on. The forces met
up at Clark's Mill about 15 miles up the river.   The good
Lieutenant Colonel gave the order "no quarter" after surrounding
the small group. They were shot at will with revolvers. "When we
dispersed and slaughtered all we could find upon the prairie it was
11 o'clock at night." The Lieutenant Colonel gives the killed on
the field as eight and several wounded. The Militia escaped all
injuries.   Neighbors in the area were left to bury the dead.
General Price was nowhere to be found.

Brigadier General D.M. Frost

Major Franz Sigel

With the coming of August in 1862, it was as if the hot sun of a
Missouri summer unleashed the fury of both armies. The war in
Missouri took up a frantic pace. Depredations committed by both
reached a new plateau of cruelty. A citizen need not by caught
with evidence.   He or she was adjudged guilty be reason of
association. Being willing or unwilling in the association was
useless in pleading your innocence. The term "guerilla" took on
a new meaning. The U. S. Army and the Missouri Militia were very
adept at practicing the very same type of warfare they had so long
condemned as wanton murder in their field reports. The Grim Reaper
now wore a uniform, rode a horse, carried a gun, flashed a gleaming
saber and rode in the darkness through Missouri's heartland.   He

could be found behind the rail fence of a neighbor's cornfield. He could also be found in your neighbor's house enjoying a friendly conversation. Sometimes he wore a blue uniform, other times he wore a gray. He was sighted as wearing the ordinary dress of a farmer. He was ever present.

August 1st...First Lieutenant Thomas Doyle (MSM) had a run-in with a force of about 400 on his expedition to Carroll County at Carrollton. The skirmish took place about five miles from Carrollton. After capturing one of the pickets, he fell back about 10 miles and camped. The next morning he moved out to find the camp of the enemy. Finding it deserted, the trail was picked up and the pursuit began again and lasted for nearly 25 miles toward Grand River. There the wagon trains, baggage, etc., of the rebels were captured. Also on the 1st of August a scouting party left to reconnoiter the country in the vicinity of Forsyth. This scouting party met the wrath of Confederate Colonel Lawther in a spirited skirmish about five miles below Forsyth at White River. In the foray the sword of Colonel Lawther and a bag of mail were taken. Also while out the little band encountered a well-known guerilla horse thief, Robert Wisener. He was killed before he could be captured and brought in. The death of Mr. Wisener, a well-respected man around Ozark, has created quite a stir among the Southern sympathizers. This same group of Militia met up with Colonel Lawther again on August 4th. The report of Colonel Robert Lawther was found inside the mailbag. It states that on the morning of the 31st of July he was encamped at the mouth of Long Creek on the White River. He reported the enemy (Militia) was encountered in front of the courthouse and secreted in some surrounding buildings. After a successful rout, the Militia took cover in the houses and stable of the town and remained there. Lawther withdrew, as he had only 55 armed men versus 150 of the Militia.

August 4th...Skirmish on Clear Creek near Taberville (Headquarters Butler, Bates County). The farm of one Gordon on Clear Creek in the corner of St. Clair County was the site of a pitched scrap. Captains J.W. Caldwell and Heath (1st Iowa), under Colonel Fitz Henry Warren, were led into a brilliantly executed ambush. To get his command in position Captain Heath had to run a gauntlet of the entire front line of the enemy which was secreted in the woods. None were visible. In doing so, Captain Heath was killed along with three others. After the sheer steady burst of fire, the invisible foe retreated without a trace through the woods. Captain Caldwell searched for their trail. The troops under Colonel Warren marched 70 miles in 23 hours. Upon facing their hidden enemy, many of his men were only armed with sabers. Carbines and cannon were nonexistent. On the 4th a scouting party started on Sinking Creek and vicinity. The same morning they surprised a camp of one Confederate command under Barnes(?). Barnes was trying to make his way through to join Colonel Coleman. They captured Barnes' private papers and killed four of his men. The Confederates are now scattered throughout the countryside in little squads, heading for West Plain, Howell County. They were supposedly moving the camp of Coleman. Colonel Joseph Porter's trail has been picked up by his pursuers in the Faubius Bottom near Clapp's Ford and proceeds until it reaches the Middle Faubius some 10 miles south of Memphis.

August 5th-9th...Skirmishes near Cravensville in Daviess County. The Missouri State Militia was fired upon by a force of 85, in ambush, under officers Davis and Kirk. On the 6th a notorious fellow named Wicklin was killed, and on the 7th Daniel Hale was killed by the command near the forks of the Grand River. The Confederate Commander Joseph Porter and his command of about 1,500 met up with Lieutenant Colonel Woolfolk on Panther Creek near the Hannibal and St. Joseph Railroad crossing of the Chariton River. Porter supposedly retreated across the river. The next day he was encountered again at Walnut Creek where Porter prepared another ambush reception at Sears' Ford. After some skirmishing, he moved his command off. This proved to be costly in life for both sides. Also on August 5th it was rumored that a Colonel Barstow (Union), with his detachment, had been captured at Montevallo. That rumor proved to be false, as he returned to camp with Coffee's (CSA) roster; however, not before he was forced to evacuate the town and make a running fight in his retreat. Colonel Barstow reports 1,500 Confederate sympathizers in and about Montevallo.

August 7th...Joseph Porter, with a command of 2,500 to 3,000 Confederates, is in Kirksville. After evacuating the town, he posted his men in the cornfields, some houses, various businesses and in the cupola of the courthouse. He didn't make it easy on his pursuers. He burned every bridge and felled large trees across the creek fords. Not being able to ascertain just where he was in force, Lieutenant Cowdrey of Merrill's Horse made a wild dash through the main street and around the square, drawing their fire in a most horrific fashion. Upon reaching safety, the firing from the artillery commenced. Shot poured into the houses and cornfields. The cannon belched a deathly flow. Many soldiers were killed on both sides. Porter, with the remainder of his force, pulled back across the Chariton River. Upon finding that many of the 15 prisoners taken at Kirksville had been captured before and having been released upon taking the oath not to bear arms again, these loyalty slips being found upon them, they were executed. Porter is supposed to have McCulloch and Franklin in his command. This was not a good camping place. No forage was available of any sort in this area. It had played the host to armies totaling over 3,000 men.

At Rocky Bluff in Platte County, skirmishing was heavy today on the south side of the Platte River about five miles from the city. From all appearances, three houses in the vicinity were being used as headquarters for the Confederates and guerillas. These were burned with the captured tents and camp equipage. The 10th Kansas then ate the captured cooked breakfast of the guerillas. Coffee's

command is now divided, part at Montevallo and the balance at
Osceola. A scouting party left Ozark for Forsyth in the pursuit
of guerillas. They encamped on Swan Creek at one Cook's place.
Cook was a well-known secesh. It appeared Cook's farm was used as
a rendezvous place for the guerillas due to the great quantity of
cakes and pies baked, obviously for someone other than the family,
which the scouting party relished! A Colt revolver and three
horses were taken from Mr. Cook.

August 8th...Major J.M. Hubbard of the 1st Missouri Cavalry (Union)
was fired upon by a force of about 1,000 men on an open prairie
near Newtonia where they were camped. Porter's stalwart
Confederate command is still being pursued. He turned near
Stockton and gave fight. Brigadier General Lewis Merrill (Union)
took 26 prisoners from Porter's command. These men were executed
by one McNeil. Colonel Oden Guitar has taken up the pursuit of
Porter. In his report of the 15th, Oden Guitar states that he has
pursued Porter 250 miles in seven days and came to confrontation
with him three times, once at Switzler's Mills, at Little Compton
and on the Muscle Fork of the Chariton. The last pursuit was 25
miles "under the lash" and accomplished in four hours. The elusive
Porter made good his escape by burning the bridge over the Muscle
Fork. He is now reported to have only about 400 followers, no
ammunition or baggage train.

August 9th...Porter's command was broken up today near Bloomington.

August 11th...A well-known Confederate commander, one Hughes,
launched an attack on the National Arsenal at Independence with the
purpose of obtaining additional arms. The command surprised and
killed the pickets before they could give the alarm. They then
entered the town by two roads and attacked the various buildings
where the command was garrisoned. A gallant stand was made by the
Federals, but being outnumbered two to one and with no prospect
for assistance, Colonel J. T. Buell commanding the garrison finally
surrendered. Hughes and many of his 800 men had been killed.
Several of the buildings were riddled with balls, and 26 of the
garrison lost their lives.

August 12th...Skirmish between Stockton, Cedar County, and
Humansville. Major Samuel Montgomery followed the Confederate
Commander Coffee to Stockton. He arrived at Stockton on the night
of the 11th, moving from Humansville toward Bolivar and then
changed his course to Stockton. The artillery and the 4th Missouri
Militia took the same road and came upon Coffee this morning just
at daylight. Fighting was brisk, with the Confederates moving now
in the direction of Montevallo. The cavalry is in full pursuit.
Also on the 12th, a skirmish took place at Van Buren in Carter
County. The surprise attack was made on a small Confederate camp,
killing two and capturing three. While there the Union soldiers
burned a mill and three houses, contrabanded seven horses, a wagon,
a team and the negro driver. Also captured was rebel mail from

McBride's camp in Oregon County which was going to Potosi.
McBridge has now gone to Batesville to organize and tells his men
he intends to take Greenville very soon. McBride now has 2,000
poorly-armed men and there are many without any arms at all.
Another expedition got underway from Ft. Leavenworth in Kansas to
the rescue of Independence. A very large force of Confederates is
threatening to take Kansas City, having already taken Independence.
August 12th found an expedition underway from Fort Gamble in search
of guerillas. The assistant surgeon and two cavalrymen were
seeking provisions and forage and were captured. They were located
and brought back to camp two days later. Besides the surgeon, they
brought in 49 prisoners.

August 13th...Having left Ft. Leavenworth on the steamer A. Majors
and arriving in Kansas City the same day, Lieutenant Colonel John
T. L. Burris, 10th Kansas Infantry, was informed that Independence
had been taken by a force of 400 led by Colonels Hughes and
Thompson. All Federal stores, ammunition, arms and much civilian
property had fallen into their hands. The Federal troops stationed
there were taken prisoner. Lieutenant Colonel Buel was taken
prisoner at his office three-quarters of a mile from the camp.
Captain Thomas (MSM) was taken prisoner at his family residence
about a mile from the camp and shot by the enemy. Captain Cochran,
at first firing, took shelter in a private house and remained there
until the fighting was over. Lieutenant Goss, who had slept in the
house of Corporal Miller upon starting together for camp, succeeded
in escaping but could not reach his command. Miller was killed.
Between 50 and 60 men managed to cut their way through and escape.
Buel is charging two of his command with cowardice, one Captain
Breckenridge who waved the white flag of surrender long before the
order was given, and Cochran who escaped to Kansas. Breckenridge
was arrested and taken to St. Louis. Buel reports 26 dead and 30
wounded. He also had learned that Kit Chiles (guerilla), Colonel
Hughes and Captain Clark are now buried at Independence.

August 14th-17th...Scouting from Ozark to Forsyth produced no
actions. The countryside is a desolate place. There is no forage
nor provisions on which troops can subsist.

August 15th...The Militia received intelligence that a large group
of outlaws or guerillas was encamped at or near the house of a Mrs.
Elliott near Linn Creek on the edge of Platte County, about three
miles south of Barry. Upon entering the neighborhood, one man was
taken prisoner, being "taken" along as a guide for the expedition.
Since the terrain was very hilly and wood covered, the plan to
dismount and surround the camp failed. Skirmishing broke out as
a result. The little expedition lost two men killed and seven
wounded. Several of these outlaws had taken cover in Mrs.
Elliott's house. There were three men in the house. The men
denied any knowledge of any camp within three miles of the place.
After the skirmishing, two of the men in the house were taken
outside and shot. The bedding and clothing were removed from the

house for the wounded Militia, and then the Enrolled Militia set fire to the dwelling and stables. The homes of Thomas Hamilton and Archibald Elliott were burned. These men had been in the camp. They took from Mrs. Elliott three or four horses and four negroes aged 12 to 20. Killed today by Colonel W. R. Penick, 5th Cavalry, Missouri State Militia, were James H. Rollins formerly of Parkville and Zack Elliott, the son of Mrs. Elliott. Supposedly with the gang are Jim Hopkins of Shapp's Cove, Holt County and J. S. Craig, a son of the "guide." All are reported to be "hanging" around Mrs. Elliott's home.

August 16th...At Lone Jack, just south of Independence, the guerillas made a successful fight with the State Militia. Major Foster with a command of about 600 men had been hunting guerillas and Confederates when he found more than he really wanted. They were estimated at 4,000, and on the approach of Foster's little force they turned and attacked him. Foster's men fought overwhelming odds for over four hours, and only after they had lost about 160 men were they finally overpowered. The National reinforcements were approaching and at this the large force retreated. The command of the Federals was actually eyeing the camp of Colonel Coffee, about one mile south of the town, and planning a surprise attack. However, when dawn came so did Hindman, Quantrill and Coffee, some 4,000 strong. The loss of life in the bloody affair was high. Of 36 men detached and supporting a Militia battery, 24 were wounded or killed. The battery guns, with horses all dead in the harness, were left behind. In a report it is told of damage to one gun and the spiking of another, but to the victor went the spoils. Union reported losses were 43 killed, 154 wounded and 75 missing. The Confederates acknowledged 118 killed.

August 20th-27th...Scouting in Wayne, Stoddard and Dunklin Counties. The scouting party started from Bloomfield with two officers, a 12-pounder howitzer and 80 men. About two miles east of Mingo Creek or 22 miles from Greenville, the infantry protecting the scouting party flank was fired upon by Confederates. The picket detail was handled with three killed and two taken prisoner. Another Confederate camp was found at Four Mile (a village on the road from St. Luke toward West Prairie).

August 21st...There is pursuit of Confederate commands and guerilla bands from Neosho heading south toward the Arkansas line. A Union scouting party camped at Daylight three miles south of Carthage. During this chase the mules and horses gave out. The artillery had to make camp at Elm Springs five miles south of Neosho. There were no horseshoes, nails or supplies and none were to be had in the countryside. Major Ransom (Union) on his way to Independence, stopped at the home of one Benjamin Rice and promptly burned his house and all of the outbuildings. Then Ransom upon arriving at Independence, took the editor, Mr. McCarty of the The Border Star, prisoner and distributed the type elsewhere.

August 22nd...Lieutenant Colonel John T. Burris (Union) moved his command today from Independence in the direction of Harrisonville. They marched about 12 miles and were near the headwaters of the East Branch of the Little Blue. Here information was received that Quantrill, Thompson and Upton Hayes were encamped about four miles farther up the stream, about 1,000 strong. The battleline formed on the farm of Charles Cowert. Because of the lack of water, the fight was called off. Union troops were unable to draw fire. The torch was applied to the farm. According to some ladies in the household, the house was being used as headquarters by these Confederate bands. Along with the house were the "immense ricks of grain and hay found on the premises." The rebels moved off toward the south. The Union troops took up position on an eminence near Hickory Grove. The rebels just kept moving south. A portion of the Federal command returned to Camp Moonlight near the Methodist Mission in Kansas.

August 23rd...Skirmishing at Wayman's Mill of Spring Creek. This mission was undertaken by Colonel John M. Glover (Union) to retaliate for the death of Lieutenant John Heusack who was killed today by Peabody. The Lieutenant's force crossed the path of the enemy at Wayman's Mills 25 miles southwest of Rolla. Prisoners were taken and were being transported under guard when an escape was attempted. Prisoners received injuries and some were killed. Captured were Robert Barnett, James Scott, Jonathan M. Stork, John B. Walthall (dead), Lieutenant William A. Edwards (dead), Elias Hopman (shot in the hip), Edmond B. Dixon (saber wounds to the head), a nephew of Honorable Thomas Price of Jefferson City and John Stephens, mostly Cole County residents. Another man died of saber wounds about the face, but he was unidentified.

August 24th...Colonel W. L. Jeffers (CSA) with 100 men attacked four companies of the 12th Cavalry, Missouri State Militia, under Major B.F. Lazear on Crooked Creek in Bollinger County after a short fight which drove them back. There was skirmishing again today at Coon Creek, Lamar. Brigadier General James G. Blunt's forces met up with some of Quantrill's men about eight miles south of Carthage. Supposedly Upton Hayes and Joseph Shelby's Confederate commands are with him. Blunt lost five men killed and 15 wounded. The 24th saw fighting near Bloomfield. Colonel Sempronius H. Boyd of the 24th Missouri Infantry (Union) was detailed there on the 21st to encounter the Confederates between Bloomfield and the Cape. Thirty men were killed and 16 surrendered. Also today a scouting party left Salem in a southerly direction toward Current River. Noon camp was made on the first day 20 miles from Salem on the Barren Fork of Sinking Creek. The afternoon trail followed five miles down Sinking Creek in a southwesterly direction, then changed course to the south six miles. This brought them to Current River. They continued down the river four miles in a southeasterly direction and halted for supper. In the evening, they resumed the march in a southerly direction six miles on the country road and halted at the house of Jackson Sugs. They searched the house but found nothing. The march continued in the same direction for another four miles and halted at Chilton's Mills. There a house was searched and again nothing was found. Next the house of Andrew Chilton was approached. In doing so, they were fired upon by someone in the house. The fire was returned, killing one man and wounding a woman standing near the man. No contraband was found in the house. The march continued in a westerly direction to the house of Cedrick Chilton, two miles farther. This house was surrounded. A search was made and three men were found, Alexander Chilton, Henry Smith and James Gallien, and shortly afterward, William Chilton. Also found was one gun, one U.S. saddle, two U.S. horses and two contraband horses. All were placed under guard. They resumed the march and halted at the house of Joshua Chilton. Three men ran from the house and were fired at. Jesse Conway was mortally wounded. Perry Chilton was shot as he headed for the brush, and Joshua Chilton was caught swimming through Jack's Ford after a pursuit of nearly a mile. The next day saw more homes searched, including the home of Andrew Marsh, suspected of being a member of Coleman's Confederate command. Horses were found. A bay mare in the pasture of Daniel Williams was said by his wife to be a stray. Another bay mare was found by Benjamin Conway. Also found were a bay mare and a horse secreted in the woods at Jackson Herring's. They took one man and the horses with them. Horses and colts were taken from Goforth, whose son rides with Coleman. Goforth escaped. The expedition ended on the 27th, and on this day they took a wagon and oxen team from Alfred Deathridge for transportation of the families of Daniel and David Smith. That evening they encamped at the residence of Joseph Conway.

August 28th...Fighting lasted one hour at Ashley between 150 seasoned rebels and 30 newly-enrolled Militia. Every man in the county is under arms. Moses Beck, one of the Confederates killed, was left on the field.

August 29th...Skirmish near Iberia, Miller County. Colonel Robert R. Lawther's command of Confederates met with Captain Long and his Enrolled Militia. One man was killed in each force. Lee Whittle of the Militia was one of these. Also today an expedition left from Waynesville. There was fighting at California House. Colonel Franz Sigel (Union) learned on the 29th that a large body of Confederates, about 300 strong, were moving through Texas and the southern part of Pulaski Counties, moving in a northerly direction toward his line between Lebanon and post at Waynesville. They were encamped about 13 miles south of the post where the Gasconade crosses the Springfield Road. Sigel deployed part of his command at the California House which is located about seven miles from the post at Waynesville, and the rest moved in search of the Confederates. The much sought after men crossed the road at midnight near the California House. Captain Murphy took up the chase for over 18 miles and succeeded in capturing Captain Peabody of Jefferson City and 28 of his followers. They surrendered to the Osage County Militia. In the skirmish seven were killed. Of Sigel's command three were wounded and one killed. McKerk (possibly McGirk?) Landing was a favorite crossing place for Peabody. All skiffs there were destroyed. Colonel Lawther was left sick in a house on the Gasconade and is now in the hands of Colonel Glover. More prisoners were brought in belonging to Coleman's band along with horses and arms. Three of the Confederate command were killed.

August 31st...Skirmish at Little River Bridge. Colonel White (CSA) fought fiercely for over an hour with Major Lippert (Union) today at a point 12 miles southeast of Pittman's Ferry.

September 1st...The 3rd Indiana Regiment commanded by Colonel Ritchie attacked and defeated a force of 600 Confederates, which included about 100 Cherokee Indians, at Shirley's Ford on Spring River. Sixty of the command were killed or wounded before they retreated. Shirley's Ford was hit again on the 20th by the guerilla forces.

September 4th...Scouts move through Callaway County. (This is also known as that of Prairie Chapel OR). The scouts divided, one part on the Columbia River and the other on the St. Aubert Road. The skirmish took place at the house of Givens. There some of Parcel's men attacked the Militia. They had stopped at Givens' house for dinner. Seven of Parcel's Confederates were killed before the hour was up and the Militia's scouts had used up their ammunition. Random shots were fired on the St. Aubert Road by the Confederates as they went in all directions.

September 6th...Captain Baird of Merrill's Horse was mortally wounded today when the command met up with Bushwhackers at Roanoke.

September 7th...Tice Kane, Bill Dunn and 80 guerillas attacked Captain Thompson's Militia at Lancaster.

September 8th-23rd...There was a large expedition from Ft. Leavenworth through Jackson, Cass, Johnson and Lafayette Counties. The command started in search of guerilla bands. They arrived at Westport, then on the 10th, moved out. They came within sight of a band on the North Branch of Grand River in Cass County, keeping up a steady pursuit day by day across four counties. They had one confrontation that lasted about 10 minutes at Smithfield, about five miles north of Pleasant Hill. The 10th Kansas Infantry, in its report, tells of burning the houses, outbuildings, grain, hay, etc., known to belong to about a dozen known marauders. They took 100 stands of arms, 10,000 rounds of ammunition, nearly 100 head of horses, four yoke of oxen, five wagons, a number of tents, dry goods and camp equipage. Also recovered was property stolen from Olathe, Kansas. Upwards of 60 colored persons followed them back into Kansas.

September 10th...Reports are in from fighting in Scotland and Boone Counties.

September 11th...Confederates made off today with a 24-pounder howitzer in a skirmish at Bloomfield. They are now headed toward Holcomb's Island with the howitzer in tow.

September 13th...Skirmish near Bragg's farm near Whaley's Mill. Brigadier General John McNeil met up with Joseph Porter's command. McNeil took 20 prisoners. Also on the 13th, there was a skirmish at Strother Fork of Black River in Iron County. In this sharp fighting five rebels were killed, seven prisoners taken, along with two rebel women and three Union men that had been held by the rebels, 35 horses, saddles, bridles and equipage were recovered. The horses were commandeered into service.

September 15th-20th...Scouting in Ralls County. The party left for the neighborhood of Ogles' Mill. The next day through the Salt River Bottoms, when near Sidney, Colonel Hayward was captured by Captain McDonald's Confederate forces. After scouting around the Salt River area, New London and Cincinnati, the commands met up again with the Confederates within two miles of Caleb Hurd's farm.

September 19th...Mount Vernon was entered by Confederate Captain Long and before any retaliation could be taken by the hidden Militia, he pulled back out. It was only after gaining the advance of the Confederates that the firing would commence. Five were killed, along with one of the Militia.

September 20th...Action on Shirley's Ford, Spring River. This report we have quoted in part.."HQ on Cow Creek. Sir; Yesterday morning at about 8 o'clock, our picket guard was fired upon, and a regular stampede of 1,500 women and children crowded into our camp for protection, making a Bull Run retreat. Everything seemed to partake of the spirit, but only after a moment when the orders were given, every man made ready for any emergency." This report is made from Colonel John Ritchie, commanding 2nd Indian Regiment. Colonel Ritchie sent out a detachment to surround the force. This worked, and he was successful in capturing the flag and killing at least two of their officers. The attackers were said to be forces under Confederate Commanders Stand Waite and Jackman.

September 23rd-24th...Major Frank J. White (Militia) took a command of 65 mounted men and a 6-pounder howitzer and set off on an expedition to Eureka in Boone County, taking a boat to Hibernia on the Missouri River and that night starting a forced march to Eureka. Confederate Captain Nevins was said to have been harassing the Union families. One aged informant spoke of the previous night of a band taking him for the purpose of hanging him; but were being scared off by some unseen noise. Captain Nevins (CSA) was captured at daybreak. He was disguised wearing a mask and had his arms upon him. Upon his person was found his oath of allegiance taken in Jefferson City, October 23, 1861. A drumhead courtmartial was held and the prisoner pleaded guilty to violating his oath and bushwhacking. The troops were then sent out to round up all the sympathizers in the immediate area to witness the execution. At noon on the 24th the sentence was carried out and the house of the prisoner burned to the ground. Then all the houses of the men who were in Captain Nevins' command were ordered to be burned to ashes. Captain Nevins, before his death, gave a list of those. The command then moved in the direction of Lindsey's Mill where an old camp was discovered. The command then marched between Eureka, Bloomfield, Claysville and Cedar Creek, arresting all prominent rebels along the way. Captain Nevins was shot.

September 26th...An unseen foe in ambush attacked near Cambridge in Saline County, killing three of the Militia. Information received put large Confederate movements operating at Fulton Landing and that a large force is concentrating on the Auxvasse near Moore's Mill. Major White (Militia) is at Millersburg in Callaway County. He will join with Krekel (Union) and move on Fulton.

September 27th...Fighting is reported 12 miles southeast of Warrensburg on Clear Fork. Confederate Commander T. C. Hawpes, Hawpes' Regiment, was ordered from Camp Coffee about five miles south of Newtonia to create an outpost there. An ideal site was found and Bledsoe's Battery was then brought up from Camp Coffee. Colonel Hawpes then placed pickets on the roads to Granby, Neosho and Mount Vernon Roads to watch for the movements of the Federals. By the next morning the Yankees were reported as moving on the Sarcoxie Road toward Granby, but when the scouts returned they had nothing to report of any signs of advancing armies. By 9:00 this same day, the Confederate pickets were fired upon from the brush two miles on the right of the road leading to Granby. Immediately seeking assistance from Camp Coffee, Colonel Cooper arrived, and the command spent the day. They returned to their camp in the evening, leaving only Colonel Hawpes, Colonel Shelby and Colonel Jones'/Jean's Regiments to defend the newly-organized outpost. On the morning of the 30th, there appearing no more sign of trouble with the Federals, Colonels Shelby and Jones/Jean also returned to Camp Coffee. Not more than an hour after making the report, the enemy tore loose with the guns and drove in the pickets. Again informing Colonel Cooper of the movements and dismounting his command, Hawpes set about defending himself. The men were placed behind a stone wall, about 50 yards below it, in the brush. Bledsoe's Battery was placed inside the stone fence. These men were the only ones under Hawpes' direct command. Shortly after getting his men into place, the Federals opened fire with their artillery batteries. One was about 600 yards west and the other the same distance to the northwest. Bledsoe's Battery gave favorable reply. After several shots were exchanged by the resounding artillery, the Federal infantry came up the ravine to

within a few hundred yards of the wall, when a young captain
belonging to Colonel Coffee's command, and not recognized by
Colonel Hawpes, in the slightest approached, but this young captain
who had represented himself as an aide to Colonel Cooper, started
cursing the men and calling them cowards and then ordered them to
come out from behind the wall and charge. That portion of the men
next to the wall were supporting Colonel Cooper's men. Colonel
Cooper's men, hearing this and believing him to be as he
represented himself, were soon all up and charging. After some
conflict with the infantry under heavy firing from the Federal
batteries, which were dangerously close, they fell back to the
position which was first assigned to them. As they were falling
back the Federal infantry charged and followed them back to within
gunshot range. It was as if all exploded now. They charged.
They were fired upon by Hawpes' men at the wall, then the men at
the wall charged past the Choctaw Regiment opened up by Bledsoe's
Battery, and both armies headed for the timber, then miles distant,
right in the face of the Federal batteries. Showers of grape and
canister now poured from the Federal cannons, falling down on the
pursuers. During this time, Howell's Battery had been planted
about 300 yards west of the town between Hawpes' command and the
Federals, supported on the right by Alexander and on the left by
Buster's Regiment, while Stephens was advancing from the direction
of Granby on the Neosho Road in the rear of the enemy's cavalry and
artillery. For over two hours the thundering batteries shook the
earth with round after round of shelling. The air was filled with
clouds of smoke laden with deadly grape and canister. Finally the
Federals started to falter and were moving back toward the outlying
brush. Hawpes' command, then all dismounted, was ordered to
support Howell's Battery and Jones'/Jean's Regiment in the pursuit
of the retreating Yankees. Just before dark the Federals opened
fire and killed a horse belonging to Jones'/Jean's Regiment.
Colonel Cooper came up with Howell's artillery, and after a few
well-placed rounds all was soon silenced. Darkness had overtaken
the day, and the pursuit was discontinued. The Confederate
commands returned to Newtonia. Thus ended the first day of
fighting known in history as the Battle of Newtonia. Heavy
casualties and severe injuries were suffered by both armies. The
deadly cannon took their toll. Colonel Hawpes remained at the
little outpost until the 1st when Colonel Shelby assumed command.
Shelby positioned his men about one and a half miles northeast of
Newtonia on the road leading to Sarcoxie. Shelby would be in
command of the scouts and all the pickets except those on the roads
leading from Granby, Sarcoxie and Neosho into Newtonia. Howell's
Battery remained at Newtonia and was supported by Colonel
Anderson's Regiment on the right and Colonel Buster's on the left.
Bledsoe's Battery was with Colonel Shelby. The various commands
remained in these positions until the morning of the 4th when they
were again attacked by the ever-advancing Federal Army.
October 2nd...Captain Cameron (CSA) met up with 80 men of the 9th
Missouri State Militia 15 miles northwest of Columbia. It is
believed that Captain Cameron is wounded and his horse was killed.

October 4th...Lieutenant Colonel M. W. Buster's (CSA) Indian Battalion took possession of Granby as ordered. Finding no water, he moved the whole command to Shoal Creek, a distance of about one and a quarter miles. One company was left to guard the road at the creek which led out of Granby on the left in a northwesterly direction. Another company was placed on the road leading to the right. A company was also placed on the main Sarcoxie Road leading out of Granby in a northerly direction. During the night, the company under Major Bryan that occupied the Sarcoxie Road, met with an assault by the enemy. Unable to maneuver the various commands due to the inky darkness, they all retreated to a more advantageous position. It then commenced to rain. According to the bugle heard, the enemy was flanking them. The men stood silent in the rain, sheltering their guns. As the large column of the enemy passed the left side, the command under Colonel Buster wound its way out and past the rear. Fearing for the town of Newtonia, toward which the enemy was now headed, a dispatch was sent ahead to warn them. The Colonel then set about to amuse the enemy for about three hours while the command at Newtonia could make preparation to defend its place and the big train that was there. The Colonel then took the road leading from Newtonia to Neosho and outflanked his aggressors. Upon arriving in Newtonia well ahead of the oncoming enemy, he found no one in command and no preparation made for the ensuing attack. After consultation with Colonel Shelby and Colonel Jones/Jean, and learning that communication had been cut from Newtonia to Camp Coffee, the little band retreated to a safer position under the fire of the cannon of General Schofield.

October 5th...Skirmishing today near Sim's Cove on Cedar Creek (this is 12 miles southeast of Columbia). Oden Guitar's command found only a handful of the Confederates still in camp. The main body had already moved northward. Those escaping had only the pants and shirts they wore, leaving all camp equipment behind.

October 6th...Eighty-eight men marched from Independence in a search and capture mission of guerillas. About four miles from town they netted their first two supposed Bushwhackers. Their horses, found in a cornfield, were also taken. The next call was at the Pruett house. He was a noted old rebel. However, they ascertained nothing as to the whereabouts of Quantrill. Scouting was continued in the neighborhood of Blue Springs. On the 6th, the mission took them to Fire Prairie and Sni-Bar in the direction of Sibley. All efforts and inquiries failed until they were within about two miles of Sibley. There the pickets were routed near the home of William Hughes on the State Road leading from Independence to Lexington. Pickets were also noted at Big Hill near Sibley on the same road, this being one of the most prominent heights in the countryside. Moving off, the scout passed the home of Mrs. Garrison about one mile from Sibley. Two horses were captured which belonged to the Bushwhackers, along with government equipment. Concentrated at Sibley they found the enemy encamped about a half mile distant from the town at a mill. In searching for a more advantageous position, they were attacked by about 130 men under Colonel Chiles and Quantrill. Hand-to-hand combat erupted. Colonel Chiles was taken prisoner and was thought to be mortally wounded. The rest of the notorious band took to the brush. A search was made but all that was found were the bullet-riddled hats, etc., of the rebels. As the going got tougher, desertion was noted on the part of the scouts. Sergeant Sheperson and Private Harrison had quit the trail. Quantrill is said to be headed now toward Lone Jack. In order to convey the dead, Captain Daniel H. David impressed buggies from William Hughes, Mr. Mellin and Mrs. Garrison. The chase was resumed and they met again on the 7th. After some hot firing, it was all over. Quantrill made his escape again.

October 11th...Captain Gabriel Kendrick, under Porter, surrendered himself, 27 men, 16 horses, saddles and as many guns and pistols. This man was said to have had a company of 120 men before the Kirksville action. Of these, 43 were killed or wounded and one-half again had been taken prisoner. Scouts were posted in Schuyler County, Clarke County and one each in Scotland and Lewis with orders to clean out the bands, large and small.

October 12th...Arrow Rock was the site of skirmishing today. The scouting party was fired upon by Jackson's men (CSA) with one man killed and four wounded. Richard Vaughn in his report of this affair echoes the sentiment of several commanders, "I shall not hereafter attempt to wage war against these men; it is idle sacrifice of men." He goes on to suggest that a levy of $15,000 be placed upon all their abetting friends in the county. The proceeds are to assist the families of the Militia, which are now destitute.

October 12th-19th...Expedition from Ozark, Missouri toward Yellville, Arkansas.

October 16th...Auxvasse Creek in Callaway County was the place of fighting and skirmishing today. A camp was broken up and the rebels are returning now to Boone in squads (I feel they are referring to the county.) Another camp was routed at Portland and the men were last seen fleeing north toward Monroe. In crossing his command at Portland, Porter pressed the steamboat Emilie into service. The Militia watched from the shore. The captain of the boat was disbelieved in his story of innocence and has been sent to Jefferson City.

October 18th...California House was the vicinity of the attack made by Porter's men. They were the same ones who had used the Emilie to cross the river. As he was trying to get across country, his trail was picked up and a hot pursuit began. Information gave the Militia the approximate crossing place near the California House,

about seven miles from camp (Waynesville), and the tactics worked.
Porter was surrounded and 20 of his command were killed. The
burial and tending to the wounded were left to the secesh of the
neighborhood. Two Union men held captive were released by this
skirmish. Also on the 18th there was a skirmish at Uniontown.
Reports from the field near Lancaster, Missouri state that Bill
Dunn and his men, 100 strong, are about three miles south of
Uniontown on the east line of Schuyler County. Dunn and his men
have now started to don the white bands on their hats confusing the
issue as this is standard for the Militia. Colonel S.M. Wirt took
10 prisoners from Dunn. The white bands were all that saved Dunn
from destruction this day. He was far outnumbered and in a bad
position.

October 20th...Confederate Colonel Dorsey moved up Niangua Creek
toward a point eight miles east of the Union post at Marshfield.
The command was organized by Majors Rucker and Hughes under Dorsey.
The large command then broke up into small squads and headed for
the mountains. On the 21st Dorsey's trail was followed over 50
miles until the horses finally played out. The local Militia was
summoned to carry on the pursuit. Confederate Colonel William H.
Todd was left behind as a prisoner.

October 23rd...Fighting at Clarkston. The Union forces by an
exerted forced march surprised the Confederates at Clarkston, 34
miles southwest of New Madrid. The first shells landed and burst
within their barracks. This killed Captain St. Clair, one
lieutenant, three noncommissioned officers, five privates and
mortally wounded two more. Colonel Clark in command was taken
prisoner, as were Captains Clark and Saterfield and 36 others.
Among items recovered were 100 stands of arms, 67 horses and mules
and a large amount of ammunition. The wagons, barracks and
magazine were burned.

October 24th-26th...Expedition from Independence to Greenton,
Chapel Hill, Hopewell (HQ Lexington). On the 24th the command of
Militia marched to Greenton 12 miles distant. The second day it
was ordered to the scene of a mail robbery by Quantrill. Mr.
Luther Green advised the detail that Quantrill had been to his
place the morning of the 22nd and had demanded breakfast. While
this was being prepared, the mail coach came by. Quantrill hailed
it down and took the mail sacks and ransacked them. After his
breakfast he headed toward Chapel Hill. There was immediate
pursuit. Upon reaching the village, Quantrill had already passed
through. They then marched to Hopewell. One Bushwhacker was seen
fleeing toward Blackwater Grove, but firing at him proved useless.
That night the command quartered in a church at Hopewell. The next
morning marching back to Lexington, upon hearing Quantrill had been
in Wellington, they moved toward that point. One person arrested
gave information that recruits were lurking around Napoleon.
Secret movements around that place netted five who claimed to be
conscripts. All persons appearing suspicious were arrested and

brought in. Captain C. C. Harvey, with the Captain's sanction, seized a carriage and two horses belonging to Confederate Colonel Reed. It seems Colonel Reed's lady had received an order from Colonel Deitzler, who was commanding at this post, to retain the property. "General Loan, thinks such property is contraband."

October 25th...Today one Boone (CSA) met up with Colonel Lazear while Boone was encamped between the waters of Pike Creek and Eleven Points. Eight of his band were killed and 18 were taken prisoner. Twenty-five stands of arms were recovered. He was chased over the hills. Crow's (?) company remains but has crossed east of the Current River. There was a large troop deployment from Camp Patterson across the Black River, which was very wide and deep, toward Pitman's Ferry in Arkansas.

October 29th...The 1st Kansas Colored Regiment was attacked by a superior force of guerillas near Butler in Bates County close to Osage Island. They charged upon them and made remarks and actions against the colored troops. They had a special hatred of them. This resulted in the colored soldiers standing their ground and hand-to-hand combat resulted. The colored soldiers refused to give an inch of ground or surrender. The losses were heavy. While Lieutenant Gardner was lying wounded and insensible, one of the murderous band took a knife and cut his gunbelt loose. The gun was then fired at the Lieutenant. Fortunately the bullet just grazed the top of his head. Lying next to him was a wounded colored soldier. He managed to gather enough strength to fire his gun. The rebel fell dead. (It is quite possible these were actually Confederate troops and not just guerillas.) Captain Crews had been killed, and one of the rebels was rifling his pockets. Another of the colored soldiers, though wounded, dispatched the thief with his bayonet. Upon the arrival of relief for the little command, the guerillas headed for the timber. The valiant command lost about 20 men. Also on this day there was a skirmish at Clarkton, Dunklin County, between some Illinois troops sent from Columbus and Colonel John M. Clark. The Illinois command, after capturing about 40 men and 60 horses, hastily retreated.

October 31st...Captain Foulk's command of Enrolled Militia fell in with a squad of guerillas, numbering 10, under Isaac Coppage, in the southern part of Monroe County. Lieutenant Gleason (Militia) surrounded the house and rushed in. Finding arms stacked in the hallway, he seized the arms and demanded the guerillas' surrender. After some demonstrations otherwise, they relented. These guerillas were under the command of Captain Williams.

November 1st-5th...Operations in Jackson County. Quantrill!! Ten more of his number are dead and another taken prisoner during a week-long pursuit. Operations began in earnest today in Boone County. Confederate Captain Cameron is being pursued by General Oden Guitar. The Captain is said to be attempting to cross the Missouri River in the vicinity of Rocheport. This report proved to be incorrect, so the country was scoured about three miles wide up to Land Mark. The party then struck out easterly toward Bethlehem. All was well until about 300 yards from the picket house. Two men were seen running for the brush. There was an immediate search. John W. Shipley was killed and his brother, James, taken prisoner. Lieutenant Colonel Williams in his report states that had he known who the man was he had captured, he would have shot him instantly. The man "was the most notorious scoundrel in Black Fork." The next day a scout was sent toward the neighborhood of Friendship Meeting House, 11 miles north of Columbia, and then east toward Mount Zion. Near Mount Zion, Confederate Lieutenant Colonel Peacher was captured. He claimed to be there for the purpose of recruiting. Also arrested were B.J. Batterton of Price's Army, who lives in Lewis County; another Confederate named Northcutt, who was with Peacher; and Frank Rouse. Informants state that Lieutenant Colonel Peacher is the ablest man in Boone County that ever joined the Confederate Army.

November 3rd...The Memphis Daily Appeal of November 3rd carried an account of the murder of 10 Missouri Confederate citizens by order of General McNeil of the U.S. Army. Also on November 3rd a skirmish occurred near Harrisonville in Cass County. Colonel Edwin C. Catherwood (Militia) returned to Sedalia where with a large supply train consisting of 13 wagons drawn by oxen. He was unaware of any of the roving bands being in the neighborhood except those he had dispersed from Pleasant Gap in Bates County. In the morning he was informed that Quantrill with 300 men was converging on him upon the divide between Harrisonville and Rose Hill. He immediately left with 150 men to overtake the train, but he was too late. Quantrill had already been there. Four privates were taken prisoner, four soldiers and six teamsters known to be killed, two soldiers and a teamster were wounded and four unaccounted for. Indications prove the men were killed after capture. The wagons were burned, but the oxen were saved. Lieutenant Newby was taken prisoner. Later after pursuing Quantrill, he was overtaken and the skirmishing broke out again. Newby was rescued. At this point Catherwood, after one more attempt to pursue Quantrill, quit the chase. His horses were worn down. Colonel Marvin and his Enrolled Militia would now take up the chase.

November 5th...Captain Martin Breeden, 8th Mo. Militia, was attacked at Lamar by Quantrill and some 300 strong. A running battle, almost from house to house, ensued. The Confederates rushed in and burned nearly one-third of the town.

December 9th-15th...Expedition from Ozark into Marion County, Arkansas.

December 13th...Charges were brought against Miss Lizzie Powell and Miss Maggie Creath. They are charged with stealing a buggy from Armstead Botts of Monroe County, then driving the buggy to Hannibal and bringing it out under the protection of the "petticoat flag" with some 50,000 gun caps and other essentials for the guerillas. Miss Creath has made quite a stir in Monroe County by traveling with Clay Price, a noted captain of the guerillas. These ladies openly declare that Jeff Davis is the greatest and noblest man who ever graced a presidential chair.

December 15th...Skirmishing at Neosho.

December 17th-21st...Expedition from New Madrid to Clarkton.

December 22nd...Missouri troops of the Department of Missouri operating on the Mississippi River were embodied in the 13th and 15th Corps, Army of Tennessee, Department of Tennessee.

December 23rd-31st...Operations in Sugar Creek Hills.

December 28th...New Madrid is evacuated by the Union. Through a mixup which was taken under investigation, the arms and stores of New Madrid were destroyed and its guns spiked with soft lead. When the orders came down, it seems there really was no order and great confusion as to who was in charge. Colonel John Scott, 32nd Iowa Infantry, did the work and was arrested for his efforts. "The abandonment of Fort Pillow (New Madrid) must be punished. General Carr reports that he communicated different orders to Colonel Scott. He should have obeyed Carr, not Daviess, and must be arrested."..Samuel R. Curtis, Major General. Daviess, according to reports, acted in accordance with the agreement of General Tuttle and General Fisk, thinking that Curtis would agree since a large force under Thompson and Jeffers was threatening to attack Fort Pillow. There was insufficient force to hold it. This investigation went as far as the Secretary of War and H.W. Halleck, General-In-Chief.

December 31st...John S. Marmaduke (CSA) leaves Lewisburg, Arkansas for his raid into Missouri.

So started the cold year of 1863.

1863

The year of 1862 dawned with renewed efforts on the part of John S. Marmaduke and Joseph Shelby (CSA). In the coming year they will each make famous raids on Missouri soil, their homeland. Marmaduke made his first from his winter quarters in Arkansas. He succeeded in regaining faith for the Southern Cause perhaps, but it was not to last long. The Federals who now had stepped up their operations across the state were in control. It took several of these raids to bolster the lagging spirits of the Confederate sympathizers in Missouri. Each jubilation was short lived. Even the guerilla bands, constantly pursued and attacked like well-sought-after prey, were now seeking a friendlier territory farther south. However, the heartland was still a very strategic point that the Confederacy needed. With it went the control of the rivers and the transportation they afforded. The countryside of Arkansas was stripped of forage. There was no food for man nor beast. Thus, Marmaduke made his play for some of the Federal riches in Missouri. Within the battle reports that are given the phrase, "they fight for bread," is repeated. Perhaps hunger did play a key roll. It is reported also that a huge train of wagons accompanied the party into Missouri. One is more than safe to surmise that these trains, or at least a portion of them, went back south into Arkansas well loaded with precious stores from the manned garrisons of the Federals. President Lincoln's final declaration of the Emanicipation Proclamation took effect. All over the United States the abolitionists rejoiced. In the new Confederate States, where conflict was waged, the slaves, some silently and some openly, gave thanks. The year of 1863 changed the nation as a whole. A way of established life was wiped from the face of the South. Life would never be the same for black or white. In Missouri the lack of slave labor had its effect, but slaves were still being sold as late as 1864. Missouri still was a divided state in loyalty, but the politicians in power held with the Union for the most part. After the Emanicipation Proclamation, slaves and former slaves could join the military service in certain states. In Missouri it was recorded that a least one slave had already taken up the cause. On August 6, 1862, in the action at Kirksville, it is reported as such by Lieutenant Colonel William F. Shaffer of Merrill's Horse. "In conclusion I must speak of Colonel McNeil's colored man Jim. To him belongs the honor of killing the first man in the fight. Armed with a Sharps rifle, he did splendid work through the entire afternoon. Whenever a rebel showed his head at long range, Jim was almost certain to get him."..and the war rages on.

January 3rd...Reoccupation of New Madrid by the Union Army. Upon arrival they found the magazine blown full of debris by the explosion when it was destroyed. The guns were spiked and gun carriages burned. The rest was in good shape.

January 6th...Beaver Station is burned by Shelby's command. This is also called Fort Lawrence on Beaver Creek, Lawrence's Mill,

Taney County.   Ten Union soldiers were killed and 17 taken
prisoner. The rest were routed. The Confederates captured a large
quantity of commissary stores, stands of arms and many wagons.

January 7th...In Ozark, Missouri the fort is captured by the
Confederates. Shelby burned it to the ground.

January 8th...Battle at Springfield. The battle at Springfield is
soundly claimed as a victory by both armies. The Federals remained
in control of the field but not without serious losses.   The
Confederate command, after forced marches of over 200 miles, was
tired and cold. Both sides mourned many casualties. Since both
sides basically report the same actions and the same results, we
are going to use Colonel Joseph O. Shelby's battle report for only
one reason. It's more entertaining than just the bare bone facts
of a battle. Colonel Shelby, I am told by others, did not write
or dictate his own reports. Personally, I like to think he did.
He was a colorful man indeed and daring in battle. One of the many
things that make me feel he actually did write the reports is it
has been said that he was a very compassionate man toward his men.
A very caring man. This is borne out in his descriptions of their
sufferings.

(This is to Marmaduke after the battle, written from Camp Carter,
31 January 1863.)

General; On the last day of December, 1862, when the old year was dying in the lap of the
new, and January had sent it's moaning winds to wail the requeim of the past, my brigade,
consisting of the First Regiment, Lieutenant Colonel B.F. Gordon; Second Regiment
Lieutenant Colonel C.A. Gilkey; Third Regiment, Colonel G.W. Thompson; the scouts, Major
Elliott, and Captain Quantrill's old command, under First Lieutenant Gregg, were on the
march for foray on the border's side.

The day was auspicious; a bright red sun had tempered the keen air to pleasantness, and
cheered the mounted soldiers with the hopes of a gay and gallant trip. The first two day's
march was long and comfortable; the third the rain commenced, cold and chilling, and
continued without intermission for three days, the grand old mountains standing bare
against the dull and somber sky, their heads heavy with the storms of centuries. The men
suffered much, but, keeping the bright goal of Missouri constantly in sight, spurred on and
on quite merrily.

For two days all went well. The third day my advance, consisting of Major B. Elliott's
scouts, came suddenly upon about 100 notorious bushwhackers and deserters, who fired
upon them quite stubbornly; but, upon dismounting several companies of Colonel Gilkey's
regiment, in conjunction with Elliott's battalion, and following them in their almost
inaccessible retreat, 20 were killed, about the same number wounded and many prisoners
taken, and this murdering, robbing, jayhawking band broken up completely and effectually.
Thus the skirmish of White Spring, successful as it was, proved to be the prelude of the
victories of Springfield and Hartville. The rain commenced now in earnest, and for three
days it's cold, merciless peltings were endured by the men without a murmur. Although the
sky was dark and barren as a rainly sea, and the keen northeast wind pierced the thin
clothing of the men with icy breath.

71

The 4th, 5th, and 6th were spent in long and cold forced marches, varied somewhat by Colonel Mac Donald's successful sally upon Fort Lawrence and your advance upon the fortified town of Ozark. Five miles from this place, by your order, I halted my brigade, and gave them time to forage their animals and cook something for themselves, which they did, and were again in marching order by 9:30 o'clock. At this place, and before we started to attack Ozark, I sent Major Elliott and his scouts and two companies from Lt. Col. Gilkey's regiment to gain a position in the rear of the town, on the road leading north, and cut off their retreat. He gained the position thus indicated, and but, gained it too late, for the Federals had left in hot haste long before Major Elliott could have possibly got around them. Upon arriving in close proximity to Ozark, and not being satisfied as to it's evacuation, I dismounted the half of each regiment composing the brigade, formed them as infantry, and feeling my way along slowly and cautiously, with numerous skirmishers, I soon found that the nest was there and it was warm, but the birds had flown and nothing remained to do but apply the torch to fort and barracks. Soon the red glare of flames burst out upon the midnight sky, and the cold calm stars looked down upon the scene. Several prisoners were taken here and any quantity of commisary stores, but, having no transportation, all except a small portion consumed by the men, were destroyed, and by 12 o'clock we were again marching northward. It was an intensly cold night, that of the 7th. and the frost hung heavily and chill on the garmets of my devoted brigade, marching on to the stronghold of the enemy with a determination in their hearts rarely surpassed.

The sun came up on the morning of the 8th, like a ball of fire, and the day was gloomy and chill; but Springfield loomed up before us in the distance like a beautiful panorama, and the men catching the inspiration of the scene, forgot all their trials, and hardships, and were eager for the rough, red fray. With flaunting banners, and all the pomp and circumstance of war, the Federals had marched gaily out to meet us, and taken their position on our front. I had dismounted, meanwhile, the First and Third Regiment, and was forming, them as infantry, holding Lieutenant Colonel Gilkey's command mounted until the position of the enemy was perfectly understood and all his motions thoroughly seen. When the plan of action had been decided upon, I then dismounted Gilkey's regiment and formed them as infantry, holding in reserve as cavalry Major Elliott's scouts and Lieutenant Gregg's company. Then forming my lines, I rapidly moved my brigade to the open plain south and southeast of the town, rested for a moment, making the final dispositions, and taking breath for the crisis. Major Elliott and Lieutenant Gregg were on the right flank, watching and skirmishing with the enemy there, and over the level earth squadrons of horse swept gaily and fantastically. T'was a bright and beautiful scene. There lay the quiet town, robed in the dull, gray hue of the winter, it's domes and spires stretching their skeleton hands to heaven, as if in prayer against the coming strife, and, drawing near and nearer, long black lines came gleaming on, while the sun shone out like a golden bar, uncurling it's yellow hair on earth and sky, stream and mountain, and lent the thrilling picture a sterner and fiercer light. My skirmishers advanced steadily and now continual shots in front tell that the enemy found and pressed sorely. On the extreme left you have organized Colonel Mac Donald's regiment into a storming party and sent it at the fort, and they could plainly be seen winding over the crest of the hill and moving rapidly to the attack. MacDonald has met the enemy and is driving them, but, they soon re-enforced, and would in turn compel him to retreat. I saw the crisis, and ordered Lieutenant- Colonel Gordon and Lieutenant-Colonel Gilkey to charge with their regiments to support Mac Donald. Gallantly it was done, and as gallantly sustained. At the command, a thousand warriors sprang to their feet, and, with one wild Missouri yell, burst upon the foe; officers mix with men in the mad melee and fight side by side; some storm the fort at the headlong charge, other gain the houses from which the Federals had just been driven, and keep up the fight, while some push on after the flying foe. The storm increases and the combatants get closer and closer.

I heard the cannon's shivering crash,
As when the whirlwind rends the ash;
I heard the musket's deadly clang,
As if a thousand anvils rang!

In this charge a regiment of Federals, just sent from their main fort were scattered and driven back, and their entire force forced into their heavy earthworks, surrounded by rifle pits and other obstructions. I cannot fail in this connection, to speak of the daring charge of Capt. L.J. Crocker, Company K. First Regiment; Lieut. William H. Ferrell of Company F, same regiment, and about a dozen other reckless spirits from Gordon's and Gilkey's regiments upon one piece of artillery, supported by a battalion of Iowans, but who fled after a sharp hot rally and suffered their gun and cassion, filled with valuable ammunition to be borne in triumph to the rear. The battle thickens; Colonel Thompson, who had been stationed on the right with his regiment, and who did not participate in the charge, but, who was watching and foiling the movements of a large body of cavalry in that direction, was now ordered up, and advanced with spirit and alacrity. The battery which accompanied the expedition from Lewisburg, commanded by Lt. Richard A. Collins, and consisting of one rifled piece and one smooth bore 6 pounder, was advanced, one piece brought up into the very town, and opening at point blank range with grape and canister. The Federals re-enfored largely, and came back with cavalry and artillery, and a hot, desperate conflict ensued; one side struggling to hold the position gained, the other to drive them from it. Bravely my fighting brigade meets the onset, and stubbornly they resist; blow falls on blow, shot meets shot. Lieutenant Gordon leads the gallant First, and they never fail. Major Shanks and Lt. Colonel Gilkey and Colonel Thompson are piloting their regimments, bravely, and well, and the contest rages, and the wild death dance goes merrily on.

Still Collins plies his lurid torch,
Where balls will rend or powder scorch;
Still Shanks and Gordon, side by side,
Like veteran heroes stem the tide.

This stern sanguinary fight was kept up for hours, and even into the night the roar of artillery and small arms was incessant. On the right, Lt. F.M. Scott made a bold and daring charge, breaking the first line of Federals in splendid style, and only retiring when accumulated numbers made it madness to advance.

About 3 o'clock, I had Major Elliott's scouts dismounted and brought up in the town, forming in the rear of and supporting Collin's iron 6 pounder, which moved along the various streets as unconcerned as if peace were made and he was firing a salute over the joyous event, although he was constantly exposed and always in range of minie musketry.

Night came down with weary, brooding wings, laid her dark brow across the cloudy sky, and threw her sable mantle over fort and wall and house and men, checking the bloody strife, and calming the furious passions that had been at war all day. I drew my brigade off calmly and cautiously, formed them in and around the heavy stockade, threw out trusty skirmishers and prepared to pass the night as best I could, although it was very cold, and the men had no fires, save the smouldering fragments of consumed houses, burned by the terrified enemy at our first approach. When all was quiet, Collins, with his iron 6 pounder and a small support made a promenade upon the principal streets of the city. Acting upon the principle of the Irishman at a Donnybrook fair, who, whenever he saw a head, hit at it, so this little party, whenever a light appeared fired at it, and it served not only to encourage our still victors, but to hold the foe, with thunder tones, that we were still victors, proud and defiant. The men lay on their arms until about 2 o'clock in the morning,

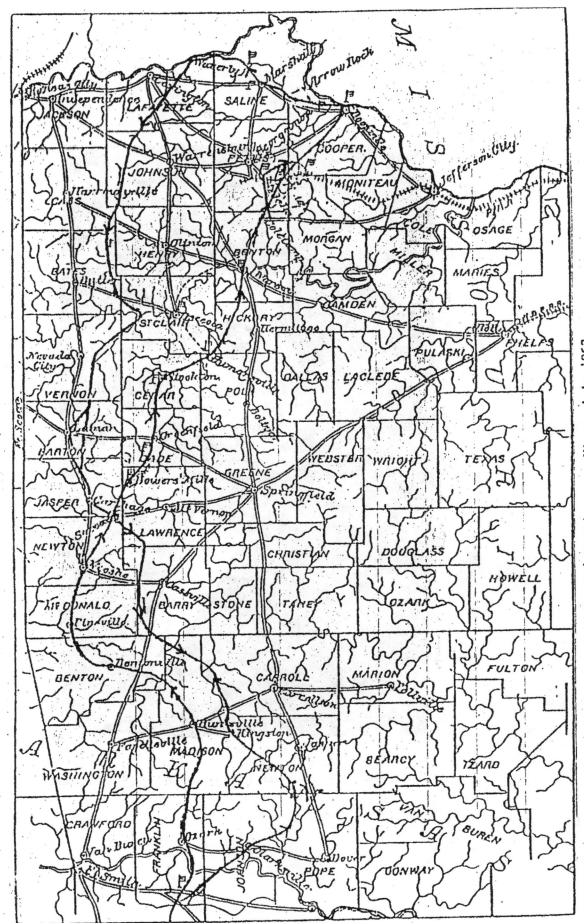

Shelby's raid across Missouri in 1863

Jefferson Davis
Confederate States Of America, President

when I deemed it best as they were suffering greatly from cold and hunger to withdraw, which was done quietly and in order. In the charge beyond the stockade, after that had been won, and almost upon the enemy's guns, H.S. Titsworth, captain of Company H, First Regiment, fell, badly wounded and has since died. The South had no nobler champion, our cause no braver defender, and he with Major Samuel Bowman, of Lt. Col. Gilkey's regiment and Lieutenant John W. Buffington, second lieutenant of Company H, First Regiment, form an illustrious trio - three of the grand "immortal names that were not born to die". Peace to their ashes! When the warfare of this world is over, when time strikes records with eternity, and mortality is paling beyond the sunset shore, and the billows of dissolution are white with the wrecks of the universe, these deathless spirits will rise beautiful from their urns of death and chambers of decay, and join the noble band of Southern martyrs that have fallen "with their backs to the field and the feet to the foe."

After the men had breakfasted the next morning, after ammunition had been distributed, and a leisurely forming of the brigade effected, we started from the scene of the hard fought battle. The mission had been accomplished; two forts had been captured, a piece of artillery taken, several hundred prisoners paroled, considerable commissary stores destroyed, and, we, after making almost a circuit of the town, with floating banners and waving pennons, left it alone in it's glory, because all had been done that could be done."

The fort Colonel Shelby refers to was a brick college used as a military prison enclosed on three sides with palisades. It was centered in the Federal front. (At least we feel this is the building he makes mention of.) The houses were burned earlier by the Federals. Visually they were unable to see the oncoming enemy on the open prairie. General E. B. Brown was shot from one of the remaining houses the Confederates occupied later. This resulted in the loss of his arm. The fighting lasted 13 hours. Federal forces numbered 2,099. Confederate estimates are around 3,000 to 4,000. Brown states 5,000. General Brown's command also consisted of what was known as the "Quinine Brigade." These were convalescents from various homes and hospitals, numbering some 300. Men whose enlistment had run out were commandeered, as were many citizens, and all were given arms.

January 9th...A Federal garrison is captured and surrendered to Confederate forces. Colonel Shelby burned the fortified post at Sand Spring. MacDonald went to Marshfield and destroyed the fort and stores, and the Federals are on the move to Rolla.

January 10th...Skirmish at Carrollton. The Confederates coming from Austin via Hartville met up with Federal resistance on the night of the 10th at Harville. Marmaduke decided to fight his way through, as he knew he was closely pursued. If he made it he would have an open road back to Arkansas. Thus, he did, fighting all the way for about five miles. The confrontation with 2,500 Federals from Iowa, Illinois, Michigan and Missouri took place at Hartville. There were many casualties on both sides. The loss of Emmett MacDonald, Major Kirtley and Lieutenant Colonel Weimer was a key blow for Marmaduke. Some of his very best were left behind.

Colonel J.C. Porter was also left behind seriously wounded. He was shot from his horse at the head of his command. There were 15 dead and 70 wounded in Marmaduke's command. The Federals sent in a flag of truce to bury their dead. Also taken by Marmaduke at Hartville were stands of arms and 150 great coats. A grand total for January 2nd-11th shows Confederate losses at 262 killed, wounded and missing.

January 11th...Skirmish at Wood Creek also known as Wood's Fork. Colonel S. Merrill of the 21st Iowa met up with the retreating columns of the Confederates.

January 13th...Skirmish at Carthage.

January 21st...Colonel Joseph B. Douglass took a Confederate camp about nine miles from Columbia. Four captains out of eight were taken but not before they had exhausted all their ammunition in the direction of their captors.

January 25th...Marmaduke's command reached Arkansas. He has this to say, "The expedition was extremely hazardous and trying one. On leaving Lewisburg and Pocahontas, the men were indifferently armed and equipped, thinly clad, many without shoes and horses, marched without baggage wagons and or cooking utensils, carrying all they had on their horses and subsisting as best they could on the country through which they marched. The horses were worn by continued and active service of many months; were, for the most part, unshod, very poor, and unfit for any service. At least 200 of the command abandoned their horses by the roadside to die and waded many a weary mile through the snow and deep mud, some barefooted, yet they encountered every danger willingly and endured all fatigues cheerfully." (This is the army that Hindman ordered to go to Missouri!)

January 27th...Colonel James Lindsay with 250 of his Enrolled Militia dashed into Bloomfield with two small pieces of artillery and broke up a small rebel camp in town.

February 2nd-13th...Scouts and skirmishes in and about Mingo Swamp. Confederate General McGee's command, at least a small portion of it, was taken today. There were three killed and two wounded. He is considered the terror of the whole country. Of the original band only three are left; Hetterbrand, Cowan and Dixon. One of the two men in the guardhouse is of a particularly bad character. He is from California. Since returning he has been involved with counterfeiting and is a slave thief. Prior to his arrest he was a member of McGee's band. This scouting mission was taken through a swamp covered with ice and the water receded from underneath, and through a violent thunderstorm that lasted two days. The trail led them to swim the Castor River and proceed to the house of S. Cato, who had been harboring the band for some months. The order was "no prisoners." Nine were killed, among which was McGee. Trying to escape through a cornfield which surrounded Cato's house, he was shot. Twenty were mortally wounded. The dead were left for their good friend's care and burial. Other information gleaned was that Colonel Jeffers is at Epsom Bottom about 150 miles below Bloomfield.

February 3rd...Skirmish at Independence. A small rebel band of guerillas was attacked. Eight were killed and two wounded. About four or five escaped.

February 19th-22nd...Scouting party in Jasper and Barton Counties. On the 19th Captain Reeder with 30 men was bringing in the worn out horses and the corpse of one of the men who had died the evening before. He crossed the line of march of Major Edward B. Eno of the 8th Militia from Shoal Creek to Fidelity. No incidents occurred. The command was then sent down Centre Creek then up the Spring River to Carthage where it encamped. The Enrolled Militia of Bower's Mills was after Tom Livingston (CSA), who made good his escape. The Militia had overtaken him with about 60 of his men on Dry Fork of Spring River. He is now headed toward Lamar.

March 1st-2nd...After swimming his command across the swollen, freezing-cold Castor River, Lieutenant Frederick R. Poole (Militia) succeeded in capturing the rebel Provost-Marshal of Bloomfield and killing a Confederate recruiting officer, Lieutenant J.D. Brazeau of St. Louis.

March 3rd...Raid by Confederates on Granby. Livingston and his followers dashed into Granby at night. Two patrol guards were captured, disarmed and probably killed as nothing has been heard from them since. Two other soldiers who were attending to a sick family a short distance outside the stockade were dragged away, pleading for their lives, and were shot and killed. Livingston rapidly went on, not venturing to attack the stockade. Livingston attacked Major Eno's command. This was the same one that had been chasing him and killed several of his men.

March 5th-13th...Operations about Newton and Jasper Counties. A detachment left camp on March 5th and proceeded to Newtonia, Newton County, a distance of 25 miles and encamped for the night. On Friday, the next morning, the detachment headed for Granby and scouted Shoal Creek thoroughly, then proceeded on to Neosho. On Saturday they left Neosho, scouted the countryside and camped at Savilla, a little village containing about a dozen houses. Each house contained several rebel sympathizers. That night the detachment lost a very valuable horse. On Sunday they went to Diamond Grove, a distance of about five miles from Savilla. The search there was unsatisfactory in locating any Confederates. It then moved down Turkey Creek and went to Sherwood in Jasper County, a distance of about 18 miles. There they remained until the next day. Striking a trail, they followed it and were fired upon by pickets. Shots were exchanged. Sergeant Fountain received a severe face wound. The rebel picket was also wounded but not seriously. The camp was located in the woods and had contained 70-80 men who belonged to Tom Livingston. They had left in a hurry, cutting halter ropes, etc. The chase began with the detachment's advance pickets and continued some three-quarters of a mile. Then suddenly Livingston turned and made the attack. The advance was forced to fall back to the main command hotly pursued by the Confederates. After a spirited firing contest, it was over. The Confederates used the attack and retreated quickly. Considerable loss to the horses of Livingston's command was witnessed in the woods after the skirmish. The next day the little detachment was furnished with 40 Indians as scouts, the trail picked up again and followed about 35 miles to Crawford in Indian Territory. The horses being played out, it was decided to return to Savilla. Hearing firing the next morning as they prepared to leave Savilla, the Indians were sent into the woods as flankers. They encountered two men from Company A who had left their commands to take breakfast at a private house, and upon returning toward camp were fired upon, taken prisoner and disarmed. One of them, badly wounded, was left on the trail. This man was retrieved and sent under guard of the Indians by wagon to Neosho. The order was issued that no one would leave the command without permission of the commanding officer.

March 9th-15th...Expedition from Bloomfield, Missouri to Chalk Bluff and Gum Slough, Arkansas and Kennett and Hornersville in Missouri. Two mountain howitzers, along with about 500 men, made this expedition "over such roads that only the swamps of the earthquake region of Missouri can produce." At Chalk Bluff a large store of corn and grain, all the buildings, and two ferryboats were burned. After proceeding on to Gum Slough in Arkansas to the fort encampment of General Thompson, they crossed again that night and camped at Kennett, Missouri. Two days were spent in scouting the country. The capture of 60 Confederates was reported by the command. The commands of Confederate Generals Thompson and Clark are now driven from Missouri into Arkansas. (The report also states, "The war steed of General Thompson, which proved to be a mare heavy with foal, fell into our hands, and the last that was heard of this doughty hero he was floating down the Saint Francis, the solitary tenant of a dug-out, quite drunk and very melancholy.") The command marched back about 46 miles to Bloomfield and encamped in position on the road from the Bluff to Bloomfield, hearing the command left at Four Mile had been attacked and forced to fall back about six miles. In all, this detail marched about 184 miles in six days. Colonel John McNeil also states, "I administered the oath to over 100 citizens, and could have done so to many times that number had they not been scared off by extravagant reports of our killing unarmed and innocent persons. The covers on the guidons, for it rained considerable amount of the time, were taken for black flags, and the story that we were marching under that peculiarly Southern emblem widly circulated. Rape and murder were charged upon us, causing the men to flee to the swamps. The women alone stood their ground, either not believing the charge or not fearing the consequences."

March 19th-23rd...The scouting party of about 75 Militia left Bloomfield to reconnoiter west of the St. Francis River. Twenty-five men were left posted at William's Crossing on the St. Francis, under the command of Lieutenant Donahoo, to guard two ferryboats. One had been captured on the Mingo and the other at Punche's Crossing on the St. Francis River, along with several canoes, all of which were floated downstream to William's Crossing, three-quarters of a mile south of the junction of the Mingo with the St. Francis River. On the 20th the command was at Poplar Bluff, camping that night at the foot of the bridge over Blackwater River on the east side of the village. On the 21st the enemy pickets were encountered. This confrontation ended in two being killed, but not until one of the two being pursued killed the horse of the pursuer. At the same instant, the rebel's horse was killed. Both horses fell close together, their riders falling together and ending up rolling over and over until the rebel picket broke free and started to escape on foot. Then he was dispatched. This affair took place within three miles of Doniphan. The telegraph was found torn down and the wire strewn carelessly along the road. Several horses were thrown by it in the charge, and some riders were injured quite seriously.

March 22nd...Skirmish at Blue Springs near Independence. Today a large guerilla force, about 12 miles from Independence, drove back a detachment of the Militia killing nine and wounding three before safety was reached by the Militia.

March 24th-April 1st...Large scouting mission from Bloomfield to Scatterville. High water caused considerable problems with this mission by the 1st Wisconsin. The enemy was in possession of the bluffs around Chalk Bluff and skirmished with the pickets. The 1st Wisconsin had to build a raft to ferry their men across. The horses refused to leave the bank due to the high, cold water. The men recrossed and a footbridge was constructed. This afforded crossing for the men. The horses swam along the side of the bridge. Arriving in Scatterville on the 28th, they located a cold camp and upon returning, the enemy was encountered. After a skirmish, the Confederates scattered. The little detail returned to camp and from there to West Prairie and on to Post Bloomfield.

March 28th...Confederates attacked and took the steamer Sam Gaty.

April 1st-5th...Scouting party from Linden to White River. Forty-one men under Captain M. U. Foster went south passed Lawrence's Mill to the head of Little Fork, passing down that stream to White River where he crossed and fell in with three armed guerillas who were killed on the spot. Recrossing the river, he traveled about 25 miles. Near the mouth of Sister Creek, he happened upon Confederate Captain John McClure who was killed in the attempt to run away. Two others were killed at the saltpeter works. Van Zandt, former clerk of the Taney County Court and a noted rebel, was killed by the Enrolled Militia a few days ago.

April 4th-6th...Second Division, Army of the Frontier, marched from Elk Creek to Camp Totten 10 miles southwest of Rolla, a marching distance of 55 miles.

April...Skirmishes in Carroll County. Four skirmishes with Bushwhackers were reported. Captain McFarlane (Union/CSA?) was reported as killed and Captain Walker is a prisoner. Confederate Captain Smith has also been killed.

April 17th...Captain Humphrey reports from his scouting mission in the White River country about 18 miles from Cassville. The enemy, 200 strong, was reported as being encamped at or near Moore's Mill on White River. Another camp is at Leashure, Wood Creek. They have been concentrating there for three days. They are reported to be part of Shelby's and Marmaduke's commands. In a skirmish that ensued, Captain Humphrey lost one man and nine are missing. Nine horses were also lost.

April 21st-23rd...Second Division, Army of the Frontier, with all the cavalry of the Division and Battery E, 1st Missouri Artillery, marched to Pilot Knob to meet a cavalry raid under General Marmaduke. On the 21st Marmaduke's command, estimated to be 2,000 to 4,000, drove Smart's Regiment out of Patterson, causing casualties. Smart has fallen back upon Pilot Knob. Fighting first broke out on Reeve's Station Road. The Confederates lashed out with six pieces of artillery and had about 1,500 to 3,000 men. The fighting continued over an area of eight miles in length. Smart burned all stores as he retreated toward Big Creek about eight miles from Patterson. Smart lost about 50 men today. Remaining movable troops of the district are being called in and placed in position at the Knob and Glover. Around 100,000 rounds of ammunition are being sent to General McNeil. Marmaduke lists his command as Shelby's Cavalry Brigade, Green's Cavalry Brigade, Carter's Texas Cavalry Brigade and Burbridge's Brigade composed of Burbridge's Missouri Cavalry Regiment and Newton's Arkansas Cavalry Regiment, in all about 5,000 men plus eight pieces of field artillery and two light mountain pieces. Of this force about 1,200 were unarmed and some 900 dismounted. The armed portion of the command carried mostly shotguns, some with Enfield rifles and Mississippi rifles and some with common squirrel rifles. He brought them all, the dismounted and the unarmed, with the hope and possibility that he could provide them both with the spoils of war, and also fearing if left behind they would desert. He split his forces and sent them toward Patterson by two different directions. First, because of forage and the hopes of picking up arms and horses along the way. They finally reached Chalk Bluff the evening of May 1st. In the report of Colonel G.W. Thompson, he lists his command as that of Shelby's, which he was detailed to take,

Lieutenant Colonel B. F. Gordon's, Colonel Beal G. Jean's and his own regiments with Major Shank's Battalion and Captain R. A. Collins' Battery of four guns. He had an effective force of 1,250 men. Upon his arrival in Fredericktown he was pleased by the capture of the "Gamble Sheriff," telegraph operator and a number of the Enrolled Militia. The detail also accomplished the burning of the Mill Creek Bridge on the Iron Mountain Railroad after a surprise attack and much confusion. They cut the telegraph wire for good measure.

April 17th-May 2nd...Marmaduke makes another raid into Missouri. This involved fighting at Patterson on the 20th and Fredericktown on the 22nd. On the 24th there was a skirmish at Mill or Middle Creek Bridges. The 26th saw actions at Cape Girardeau and Jackson. The 27th saw skirmishes at White Water Bridge and Jackson. On the 29th there was action at Castor River, and on the 30th there was fighting at Bloomfield. The command of Marmaduke then crossed back into Arkansas and fighting continued for two days at Chalk Bluff, St. Francis River. Union losses from this raid are listed as 129 killed, wounded and missing. The Union brought out the gunboats for this fight.

On the 26th...General McNeil makes a report that he was attacked by about 8,000 under the command of General Marmaduke at Cape Girardeau. Two steamers full of reinforcements arrived today. The gunboats are in reserve and readiness. By the 26th, General McNeil received by flag of truce a demand for surrender within half an hour signed by General Sterling Price. It is thought that Price is not with the Confederates. Eight hours later the firing commenced in earnest again, and Price indeed was not present. The thought was that if the note was written and his name added, it would bring about the results of a surrender.

The 28th finds Marmaduke's command building rafts to cross the river. Retaliation is planned at the ford. Larger, longer-range guns are being brought up. The Confederates showed eight pieces of artillery. The two columns of the Confederates encamped at a place four miles from White Water. They succeeded in destroying the bridge across Crooked Creek between McNeil's Brigade headquarters and William's Ferry. McNeil needs more support for his flanks. The Confederates are now only five miles ahead of him.

May 1st found the command of General McNeil driving Marmaduke ahead of him. He peppered the rear guard with howitzer fire. This pursuit started on the 27th with constant pursuit. The first day of pursuit was over 16 miles, reaching the White Water. The bridge being totally destroyed, it was rebuilt the next day. Following rebuilding the bridge, the command marched 32 miles over very bad roads. They encamped about three miles from the Castor River. (The Castor is located about six miles from Bloomfield.) The Confederates being encamped on the river edge, Lieutenant Poole (Union), who had been itching to make an attack, took it upon himself and five others. In this foray two Texans were killed and Lieutenant William Bast of Thompson's command was captured. Upon hearing the enemy were probably not able to cross the river due to the recent heavy rains, scouts were sent to ascertain more information. The scouts reported back the Confederates had been crossing the river all night, many of their men drowning in the swollen river. They now were waiting for the Union troops on the opposite bank. The long-range guns were brought up and the places of hiding became so much brush. The Confederates moved on and took up a strong position at Bloomfield. The next morning as dawn broke the spirited firing commenced. The thundering of the big guns of McNeil's artillery broke the silence at 5:00. The shelling continued within the town and at the ensconced Confederates until about 10:00 when the Union, with all they had, entered the town from the north. The rebels exited by the south road toward Chalk Bluffs. Following them another attack was forced, and this attack continued through one position after another for 20 miles. Finally they crossed into Arkansas. Marmaduke reports losses at 161 men of his command.

April 18th-21st...Back in Missouri a scouting party was sent from Salem to Sinking Creek, Current River, and Big Creek, Shannon County.

April 19th-20th...Scouting near Neosho. A small detachment of 30 men, 8th Missouri Militia Cavalry, went in the direction of Seneca Mills in search of notorious Bushwhackers, encamping at Scott's Mill. One of the party discovered some of those desired and two of them were killed. Also located in a pasture near Cowskin Prairie was a number of cattle intended for the Confederate Army. More Bushwhackers were ousted from several houses and killed.

May 3rd-11th...Scouting in Cass and Bates Counties. Confederates Jackman and Marchbanks were located, and a hot pursuit and skirmish followed. The scouts also took a few yoke of oxen, mares and colts, young horses one and two years old, cows and calves and young cattle, in all about 350 head. Also taken were about 300 sheep. This is believed to be the property of Bushwhackers and Confederate sympathizers.

May 4th...Operations around Lexington. Captain Morris, 4th Missouri State Militia, returned with 27 prisoners taken near Wellington. From the reports around Lexington, it appears that four or five men were considering robbing a boat. A citizen named Chancellor talked them into relenting. They opted to send a man upstairs for cigars and a can of whiskey. These men were later seen eating lemons and smoking cigars as they went into the upper Missouri bottoms. Their movements were followed about daybreak at Totetes above Wellington on the Lonejack Road. They were heading south. An order was also given on the 4th ordering all the men who were not friendly toward the U.S. Government out of the town of Lexington. Those not taking part were placed under arrest and their businesses closed. This is in reaction to the reformation of the county. Lieutenant Colonel Walter King's most trusted spy, John DeCourcy, brought news that Quantrill is at Lexington, coming from Price to conscript, and has about 40 men with him. He has joined up with Reed's, Jarrett's,, Todd's, Younger's and Clifton's gangs. They are now about 125 strong. He has orders from Price to stop bushwhacking and horsestealing. Price reportedly will invade Southeast Missouri and Quantrill is to annoy the Kansas and Missouri borders. Quantrill seems to be rather elevated in his purposes by his six months in the regular army. Lieutenant Colonel King will send a man into Quantrill's camp under cover.

May 5th-9th...A Confederate camp was discovered on Centre Creek near the town of Sherwood. A detachment of the 2nd Kansas Cavalry was dispatched to attack and disperse them. After adding reinforcements from the 1st Kansas Colored under Lieutenant Daniel C. Knowles, the camp was broken up and Knowles attacked another one closer to the town, taking a few prisoners and some 50 head of mules and horses.

May 6th-19th...Confederate Major Tom R. Livingston met up with a scout from his enemy while he was en route to Missouri from Creek Agency, Indian Territory, toward Jasper County. He had crossed the Verdigris River at Sandtown, camped for one day at Union Saline Salt Works, and from there moved up the Texas Road. Arriving at the house of Captain Martin on Cain Creek, the scouting party was met. They came from Fort Scott. Skirmishing ended up with one of the scouting party dead and one wounded. Major Livingston then made his way into Jasper County. On May 15th, as he crossed the timber of Centre Creek about 10 miles southwest of Carthage, he encountered a scouting party of about 125 Militia from Newtonia. Sharp fighting began and the Militia was forced to give way. Livingston pursued them about three miles. The Militia lost, according to Livingston's report, 13 killed, four mortally wounded and four prisoners. After the chase Livingston retired to Twin Groves about three miles distant. The next day, the 16th, the Militia was reinforced to about 400 and Livingston moved on to Spring River but was not pursued. On the 18th Livingston's scouts reported 60 negroes and white men belonging to Colonel J.M. Williams' Negro Regiment, with five 6-mule teams, foraging upon Centre Creek Prairie. Ordering out some 67 of his best mounted, the quarry was found at Mrs. Radar's house, and they pillaged her premises. They were routed and chased about eight miles to the crossing of Spring River. The Union loss was 23 negroes killed and seven white men. Also captured were some 30 mules and five wagons, arms and ammunition. The following day the Union troops returned with about 300 infantry and two companies of cavalry. They burned the town of Sherwood and 11 farmhouses in the vicinity. Into the house they put 10 of their dead (negroes), who had been left on the field from the preceding day, and the body of Mr. John Bishop, a citizen prisoner whom they had murdered at the house of Mrs. Radar.

They then burned the premises. They rode away to their camp at Baxter Springs (Livingston's report).

May 9th...Skirmishing in Stone County. The scouting party of Captain Moore (Provisional Regiment Enrolled Missouri Militia) came upon a party of Bushwhackers, some 50 in number, who were driving south stock which they had stolen from the farmers in the area. The stock and mules, blankets, overcoats, etc., will be returned.

May 13th-18th...Scouting from Newtonia to French Point and Centre Creek. Major Livingston and about 100 splendidly-armed men were attacked near the Centre Creek lead mines. They had taken refuge behind an old log shop. The fighting was described as hand to hand, both sides in the brush for a while. The guerillas were wearing Federal uniforms, thus they were taken as friendly. A most serious fight took place before things were under control. Captain Cassairt's (Union) men took off to safety in the hills. They were finally rallied and brought back. The good Captain threatened to shoot the first man who dared move another step in retreat. Captain Henslee's (Union) horse became most unmanageable at the noise of the firing and could not be reined. It dashed right through the rebel camp with the Captain hanging on. Then the horse barely under control, the Captain raced madly back again through the camp in order to save himself and not be cut off and run down. The Captain taking advantage of the surprise, used his revolver to the best and dispatched at least one guerilla on the return trip. It was reported that 50 guns, no less, were fired at him upon his unexpected thrilling ride. He escaped unhurt. It also was reported by some ladies that they were present when Major Livingston buried some 12 of his dead, all in one grave. Livingston had to pass by Captain Ballew's Artillery guns at the only crossing open to him. The guard at the guns became scared and fled his post enabling Livingston to make good his escape. Killed Militia were Charles Crude, Winster C. Donley, Henry C. Maxey and Horace Palmer. Palmer and Crude were killed after surrendering and taken prisoner. Of Private Palmer it is said that after the retreat of some of the command, "I didn't volunteer to run; right here I'll die." He then dismounted, tied his horse to a tree and got off 18 shots before he was taken. This took place 4 1/2 miles east of Sherwood and 1 1/2 miles from French Point.

May 15th...Skirmishing at Big Creek near Pleasant Hill. Sixty men of the 6th Kansas met up with Confederate Colonel Parker, killing two of his men and capturing some horses. Three houses were burned on the Little Blue by the guerillas, and they were reported as heading east. This party was followed and at night they came upon the camp at Big Creek near Pleasant Hill in Cass County. There six more of Parker's men were killed, more horses captured and the camp torn up. The next day Parker lost two more killed. He was pursued then to the Sni, where it was ascertained he met up with Quantrill.

The pursuit stopped there, supposedly from lack of manpower. It was pouring rain and the horses gave out from the chase.

May 18th...Captain C.F. Coleman of the 9th Kansas Cavalry and a small detachment made a descent on Hog Island in the southern part of Bates County and found himself about 300 Confederates. They had created a small breastwork and were preparing for defense. Three of their number were killed and five wounded. Captain Coleman also lost one man in the affair and destroyed about 2,000 pounds of bacon and a quantity of corn that the Confederates had diligently gathered. The Confederates are said to have removed now to Henry County. (The location of this skirmish is also described as eight or 10 miles south of Butler over the main branch of the Osage River.)

May 19th...Skirmishing near Richfield in Clay County. (This area in the report is called "Fishing River Bottom.") A command of only 36 men total split up and went their separate ways for this ill-fated scouting mission. Lieutenant Louis Grafenstein and 16 of the men were sent to the lower bridge with orders to remain hidden and guard the roads on either side of the river. These men were not mounted. The Lieutenant and Captain Session were ambushed. It seems that 16 Bushwhackers made their appearance two miles east of town (must be Richfield?) in the afternoon of Tuesday the 19th. Two of them went to a house in the neighborhood, acting as if drunk, swearing they were Quantrill's men. The men at whose house they were, started immediately after they left and reported to Lieutenant Grafenstein, as above, and the Lieutenant and Captain Session went to look into the matter, taking with them three men. After arriving at the place, about 1 1/2 miles, they were fired upon from the thick brush. Captain Session and Private Rapp fell at the first fire. The Lieutenant was soon hit and had to stop. The three remaining were then rushed by a party of "marauders." Rapp was robbed and left for dead, and Captain Session was then shot again two or three times through the head and the Lieutenant, after surrendering himself, was cooly shot twice through the head. A woman nearby begged frantically for his life. Their bodies were stripped and plundered of belongings. The gang then went in pursuit of the two remaining number of the little squad. They somehow had managed to escape. A party passing by brought in Private Rapp and had his wounds dressed. The gang of murderers, hearing that Private Rapp was still alive, went directly and shot him three more times, leaving him for dead the second time. He will yet recover. Then a general pillaging of Union and Confederate sympathizing citizens began, with little distinction between choice of whom. There were only 16 or 18 of the Bushwhackers, and they were under the command of Ferdinand Scott. He was recognized by some who knew him well. Also identified were Frank Turner, L. Easton, Frank James, Louis Vandever, Louis Gregg, a man named Churchill and Moses McCoy, husband of the woman on parole (St. Joseph?).

May 21st-30th...Scouting party from Cassville through Northwestern Arkansas into Newton and Jasper Counties, including skirmishes at Bentonville and Carthage. The scouting party left Cassville on the 21st, went to Bentonville and there surprised a Confederate force and broke up the camp. Hearing that Coffee and Hunter were at Pineville, the party went in pursuit in that direction and followed their trail from Pineville, via Rutledge, then west of Neosho to Diamond Grove and west of Carthage about 10 miles, where the fighting began. They encountered Coffee with about 100 men under his command. Hunter had gone north in Cedar County with about 100 men, and Major Livingston was not to be found.

May...Confederate Captain T. Reves reports that on a trip near Patterson they found a scouting party starting in the direction of Doniphan. They succeeded in dispatching one of them, wounding others and taking six horses. They captured about 22 horses from the Union soldiers and then fell back to the Current River about 15 miles above Doniphan.

June 1st...Captain Steinmetz with 15 men ran into a camp of men led by Confederate Commanders Jackman, Pulliam and Todd about three miles north of Rocheport at sunrise. The Militia were soundly fired upon and driven back to about three miles from Fayette. Four of the Militia are reported missing. John Vance was captured. William Hensley supposedly has been killed. Captain Steinmetz went on to Fayette to get help and has returned to pursue. Colonel Green (Militia) has been ordered to arrest Jackman's family. They are to be held for the safe return of Sergeant Vance. Pulliam's command has been pillaging in Pike and Lincoln Counties. The commands on the 1st were located in a pasture on the farm of John L. Jones about three miles northeast of Rocheport. A skirmish ensued upon this property. Also today a skirmish took place at Doniphan near Ponter's Mill involving Reves and Porter. (See last entry for May details are given as to the exact location of the skirmish at Doniphan as; "marched back to Carter's Mills about three miles from our position and took the Doniphan road, kept it 10 miles; there left it and camped at a small farm about 1 1/2 east off the road. The farm being about 16 acres, cleared, running east to west and surrounded on all sides by very steep hills, densely covered with thick brush. At the west end of the clearing was a very large log barn, the fence surrounding three sides. The fighting took place about the barnyard of this farm and a fence along the edge of some woods to the edge of the barnyard." Another report states that a command left from Carter's Mill and marched some 14 miles to the road that led them to the farm.] (Other information listed, "Reves was encamped at or near Ponter's Mill on the 30th of May. Below Ponter's Mill, there is a junction of three roads, one leading to Doniphan, one to Pitman's Ferry and one out to the so-called Glass Settlement." June 1st also saw action at Waverly in Saline County.

June 20th-23rd...Scouting from Waynesville. Captain Josiah Smith's little squad of eight Militiamen lit into a large party of 26 Bushwhackers. They captured one who was turned loose on the parole of a man signing himself S.S. Tucker, but whose real name is Benson Woods. The 20th found the little command scouting between Robideaux and Gasconade to near the line of LaClede County. On the 21st they found sign of a band. On the 22nd the little command was reinforced. They now numbered 27. The trail was found and followed. About noon of this day, upon encounter, a stage robber named Casey is now not among the living. A local citizen, William Wilson, had joined the command and showed true spirit chasing this outlaw band. On the 23rd the trail was again found of the two who had escaped on foot. After trailing them about 25 miles, they were discovered entering their old camp in Wright County about 10 miles southwest of Mountain Store and were taken prisoner. Recovered in this scouting mission was a large quantity of clothing, among other items, that had been stolen from Mr. Stith's store near Lebanon. Information gleaned from Casey before he expired, was that a man named Frick killed a man by the name of Sherwood on the Gasconade last week.

June 23rd...About 125 effective Union men and two companies of infantry from Independence went to the Napoleon Bottoms, about 14 miles from Independence, as it was reported as a district infested with guerillas. The guerilla camp having ample notice of advancing trouble, fell back to the vicinity of Sibley, the cavalry pursuing them. Upon reaching the outskirts of Sibley, the Union command met with vigorous fire. Sibley is a general place of resort for the guerillas. They fire at all the passing boats, the object being plunder, using the houses as shelter. The town was thus accordingly then burned. The only exception being one or two houses that were left standing which were the property of Union men. The town of Butler in Bates County was burned by the guerillas on June 21st. Nearly all the Union families left there. Some went to Germantown in Henry County, the rest to Kansas. No Union families remain in Bates County. (In the report of Sibley mention is made of the house of Mr. Robertson. It had been a noted guerilla habitat on previous occasions. This house was mentioned as being torched as more guerillas were found there again. We take this house to be located on the return trip possibly toward Kansas City?) Also on the 23rd there flared another skirmish at Papinsville. The Militia from Germantown (Henry County) followed a detail of Confederates, about 50 in number, to the Osage River near Papinsville, Bates County. There they crossed heading southward. Pursuit and skirmishing followed about 12 miles south of the river. Each side lost one man.

July 3rd...Lieutenant William C. Bangs (Militia) on a scout from Salem marched to within four miles southeast of Salem and struck a trail. Following it northward about 12 miles through the brush, he surprised a party of 14 Bushwhackers grazing their horses. When he left 10 of Colonel Freeman's command under Captain Lamb were dead. They had been after salt for Captain Lamb's father who lives near the Meremac River. The salt is being brought in from Rolla by the women of the neighborhood.

July 4th...Affair at Black Fork Hills. Brigadier General Oden Guitar took prisoner a man by the name of Palmer of Pulliam's command noted as notorious. Twenty others also were taken prisoner.

July 7th...Dashing madly into a reported Confederate camp located at the junction of the Marmaton and Osage Rivers, Major E.A. Calkins of the 3rd Wisconsin wounded a noted guerilla named Pony Hill today. The engagement lasted over 1 1/2 hours.

July 12th...The Militia under Captain Henry S. Glaze, with Sergeant Zimmerman and 20 men, were attacked at the house of John Watson about 3 miles east of Switzler's Mill, Chariton County. On the previous night they had taken Mr. Watson's son prisoner, and during the night he made good his escape. Knowing he would bring the Confederates, preparation was made to receive them. They came, led by a man named Holtzclaw from Howard County. Fighting lasted a short while before Holtzclaw retreated. The pursuit was taken up by Lieutenant Smith and Captain Denny. Firing can be heard in the direction of Beckelheimer's Mill.

July 18th-26th...Scouting party from Cassville to Huntsville, Arkansas.

July 24th...Fifteen negroes were taken prisoner and were on horses ready to be carried off in Dade County when Captain E.J. Morris (Militia) attacked a band of guerillas. The negroes were released, about 10 horses were captured and one man killed and several wounded by this little group of Militia.

July 27th...Three men are missing from a scouting party of the Enrolled Militia at Cassville that happened to meet up with a band of about 20 armed Confederates.

July 30th...Fifteen men (Militia) left the post at Lexington acting as escort for the paymaster, Major Smith. They were en route to Marshall in Saline County about 20 miles distant. The Enrolled Missouri Militia, having arms under escort for Freedom Township in this county, left the train about 20 miles below Lexington. The paymaster's escort continued for about another five miles and put up for the night. The next morning it was attacked by about 100 Confederates under Blunt and Graves. The paymaster finally reached his destination after much sharp fighting and with one man mortally wounded and seven horses lost.

August...Confederate Lieutenant William J. Preston visited Greenville with the intention of destroying 30 wagons of commissary stores deposited at the Widow McMinn's near Hog Eye, Bollinger, County. Upon arriving he found the wagons had already been destroyed and the owners left in haste. Proceeding on to Patterson, he caught a sutler's wagon loaded with goods, a Federal Captain paroled by Colonel Greene, three privates of Leeper's Company and the Deputy Provost-Marshall and enrolling officer. There were also two squadrons awaiting his arrival in ambush. Electing not to accept the invitation, he moved on toward Van Buren with the intention of attacking a squad near Barnesville which, however, withdrew to Ironton. He did succeed in interrupting the Congressional election and enrollment. Advance scouts are as far as Lebanon in Laclede County. Lieutenant Colonel Preston now moves on August 6th to the intersection of the Thomasville Road and Eleven Points for forage.

August 1st...On Friday July 31st word was received by Captain Charles F. Coleman of the 9th Kansas Cavalry that a large train was to be robbed was encamped in the vicinity of Westport. He sent word to the commanding officer, Lieutenant Brown, at Westport of this and requested him to come and guard the north side of the train and Captain Coleman would take the other. No reply was received from Lieutenant Brown. Captain Coleman and his men were secreted in their prechosen position about 30 minutes when they saw a band of men approaching the train from the east. By their actions, they took them to be guerillas. Immediately ordering an attack and pursuit, it was discovered this was the command of Lieutenant Brown. All operations then were ceased for the night and both stood vigil. The guerillas approached during the night and a hot pursuit was taken up. The next day they were finally stopped at the house of Mrs. Taylor on the Little Blue. After a couple volleys and leaving four of their dead behind, the guerillas scattered into the woods. Round Ponds near the Castor River was the sight of a disaster and death today. General Davidson's (Union) train of about 30 wagons was attacked near Castor River and totally destroyed. Ten of his command met an untimely death outright, many others were mortally wounded. The mules were recovered, but all the horses were lost. This attacker was one Bolands and only 12 men. Surprise was the key element. The trains had camped for the night at the edge of the woods near the river affording any enemy perfect ambush of the sleeping men. No escort guard was with the train. They had about 20 armed men besides the 40 drivers. According to reports of the sergeant who escaped the attack, sentinels were posted but were killed. The train being parked too near the woods, they afforded the enemy cover. At the onset of firing, the teamsters fled to the swamps for safety. A last report gives 65 wagons destroyed by fire, 19 horses and seven pistols taken. All horses that could be led were taken of the 400 head in camp. In retaliation all the boats above and below the river have been sunk, with the exception of one at Jacksonport. The order was not obeyed to sink it. (This all took place on the road between Cape Girardeau and Bloomfield at Round Ponds.)

August 2nd...One hundred men, a detachment of the 1st Missouri State Militia, on Sunday evening of the 2nd had a skirmish with Confederate Commanders Marchbanks and Hancock at Stumptown on the Double Branches, Bates County. Private John S. Luyster was killed. There were no casualties among the Confederates. The next day the little band was pushed into crossing the Marais-des-Cygne or Big Osage at a very uninviting place, following in pursuit to the banks of the Marmiton (southwest branch of the Osage) where they found crossing impossible due to high waters.

August 6th-9th...Scouting from Greenfield to Golden Grove and Carthage. In the brush on Horse Creek and at the crossing from Horse Creek to Golden Grove, Captain Jacob Cassairt (Militia) surprised a Confederate encampment under Captain Osburn, which numbered only six. The Captain and a recruiting officer named Bebee were killed and three others unidentified. On these three days there was also a scouting party from Lexington which went to the vicinity of Hopewell. One hundred fifty men made up this command, and they were accompanied by three pieces of artillery. This march headed toward Wellington. This was not a pleasant fall march. It was very dark and raining in torrents. They passed through Wellington before daylight, after some delay at crossing the Big Sni just east of Wellington, and continued the march to Texas Prairie. At about 11:00 they reached Eagin's Point. There a small band of Bushwhackers fled at their approach. Losing them and returning to the trail, another Confederate detail of about 30 in number crossed the trail in front headed toward Eagin's Point. Scouting parties were sent out as far as Lick Skillet about three miles northeast of Eagin's Point. The search for the home of Seacock, where one Kogin lives, failed. The scouting party encamped that night on Colonel Elliott's (CSA) place. The next morning the line of march continued in the direction of Round Prairie. Seeing no sign of activity, they turned east to Chapel Hill and then to Hopewell. The Confederates appeared to be encamped near Davis Creek on the waters of the Sni and in Greenton Valley. One reconnoitering party killed two of them. The command directed about seven families who have been harboring and fleeing some of the more influential rebels, to report to the post at Lexington. Two companies had come into the area to "escort" out Quantrill and Graves, but Graves was accidently killed by his own men on the night of the 7th on the Sni west of Hopewell.

August 6th-11th...Skirmishes during a scout from Houston to Spring River Mills. Starting August 6th from Houston, 270 men under Lieutenant C. Stierlin reached Hutton Valley with nothing of importance happening. About 15 miles from the valley on the next day the advance came upon a Confederate detail. A running fight ensued and two Confederates were killed. The party made camp that night about 15 miles southeast of West Plains. The next day, the 8th, after advancing about eight miles in a southeasterly direction, the scouting party was again fired upon by 25-30 Confederates settled in upon an eminence. Eight more were dispatched this day. After this little foray, advancing another two miles, there was found posted on a fencepost a poster that was encouraging enlistment in the Confederate Army. This poster was located at Gouge's Mill. At the mill site were found five Confederate officers. Two belonged to Burbridge and the remaining three to Freeman's command. The mill was found to be a rendezvous point for the Confederates and the local guerilla band, complete with a blacksmith shop and a gunsmith shop, which they used to repair their guns or get their horses reshod. The place was burned to the ground. Leaving there and going about three miles toward Spring River Mills, the advance was fired upon from an ambush in a cornfield. A running pursuit commenced. This brought more men down, along with a very fine horse belonging to Nick Yates, who was with them. Continuing on to the mill, the Lieutenant and command reached there about 4:00 in the afternoon. He found that Freeman had kept his fine camp there and had only moved out about two weeks before. The premises with all contents of corn, flour and grain was reduced to ashes. Removing another four miles on to a house, they made camp. At this house was found a "notorious den," one Minié ball and several small bird rifles. Also found was unserviceable United States horse equipment. He applied his infamous torch to this house, also.

August 8th...Balltown was the sight of a rendezvous for the Federal commands from Fort Scott, Kansas, Drywood to Nevada, and from Lamar. All met and started from Balltown on the morning of the 8th. Finding that the enemy had removed to the vicinity of Horse Creek, they hoped to check his advance at the recesses of Clear Creek. Upon proceeding a little east of the southern course toward the head of Clear Creek and down the creek a short distance, the fresh trail appeared. Following and turning again at about 100 yards, they ran into five of the enemy advance guards. Three of them, being mounted, escaped and after a fast chase for over two miles, they were dispatched as were the other two who were on foot. Going down the creek another mile, they came upon a house. A man ran out under cover of darkness and escaped into the brush. The next morning the command was divided and Lieutenant Pond took one side and Captain Robert Carpenter took the other. The Captain came up empty handed; not so with the Lieutenant. He took the south side and found their camp, complete with secreted horses. The occupants had departed. He remained hidden near the camp for the night, and the enemy failed to return. It should be noted here that Colonel Brag was to accompany this detail and failed to appear. Had he followed orders, he would have found the enemy encamped on his direct route.

August 9th...Garden Hollow is the site of Confederate Commander Coffee's camp. Captain C.B. McAfee got within three miles of the enemy camp near Pineville today. Fighting erupted. Coffee is reported to have about 300 men encamped there.

August 9th-18th...There was a scouting party from Cape Girardeau to the Ash Hills and Poplar Bluff and fighting on the 13th at Ash Hills. This party went to the defense of Bloomfield, which was thought to be in grave danger from attack. This rumor proved to be false. They moved toward Pocahontas through Ash Hills, then in a roundabout way to Poplar Bluff. At the skirmish, which took place in the Ash Hills country, Major Frederick R. Poole was shot through the leg and then, at the same instant, his horse was shot and fell upon him wounding him considerably. No doctor being available, he had to endure this for another five days. (The command rode the first day from Bloomfield and rested at Camp Poole near St. Francisville, then crossed the St. Francis River at Indian Ford and proceeded down the Ash Hill Road about 10 miles along the west bank of the St. Francis and then entered the Ash Hills country.) On the morning of the 15th they marched on the west side of Black River, about 6 miles, crossed the ford and proceeded in the direction of Greenville, encamping at Camp Law on Otter Creek 25 miles from Poplar Bluff. On the 16th they passed through

Greenville and went into Camp Rogers 18 miles from Dallas and 25 miles from Camp Law. On the 17th they left Camp Rogers and marched to Camp Thomson within 23 miles of Cape Girardeau. Foraging through the country just passed through is out of the question. The roads were very nearly impassable.

August 10th...Pleasant Hill has been evacuated by Federal troops, which a few days before had been burned by the Confederates. The 1st Missouri Militia now occupy the town of Dayton, marching there from Germantown in Henry County. On the march they were attacked by a small band of guerillas. Scouting details now have been sent to Napoleon and another to Trading Post in Kansas. Also on the 10th, the pursuit of Colonel Coffee (CSA) has lasted for three days and two nights, and he was finally met with at Pineville in McDonald County.

August 14th...On the morning of the 14th, while on a scouting mission, Colonel James McFerran (Militia) with about 65 men, passed up Davis Creek to near Hopewell and then down the Sni to Wellington. They ran into only small bands of guerillas and chasing them, caused the death of only one. It wasn't so quiet near Houston. A Union man named Hackwerth, living at present near Salem, with the assistance of a man named Johnson, had gone to the Casto Valley to round up Hackwerth's cattle. They were taken prisoner by a small detail of about five rebels. A pursuit was organized and the trail was struck about 25 miles southeast of Houston at Spring Valley. Following it for two days and finally overtaking the small command, they killed two of the rebels and captured one horse. The Confederates then scattered to the woods on Jack's Fork, where all traces of them were lost along with the three Union men they held as prisoners. Sergeant McDowell (Militia), as he rode through the country, made known to the citizens they would be held responsible for the safe return of the three men or they would suffer the consequences.

August 17th-26th...Union expeditions left again today from Cape Girardeau and Pilot Knob to Pocahontas, Arkansas. The well-known Confederate General Jeff Thompson and his Adjutant General, Captain Kay; a medical director, Dr. Frame; a captain of artillery; a lieutenant of cavalry and a captain of ordnance plus about 50 soldiers, were captured without a shot at Pocahontas. This was accomplished by Captain Henry C. Gentry, 2nd Missouri State Militia Cavalry. General Thompson was taken prisoner in his office, which was located in a lower room at the St. Charles.

August 23rd...Bennett's Bayou was the site of action near its mouth today. Confederate Lieutenant Biffles was killed about sunset in the skirmish that ensued when the commands met. Captured were Captain Henderson Green and a member of the Legislature of 1860-61 from Christian County. The scouting party then moved toward Big North Fork and ran head on into Captain Vanzoot's Confederates. Both sides suffered the loss of two men and several wounded.

August 25th...An escort of about 14 men from Lebanon (Militia) to Waynesville was attacked by about 25 to 30 Confederates. A command of about 35 men has been sent to the California House and another 14 men in another direction after this Confederate command. A citizen, Mr. McCain, brought in the wounded and killed. Also today Lieutenant J.G. Lindsay had a fight near Independence at sunrise.

August 25th-28th...Scouting from Sedalia and skirmish at Clear Fork. Captain Ferguson (Militia) reports that on the evening of the 25th a command of Confederates, about 30, were met at the head of Clear Fork Creek in Johnson County and a fight ensued. The Confederates made good their escape after some heroics by Lieutenant G.W. McGuire (Militia). The Lieutenant only had 22 bullets, firing them all at the fleeing rebels. He received two shots in his coat from pistols and one from a shotgun, but still he kept on with the pursuit.

August 29th...Captain Lyman D. Rouell, 2nd Colorado Infantry, burned the regular boardinghouse of some Confederates along with about 100 bushels of corn they had been feeding their stock. The scouting "party" took place at Blue Timber, about 15 miles from Hickman Mills. Crossing the Blue and discovering a trail of a single horseman, they followed right into a camp of eight Confederates holed up in a house in the timber. Several were killed.

August...A court martial was held in Marshall for Dr. Benson who had been captured by some Union soldiers. It was charged that he had been with Quantrill at the burning of Lawrence, Kansas. This was proved, and he did not deny it; however, he stated he was there in the capacity as a surgeon only. The verdict of guilty was passed. He was sentenced to be shot, next being taken to the graveyard north of town where he was then seated in his coffin. The sentence was carried out. Doctor Benson was on his way to surrender when he was captured by the soldiers. He had been convinced to do so by some Union friends. Also in 1863, the actual date not know (Saline County History), a Reverend Kavanaugh was shot and killed by Federal authorities for being an active Southern man. Also in 1863 in Saline County, James E. Elson of Miami Township was killed by guerillas. He was a Union soldier and had been captured by them. Asking for a drink of water, he was taken to the river in the Petit Saux bottoms, and while kneeling over the river water, he was murdered. In 1863, one Asa Huff of Captain Garrett's Company, Shelby's Regiment, was left behind as his command stormed through the county during the famous Shelby Raid. He remained at and around home in Cambridge Township until July of 1864, living a great deal of time in the brush in a sort of cave dugout, in the company of a man named Norvell. One day Huff took sick and a doctor was summoned, but the doctor refused to prescribe for the invalid until he had informed the Federals of Huff's whereabouts. The Militia went out to the cave and paroled him.

As soon as his sickness was over, they took him to Marshall and there shot him dead. Also reported is that a man named Flannagan was also shot that day by this same detail of Militia.

September 4th...A band of guerillas led by a notorious man named Rafter, dashed into Quincy, at once firing into a quiet bunch of citizens in front of the store. They killed Mr. Thomas and wounded a soldier who just happened to be in town. The stage had just arrived and had three or four soldiers from the 18th Iowa as passengers. They took refuge in a house. Rafter, in person, went in after them. As he burst through the door, one of the soldiers took aim and shot him twice and he fell. The Iowa soldiers were taken prisoner and carried off. It is quite probable they have since been killed by their captors. It is also reported that one Mattox (CSA) is terrorizing Johnson County. On the 8th the bodies of the Iowa soldiers had been located about six miles from Quincy. One was found dead and one mortally wounded.

September 4th-7th...Scouting parties worked from Cold Water Grove to Pleasant Hill and Big Creek. The chase is on again for Quantrill.

September 5th...A Union command left Springfield on August 31st and arrived at Cassville on September 1st. They were joined by an escort party, and all made their way to Bentonville, Arkansas.

September 6th...There was an attack on the Union supply train between Fort Scott, Kansas and Carthage. Four men were sent as escort for Joel P. Hood on official business from Carthage to Fort Scott. Starting back, they overtook and joined up with a small wagon train of about four wagons loaded with dry goods and groceries destined for the post at Carthage. They traveled together until about eight miles from the post. Suddenly they were attacked by superior numbers and two wagons were lost and one of the escort party killed. The man who had been killed had been home on furlough and was just returning to the post and his command. Reinforcments were dispatched to the aid of the train and two of the wagons were regained. Several of the attacking Confederates were killed. Joel P. Hood killed the Confederate captain named Turk. Each side holds a prisoner belonging to the other. Part of the Confederates belonged to Coffee's command and the rest were just deserters. The latest attack was led by one Meadows.

September 7th-19th...Expedition from Springfield into Arkansas and Indian Territory and skirmishing near Enterprise, Missouri. The expedition went to Cow Skin Prairie and crossed the Cow Skin. On the prairie they learned that Coffee had been reinforced and had moved his command to Enterprise about four miles beyond Elk Mills, and it is reported to be 1,000 men strong. Dismounting his command upon entering the town, Colonel M. LaRue Harrison, 1st Arkansas Cavalry, started shelling the town. Enterprise suffered the brunt of the big guns.

September 12th...Information was brought to the post at Houston (Militia) of a small band of guerillas, six men with five horses, who just passed a house about 10 miles south of the post. Captain Richardson took up the pursuit, following them about 57 miles without stopping. He finally found them asleep in the woods. Three attempted to escape and were killed. They were William Lingo of Waynesville, Lieutenant Obe Moss of Pulaski County and Jacob Bottom. Oscar D. Blount of St. Louis was wounded in the thigh. Captured with the men were 11 horses, two of which were the stage horses, and three were taken from a wagon on the road near Rolla. Also captured were seven citizens, saddles and three bridles, one of these belonged to the stage company, 32 pairs of shoes, 17 pairs of women's shoes, two bolts of domestic, three sacks of coffee and one United States newspaper bag and a set of stage lines. The wounded man, Blount, gave them information as to the local men who have been harboring them. He named Andy Hall, who lived close to Judge York, and a man named Purcell who lived close to Licking. William Lingo also was keeping 13 horses and a great variety of other stolen goods at the house of John King close to the Arkansas line. Lee Tilly, son of Tilly near Waynesville, also has a number of horses and other articles secreted in the vicinity.

September 13th...Attack and skirmish near Salem. Colonel Freeman and his men made a bold, stubborn attack on the post at Salem, killing one man and making off with about 10 guns, hats and boots, part of which they left behind in the confusion. After the struggle, the pursuit followed the estimated 300 Confederates. Colonel Freeman did not keep to the roads but went right over the mountains and through the woods. It was upon one of these mountains that he made another stand. The base of this little mountain was surrounded by flanks of troops of the Missouri Militia. Freeman left 14 dead on the field and many wounded. Two men reported as residents of Salem, William Orchard and a man named Duckworth, were with Colonel Freeman's command.

September 15th...They have chased Quantrill for a week around Pleasant Hill. Now, unable to find him, they feel he is encamped on the Blue or Sni-Bar Creeks in Jackson County. After moving the search to where he supposedly was, they found him, camp and all. Two of Quantrill's men departed this life on this day. The camp was ransacked and destroyed. It is reported also that the flour mill at Lone Jack has been destroyed by Bushwhackers.

September 15th-18th...On September 11th Captain E.J. Morris (Militia) was sent to the head of Cedar Creek to assist a Union man in moving out. A small band of rebels attacked them and caught Private Samuel Downing and murdered him. He had 32 bullets shot into him and was beaten with his musket. By the 15th a detachment set out from Greenfield to avenge this crime. In this little get-even foray they killed only one rebel, but burned everything from a pigpen to a mansion on Cedar and Horse Creeks. The band that killed Private Downing has headed south. "I think as soon as I get shut of the rebel women in these parts, we will have peace." signed by Major Wick Morgan.

September 22nd-25th...Scouting party in Lafayette County and a severe skirmish in the brush on the Tabo. The guide, Mr. Sullivan (Militia), was mortally wounded.

September 22nd...Shelby's (CSA) command sets out from Arkadelphia, Arkansas for a raid across Missouri.

September, 1863...Terror was to ride across Missouri in the form of Colonel Joseph Shelby. He at this time in 1863 was with the Trans-Mississippi Department of the Confederate Army in Arkansas. He selected a body of tried and true men from Missouri cavalry regiments to go on an invasion up through Missouri, into the country where he had formerly lived and where most of his men called home. The object of the incursion through Missouri was to obtain recruits for the Confederate Army. Many remained in Missouri who were strong sympathizers of the Southern Cause. Some of these Missourians had already seen service, more or less, and were home on parole. Another object was to capture supplies from the Federals and to let the world know, and especially the people of Missouri, that this portion of the American soil was still claimed as a part of the Confederate States and was not expected to be abandoned. The presence of a strong Confederate force was thought to be necessary to restore and maintain confidence with those who had begun to doubt the success of their Cause. Just how many men Shelby left Arkansas with cannot now be known. The number is placed at near 800. It is said he gained about 600 men on the raid. How many just rode along for the fight cannot be, or probably never will be, ascertained. There were Shelby's Regiment commanded by Captain George P. Gordon, Shank's Regiment of Cavalry commanded by himself, Thompson's Regiment commanded by Lieutenant Colonel Hooper and Elliott's Battalion and two guns of Collins' Battery in the charge of Lieutenant David Harris when the expedition started. They were afterward joined by Colonel Coffee's and Colonel David Hunter's Regiments, making a force of about 1,000 men. One of the gun was a 10-pounder steel Parrott captured at Springfield from the Federals and the other was a 6-pounder brass piece captured from the Federals at the Battle of Lone Jack in August of 1862. (Extracted Saline County History)

He was met in battle by Missouri Militia from all across the State. They seemed to come from every corner and criss-crossed the path of Shelby many times in an attempt to block his pathway. It is virtually impossible to be accurate as to where these men were. They moved back and forth several times each day, and just traded places many, many times retracing their daily movements, when Shelby slipped by. The estimate is placed at about 2,400 of the Militia and 2,000 Enrolled Militia were called into action, along with at least 1,000 more men of the various commands called in.

Shelby had about, as stated, about 1,000 men. One cannot imagine the terror that fell upon the innocent citizens when an army of this size rode across their yards or their farms. The corn was about ready to be brought in. Forage would be very necessary to sustain this many men. When this raid was over, one end of the State to the other was laid to waste. It was stripped of all. Shelby makes mention of this in his report of the desolation of the border counties of Kansas and Missouri.

To venture such an undertaking took a man of steel and men of iron endurance. Shelby and his command were such. A daring man who took daring chances, he led them across the State from border to border and back out again. If he failed to get the attention of the world, it really doesn't matter. He most certainly got the attention of the citizens of Missouri and the Federal authorities. The spirit of this man and his men lives on today, with no little pride. He was and still is a hero to many.

Due to the retracing of the many Federal/Union commands back and forth, and in order to let you know what happened, we will use portions of Shelby's report. All commands agree as to the sequence of events. The victor is according to your judgment.

September 21st...The Confederates received their final orders from General Sterling Price. The long gray line was underway. This march would carry them about 1,500 miles. It would cost 125 Confederate lives from Shelby's command alone. The other figures are not available. By October 2nd, he had planned to take Neosho. Colonel Coffee's men caused a valuable delay by arriving in small squads. That night they camped at Pineville. At daylight of the 4th he started the mighty army toward Neosho. There 300 Federal cavalry were stationed. Surrounding the fortifications, they succeeded in taking it. The Federals made a wild dash with Thorp hot on their heels. They made it to the courthouse, and there made a stand against tremendous odds. The courthouse was a strong brick building, pierced and loopholed for musketry. The Confederate cannon belched its destruction and two balls went crashing through the walls. Surrender followed. The captured Federals were paroled. The company then moved toward Sarcoxie, resting on Jones Creek about five hours. On the 4th they passed through the blackened town of Sarcoxie and then to the town of Oregon, or Bower's Mills, a favorite meeting place of the Militia. This place was "swept from the face of the earth." Approaching the town just before daylight, and by day's light, the sleepy town was surrounded. Shelby captured the contents of several stores, a quantity of small arms and destroyed their strong fort. That night they rested 10 miles north of Stockton. At the town of Stockton, the fort was burned and the entrenched Militia driven out after some hard contesting. Shelby states that all along this road the inhabitants had their household possessions piled outside, awaiting the torch, being told that the command was laying waste to the countryside. Also on this route, every house that had belonged to a Southern family had been burned and the family effectually destroyed. On October 6th the command passed through Humansville. There Shelby met head on the command of Brigadier General John McNeil and a force of about 2,000 men. They managed to hold him (McNeil) in check until the last of the column passed through town, but not without losses to both sides. While at Humansville, Shelby sent a small force of 10 men into Osceola and burned a fortified Federal structure there. The night of the 6th they encamped within 10 miles of Warsaw. This day on the road, they had captured about 30 government wagons and picked up many prisoners. On the morning of the 7th he reached Warsaw and found the Federals ready to do battle. They were disputing Shelby's crossing the river. Part of Shelby's command (Gordon's Regiment) was sent to cut the Federals off from the road toward Osceola and another battalion to the east. Hooper's Regiment was dismounted and formed into a line of battle and charged straight for the ford, which was about two feet deep. The men dashed across the river, anxious to do battle. (In reading his report, you can very well imagine the spine-chilling Confederate yells and the confusion that broke out with this charge through the water under fire of the Federal guns.) Shelby managed somehow to virtually pull off this crossing and captured some government stores in the process. Shelby describes it as a "well-provisioned fort."

The safe passage through Missouri was near an end. So far he had managed to head off the local Militia, but the wires started humming with the news of his invasion upon the fair state. The railroads, loaded down with men atop and inside the cars, were bringing the forces to bear upon him.

On the 8th and 9th he marched "leisurely" through Cole Camp, "the cradle of most liberty in Missouri." (I rather doubt he went at a leisurely pace. Lieutenant Colonel Bazel F. Lazear, with 700 men and three pieces of light artillery, was following him from Cole Camp, another 300 men were added to Lazear's force, making the odds more even.) He also passed through Florence, another "beautiful little town." "Vast herds of horses covered the prairies, a sight most refreshing to my grim old dragoons, and during the two days, vast quantities of good Union steeds were changed into Rebel chargers." By daylight of the 10th the town of Tipton was surrounded and taken by Shelby, hotly contested by local Militia, just missing the advance of the Federal forces approaching from Sedalia. The previous night a detachment of 100 hand-picked daredevils was sent under Captain James Woods to attack and destroy the Lamine Bridge "at all hazards." Forty Federal officers and men guarded this bridge from a solidly-built blockhouse. Before the sentinels could give the alarm, Captain Woods and his daring little command were dispatched. Giving a wild yell, the Confederates charged headlong upon the fort. It was a brief but vicious, bloody encounter. Within five minutes the Confederates were in control of this fort and all its stores. (Shelby estimates its value at $400,000.) It was falling into its own ashes when Captain Woods broke camp the next morning. At Tipton, scouts were sent 30 miles in either direction to wreak ruination upon the railroad, telegraph and to just generally tear up the countryside. Railroad ties were torn from their anchors, wire rolled up and cut, cattle stops and water tanks torn down, railroad bridges destroyed and burned and, by 4:00 in the afternoon, Shelby was off for Boonville, having also entered Syracuse and stormed the town, all in one day's work. Just on the outskirts of Tipton Shelby met up with Colonel T.T. Crittenden, and a great battleline was drawn by about 1,000 men. Determination was the word to describe both Crittenden and Shelby at this moment. Shelby needed to get through and Crittenden disputed his passage. Shelby, rather than spread out his command, drew them up by eights, closed ranks and headed for the middle. Unprepared for such an attack, Crittenden, who was taken by surprise by the outrageous tactics, gave passage reluctantly. This night Shelby's command camped on the farm of Judge Nathaniel Leonard south of Boonville in Cooper County. On the 10th the Federal forces were amassing toward Boonville and the reports are numerous. (One can readily assume some of the men who had joined up in this infamous destruction just kept after it and left the main body of the Confederate command, continuing on their own. Shelby's reports never mention discipline problems with his commands, so one cannot readily consider them to be realistic in that sense. This leaves credibility to the numerous reports of the Federals of the raid. Shelby's command was virtually strung over miles.) At this point all men, Confederate and Federal, were traveling light for the sake of speed. Sunday morning dawned clear and found Shelby still within 10 miles of Boonville. Fast approaching to counter Shelby was General Oden Guitar. Delayed repairing a broken axle, Shelby again lost valuable time in getting his forces deployed at Boonville, but while at work repairing the gun, a flag of truce appeared from Boonville asking for mercy and protection with the offer of unconditional submission. By 11:00 Shelby had entered the city. He knew full well that the citizens, along with the local Militia and other interested persons, had been armed the previous night. It is reported the mayor of the city requested the peace. By now, drawn up across the vitally-important river, in command of the ferryboat, was General Oden Guitar with his men. Placing the ferry behind a midstream island for protection, the battle began. The boat was safely out of firing range and was not to be taunted into approaching closer. It is here the cannon breaks down again and on the horizon a huge blue cloud is forming in the shape of General Ebert B. Brown with about 4,000 men fast approaching from Jefferson City to the rear of Shelby. General Brown drove in the pickets and, again, Hooper's command was dismounted and forced to hold the Federals back while the gun repairs progressed. This skirmishing, sometimes very hot, lasted until 10:00 in the evening. Shelby camped for the night about four miles outside of town. That day he had taken valuable arms and all the stores he could carry. The morning of the 12th Shelby's pickets again were driven in by General Brown. Shelby decided to make a stand, located an advantageous position and waited for the approach, but Brown did not accept the invitation. Shelby then moved his force onto the main Marshall and Boonville Road. Traveling for about two hours without incident, he was again attacked by Brown, driving in the rear guards. Again, the defensive was placed into action. Deploying Major G.P. Gordon's Regiment to the west side of Lamine River with its rugged and precipitous banks, a well-played ambush was planned. Another two companies were deployed behind the east bank making it secure. General Brown, seeing the rear of the retreating Confederates, fell right into the trap. Shots echoed and careened into the hapless men, horses fought the bridle and reins churning up the water, hooves lashing out. Men fell off into the riled muddy water. There were yells like no other earthly sounds ever heard by man and smoke, heavy and unmoving, dropped a wistful blanket enveloping the carnage beneath it. On this horrible day in Missouri history the waters of the Lamine ran red. Trapped, General Brown had no other course but to save his men and get out of the trap. Many were left behind. General Brown rallied his valiant soldiers and struck Shelby again in his rear. This well-executed fight took place at night with General Brown enforced with artillery. The same day near Jonesboro, at the crossing of the Blackwater, Brown made a furious onslaught. Both sides suffered losses before Shelby moved in the direction of Marshall, and Brown backed his men up. Shelby encamped that night within six miles of Marshall. The next day, the 13th, found Shelby entering Marshall. Here General Thomas Ewing awaited him with about 4,000 men. General Brown was in the rear. It was here, between the two large Federal forces, Shelby made his stand. (The casualty numbers that occurred from this battle have been contested for years. We will make no attempt to

100

give any but, due to the vast number of those actually involved and the circumstances under which they fought, Shelby's men must have been exhausted and Ewing's primed for the fight. One is safe in assuming many casualties occurred.) General Brown, smitten twice already by retreating to some extent, it was nothing less than an all-out stand. Ewing had chosen a great vantage point. He was amassed on a high point looking down on his foe. Shelby, determined to hold them, ordered the bridge that he had just crossed burned in his rear, and then deployed his various commands. The battle raged on for hours. First one, then the other, having the upper hand. Shelby finally gained entrance into Marshall. Shanks had held General Brown's men in check for several hours. Brown, finally getting an edge, joined commands with Ewing and this combined total manpower and weapons placed the odds at eight to one. Shelby's cannon became useless, so he retreated. Forming his men on the retreat into regiments, playing for time, he managed to gather the remnants of his men and get away, abandoning the broken cannon. By the time he had accomplished the regathering and reformation, he was almost surrounded by the amassed Federals. His only opening was to his right, through the thick-matted undergrowth, but the way was almost impassable for cavalry and directly in front was a deep, wide ravine. Feinting to the left with all his strength, he forced the opening wider and made the slip through. The wagons passed safely through, but the head of Hunter's Regiment became tangled up in the underbrush. The Federals, seeing this gap in the retreating line, took advantage and divided the force. Dashing away by a direct angle, they made good their escape. Shelby, on his way, retreated toward Waverly. The others were out there somewhere, and the Federals were directly behind. For over eight miles they pushed hard at Shelby. At Germantown the Federals made a desperate attack but were driven back. At 3:00 Shelby passed through Waverly then turned directly southward. At Hawkins' Mill, finding the wagons troublesome and having no ammunition left except what the men could carry, the wagons were pushed over the steep embankment of the Missouri River. The 14th, 15th and 16th were spent in constant travel, still hard pressed by the Federals that appeared at every turn, anticipating his route of return to Arkansas. At Warrensburg, about 2,000 fully-armed men had waited for his arrival. With the ragged, tired soldiers trailing behind, Shelby slipped passed them without incident. Realizing the slip, the Federals advanced on to Johnstown, and there the attack was made. By nightfall Shelby was within eight miles of the Osage River. Traveling hard on the 17th, 18th and 19th and fighting once at Carthage, he crossed the Springfield Road three miles east of Keytesville, all the time followed and constantly pushed and harassed by a large Federal force. Finally on the 20th, Shelby was rejoined on the banks of the Little Osage in Arkansas (?) by Hunter, Hooper and Shanks, with whom he had lost contact at Marshall. They report they crossed the railroad four miles from Tipton, which entire road was then heavily guarded by Federal infantry; charged a herd of 400 mules and captured them within eight miles of Syracuse; took over 50 prisoners; destroyed 20 wagons; tore up the newly-laid railroad track and again damaged the repaired road; fought at Florence, Humansville and Greenfield; crossed the Osage at Duroc; charged and defeated a detachment of the 1st Arkansas positioned two miles south of the river. Their now broken gun was abandoned at Humansville when the eight large horses fell in their traces from exhaustion. The raid was over. While the Federal soldiers pursue Shelby into Arkansas, the citizens of Missouri are again faced with the devastation, the healing of old wounds, the burying of the dead, the healing of the sick, and the search for food. This raid had taken its toll.

Yes, the raid was over, but life in Missouri had progressed in the same fashion before Shelby's arrival.

September 27th-28th...Captain G.F. Earl, 9th Kansas, reports that he met up with a small party while on a scout through Bates County at the crossing of the Marais-des-Cygne River south of Butler. The colonel of the party escaped with about 40 of his command. He is thought to be Marchbanks. It is reported that a number of families still inhabit the houses in the timber and that the town of Butler has been burned, this time to the ground.

September 29th-October 26th...Expeditions from Pilot Knob to Oregon County, Missouri and Pocahontas, Arkansas. Prisoners taken were reported to be part of Reves' and Crandall's commands that were taken by the scouting party to Smithville, Arkansas and are now at Pilot Knob. Dr. Pollock (Union) is thought to have been wounded and taken prisoner. By the 30th the scouting party which left on the 29th had sent a detachment via Eminence to join again at Alton. The other command was to take a lower route following the Van Buren Road and camped that night at Hen Peck Creek (MO/ARK?). By October 1st another detachment was to go lower and cross Eleven Point River at Boyce's Mill and then proceed to Alton. The main force of the command crossed Current River, encamped at the head of Pike Creek and the following morning removed to Alton. Scouting the next day concerned the area of Simpkins' Mill, Boyce's Mill and Boyce's Ford. It was on this route that Confederate Lieutenant Duckworth and his command were encountered. By the 5th the scouting party is heading south through Arkansas.

October 2nd...Quantrill started today from the Missouri River and this night camped on the Grand River, then marched to Osage. The march continued each day, taking a due southwest course, leaving Carthage 12 miles east, crossing Shoal Creek at the falls, then going due west into the Seneca Nation. On this trip to the Canadian River Quantrill had a major clash with Union Brigadier General Blunt who was escorting a large train from Fort Scott, Kansas to Fort Smith, Arkansas. It included Brigadier General J.G. Blunt, his staff and bodyguards and about 125 men. In this raid the escort of Blunt faltered and gave way, retreating in great haste. Quantrill captured the buggy belonging to General Blunt, his sword, his commission and all his official papers concerning headquarters, etc. Among those reportedly killed were General Blunt, Majors Curtis, Sinclair and B.S. Henning, Captain Tough and three lieutenants of the staff. Quantrill used his old ploy of wearing Federal uniforms and carrying a Union flag when making his approach of the enemy. Quantrill also states that he had killed William Bledsoe, and John Coger was seriously wounded. When this band entered the Indian Nation, they reported taking 150 Federal Indians and negroes prisoner but brought none of them through.

October 4th...The Widow Wheeler's property, southeast of Neosho, was the site of a skirmish. A band of guerillas operating in that vicinity was discovered by a detail sent to the area of Turkey Creek to escort some moving families out of the neighborhood. Twenty-nine men started on the trail of about 40 well-armed rebels. The trail led to within one mile of Shoal Creek, 15 miles from the starting place. Here the trail was lost. The detail camped five miles south of Baxter Springs. The next day the trail was struck again, following about 30 miles, and it was on the Widow Wheeler's land they had made camp. A spirited skirmish erupted. After a running fight and chase of about four miles, 10 of the rebels were killed and a good many more wounded. Upon their return toward Neosho, the detail passed the home of Mr. Wade and found it in flames. They then learned the town was full of Confederates thought to be Shelby's advance guard.

October 13th...Confederate General (Colonel?) Waldo P. Johnson (MSG), who succeeded M. Jeff Thompson, with authority to organize a force in Southern Missouri which, "from friendly trees" might shoot Union soldiers and citizens, is said to have abandoned the enterprise and would be very glad to again represent Missouri in the service of the Union. This man had been a very influential lawyer within the State previous to the war.

October 18th...Lieutenant Michael Eddleman (Militia) discovered while on an escort duty with the enrolling officer of Shannon County, that as he proceeded to the southeast part of the County on Jack's Ford of Current River to Man's Creek, the road had the beaten-smooth appearance of having been ridden over by a great number of horses. After crossing the creek and gaining the top of the hills, he found the roads strewn with bits of forage and here seemed to be regular picket posts. Traveling a short distance he chanced upon a Confederate command of about 20 to 30 men. Four of their saddles were emptied. The rest escaped. After enjoying the forage, the command returned to Salem.

October 19th...Scouting in the Honey Creek neighborhood near Clinton, Colonel Henry Neill surprised four Confederates just as they finished a nice dinner that had been provided for them. Killed were Thomas Banks, Joseph Gibson, Riddle and Hogle. Confederate Captain T. Alexander has departed this life at the hands of Major A.J. Pugh. Captain Alexander was of Waverly.

October 21st...Four more Bushwhackers lost their lives in the neighborhood of Greenton Valley near Hopewell.

October 22nd...MUTINY AT BLOOMFIELD!! A courier brought in a message signed by all the officers (Union) at Bloomfield, with the exception of two. They state they are not in revolt against authority, but believing that they were commanded by a traitor and that the post of Bloomfield with all the stores, troops, arms, etc. was about to be betrayed and sold into the hands of the enemy, they thought it their imperative duty to seize the commander and commandant. If the charges can be proven, it will go far to justify apprehensions. The statement was made in headquarters at Cape Girardeau that Bloomfield is sold and in a short time will be in the hands of the enemy. It was already sold once to a woman. Supposedly some sort of conspiracy is suspected of Major Samuel Montgomery, Commander; his son, Captain R.H. Montgomery and Dr. T.W. Johnson. The charges were signed by Captain William H. Crockett, Captain John H. Paynter, V.B.S. Reber, Second Lieutenant Luther D. Potter and Second Lieutenant E.J. Burross, all of the 6th Missouri Cavalry. Headquarters sends down Lieutenant Hiller to take command. The company officers were arrested and sergeants placed in command of the various companies in their stead. Major Montgomery has made notice to his commander at headquarters that posted outside his door Lieutenant Reber had placed a battery aimed at the door. They have taken over the telegraph operator and all instruments. Captain Crockett is in command of the mutineers. The whole battalion supporting the charges is drawn up in a line before the Major's headquarters. Since the arrest of Major Montgomery, Lieutenant Reber has been very drunk. The battalion of men, not realizing what they were called out for and upon finding out, have left the cause. The telegraph operator told them in so many words "to be damned" when threatened with death if he used his instruments. The accused will stand trial, and Major Montgomery is still in command.

In a court-martial held in January of 1864, all the charges were dropped against J.H. Paynter, E.J. Burross and Luther D. Potter. About 35 members of the Missouri Legislature petitioned President Lincoln, and he ordered the charges and sentences of dismissal from service to the United States be dropped. The men had charged their commanding officer with indiscriminately allowing rebel deserters, large numbers of whom came into the post from day to day, to return to their homes without giving bond or oath. The Major replied it was an experiment. The second charge was his habit of associating constantly while at Bloomfield with the most dangerous and notorious rebels, some of whom have been known to act as spies. The third charge was his habit of cursing and abusing many of the highest military and civil officers of the government, including the President and Governor Gamble, in the most profane and bitter terms in the presence of such associates as have been described, while he kept himself isolated from his commanding officers. The

fourth charge alleges that in the sale of contraband goods he
favored a notorious Secessionist who at one time sported a
secession badge in his hat. The fifth charge made was that he had
married one of the two most notorious rebel women in the country,
who was known for carrying dispatches and writing ballads for the
rebel army. The Major must have known of her exploits. She
boasted, at a time when the enemy was supposedly marching on th
post, that she ruled the place and although the 6th Missouri
Cavalry was holding the post now, that her Southern friends soon
would do so. Knowing as he must of these rumors, he neither said
nor did anything to remove the impression made by them on the minds
of soldiers and citizens. The judges decided the men had acted on
their instincts and had no mutiny in mind, only the preservation
of the United States. William H. Crockett and Reber evidently were
dismissed from the service.

October 26th...On the 25th a scouting party was ordered south from
Waynesville with about 15 men to gather information concerning
Benjamin Moore (CSA/Guerilla/Union?) whether he was taken prisoner
or killed. Supposedly he was killed. During the night the camp
was approached by an unknown, and the guard was slightly wounded.
The next day the guard was sent to Waynesville with seven of the
men, the party proceeding on to the home of Hiram King. He learned
that Benjamin Moore was taken prisoner, afterward escaping or was
paroled, he knew not which. Being near noon as they awaited their
dinner, about 20 or 25 men came on a charge out of the brush toward
the house. The soldiers moved to a smaller adjoining log house,
with four or five feet between the structures, and prepared to give
them a nice warm welcoming reception. After some shooting, the
family of the house was placed under the floor in the cellar for
protection. The fighting grew hotter. After many tries at
dislodging the soldiers, the building was fired. Knowing the house
was afire, all identification papers as to who they were went up
in smoke. The little bunch changed their names and ranks to avoid
detection. The Bushwhackers had sworn that should they ever catch
Frank Mason, Michael Williams and Lieutenant Twyford, they would
burn or shoot them full of holes. (Lieutenant Twyford was in
command of the men in the burning house.) Finally with the roof
ablaze, the white flag of surrender went out. The family was fine.
At 3:00 they surrendered their arms. They were stripped of their
clothing but were given old clothes to put on. They were then
marched until dark and encamped within 12 miles of Waynesville.
The next day they were paroled. It took a day of solid walking
over areas with no roads, through the brush, being scratched and
with very sore feet, they arrived in Lebanon on the 28th tired and
hungry.

October 26th-November 12th...Scout from Cape Girardeau to Doniphan
and Pocahontas, Arkansas. A party of 250 Militia started from Camp
Lowry in the direction of Doniphan. When near Greenville, 75 men
were dispatched to guard the election polls at Poplar Bluff,
scouting on the way, then on into Arkansas.

October 27th-November 15th...Expedition from Cape Girardeau to Clarkton. The detail commanded by Captain Henry C. Gentry, 2nd Militia Cavalry, left Cape Girardeau on October 27th and arrived that evening four miles west of White Water. The next evening they encamped at Bloomfield and on the 29th at West Prairie. On the 30th they moved to Four Mile in Dunklin County. There they arrested and later paroled Confederate Captain Whitacker and Lieutenant Walker. On the 31st they encamped at Clarkton. November 1st found them at Kennett. On the 3rd they moved back to Clarkton to protect the citizens who wished to vote, none availing themselves to do so.

October 29th...Stragglers from Shelby's command were sighted about 15 miles south of Warsaw. A detachment of about 25 men was sent to bring them in. Two or three were killed and 10 or 12 horses were captured. Captain Squire A. Ballew commanded the post at Warsaw.

October 29th-November 5th...Scouting by the Militia from Pilot Knob to Alton and Doniphan. Leaving on October 29th at 9:00 in the morning, the party arrived and encamped that night on the Little Black River on Buford's farm. The 30th was a terrible day as snow and rain fell all day. They camped that night on Hen Peck Creek then to Eleven Point River and camped near the farm of Confederate Commander Lieutenant Huttleson. From there they went on to Simpson's about four miles from the town of Alton in Oregon County, then into the town for the election. The election passed without incident. Lieutenant Bricker (Union) was much mortified by the results (?no clues?), "but the thing was done and could not be helped." That evening they made camp on the farm of Mr. Saunders. Daybreak of the 4th found them moving through the hills toward Doniphan in Ripley County. On the 5th they passed through Doniphan and camped again on the Little Black, then to Otter Creek, Bailey's Station and Pilot Knob. On the expedition a man named Farmer was found who had taken the oath at St. Louis and had a copy dated April 14, 1863 on his person. He also had a certificate that stated that William W. Farmer had furnished a substitute in the person of Jesse Hollice of Oregon County, Missouri; age 15 years, 5 feet and 7 inches in height, dark complexion, dark hair, hazel eyes, and by profession a farmer. This certificate was dated September 7, 1863 and signed by Major Lee Crandall, Commanding. The Captain goes on to state in his report, "I am of the opinion that the women in the region (area scouted) are even more dangerous and treacherous, and, in fact, worse than the men, as we found in their possession a number of newly made rebel uniforms," signed by Captain Robert McElroy.

November 4th...Brigadier General Egbert B. Brown located another band of stragglers from Shelby's command near the Sedalia Road, about 12 miles east of Lexington. Two were killed and four horses and equipment were captured.

November 4th-6th...One man belonging to an expedition of the 8th Militia was killed when he encountered a small detail of Confederates. It seems they had been plundering the town of Neosho, the booty being recovered. On the 6th the detail went down Butler's Creek and ran into another detail of Confederates killing eight. The number of wounded is unknown. It is reported that at least 200 Confederates have divided into small squads and are operating in this area.

November 4th-9th...Scouting party from Houston to Jack's Fork. Leaving the morning of November 3rd with 25 men, First Lieutenant John W. Boyd, 6th Prov. Enrolled Missouri Militia, set out on his gruesome mission. Boyd was pleased with his ensuing exploits. He started in the direction of Spring Valley, marched that day about 25 miles, without discovering anything worthy of note. He visited the residences of Benjamin Carter and Wilson Farrow, who had been engaged in the burning of Houston. They were apparently gone. He had Carter's house burned. On November 5th he divided the scout. Ten men were sent under Sergeant Basket, Company I, to march by way of Bay Creek to Jack's Fork. Lieutenant Boyd proceeded with the balance of the command by way of Leatherwood or Wollsey's trail; struck a fresh trail of horses; followed them on Jack's Fork to the residence of Miles Stephens and brother, Jack Stephens, whom he was satisfied were Bushwhackers. He burned the house. He heard that Fed Taylor had been at Stephen's place last week with 25 men. He proceeded down Jack's Fork ten miles, having marched 30 miles that day and camped at Widow McCormick's. Boyd had positive evidence that the widow had kept a general rendezvous for Freeman's and Coleman's Confederates. On the morning of the 6th he burned the buildings. Learning from the widow's son, a young lad, that on the previous evening James Mahan had got him to give news of their approach. He sent back and took Mahan prisoner then went down Jack's Fork to the mouth of Mahan Creek and turned up said creek on the Thomasville Road. Prisoner Mahan attempted to escape and was shot by the guard. Boyd camped at William Mahan's that night, having marched some 24 miles. On the morning of the 9th, he marched up Mahan's creek. About 9 o'clock, some 20 men were discovered on a bluff above them and shots were exchanged. Upon approaching the bluff, they saw the men had already gone. Boyd proceeded a few more miles and met three men who started to escape upon seeing the soldiers approach. He killed two of them, whom he ascertained from papers found upon them, as being William Chandler, supposed to live in Dent County, and a man named Hackley, who had in his pocket a discharge as lieutenant from Company F, Mitchell's Regiment, Confederate Army. He also had letters from citizens of Arkansas directed to persons in Dent and Phelps county. Two miles farther on they captured William Story on a United States horse. He was recognized as being a notorious horsethief and house robber. He tried to escape and was killed. That night Boyd camped at Morgan Dean's on Birch Prairie. On the 8th he started for Houston, about 5 miles, and there captured William Hulsey, James Hulsey, William McCuan and Samuel Jones at the house of James Harris, all well provided and packed, going to Freeman (Confederate officer). One of them had a horse which had been stolen sometime since from one of his men along with goods of different kinds. The first three, the Hulseys and McCuan were killed. Jones, on account of his extreme youth and apparent innocence, was brought in as a prisoner. About five miles further down the road, at the house of Jack Nicholson, a known rebel and Bushwhacker, they captured the said John Nicholson, Robert B. Richards, alias Bruce Russell and Jesse Story, all of whom were killed. Boyd then marched by way of McCubbin's Mill to Spring Valley and camped at Wiley Purcell's. He arrived back at the Houston camp on the 9th. He and his men marched in all 145 miles, killed 10 men and returned with one prisoner and burned 23 houses.

A court of inquiry was sent to Houston to investigate this mass burning and killing. It was then reported by Lieutenant Boyd that it was under Captain Murphy's orders to "clean them out," and that he did so. The court changed its mind. It was not adjudged after investigation as wanton killing or burning!

November 10th-18th...Expedition from Springfield, Missouri to Arkansas. This command of about 200 men of the 6th Missouri State Militia and 11th Missouri Cavalry marched to Linden, then southeast to Forsyth where the train was left, then south across White River to Carrollton, Arkansas.

November 23rd-29th...Scouting party leaves Houston again under command of Sergeant Basket to rescue two men who have been captured from the command of Captain Richard Murphy. (Murphy ordered the mass burnings on the last expedition out.) After a chase of two days, the party gave up. On the 24th, while two others of his men were riding about four miles from the post, they were met by what they supposed were three Federal soldiers, being dressed in Federal uniform. When they were in the act of passing, however, the three men drew their revolvers. The luckless two were taken to the brush, deprived of their horses, equipment, arms and clothing, with the exception of their underclothing. Afterward they were sworn and allowed to return to camp. Scouting parties were sent in every direction for 20 miles. Sergeant McDowell found a trail of six horses and commenced pursuit. The trail led about eight miles in the direction of Big Piney. There they suddenly came upon three Bushwhackers at the house of one Blankenship. Two escaped and Blankenship finally fell with 12 bullet holes in him. In the skirmish Blankenship wounded Private Henry J. Rennison. The wounded soldier was left behind at the home of Mr. Bradford, near Licking, but died the next day while being transported in an ambulance to the post.

November 30th...Attack on Bloomfield and pursuit of the Confederates to Brown's Ferry, Arkansas. About 500 Confederates surrounded the post at Bloomfield about 7:00 in the morning of the 29th. The Federals immediately opened fire with their two small howitzers, throwing shell into the Confederate ranks. This disgorged them from the hills surrounding the little post and forced them to the ravines for safety. About 8:00 in the morning they sent in a flag of truce demanding surrender and stating that the post was completely surrounded and all communications cut off, etc. It was signed by Major Lee Crandall, C.S.A. The Federals were ready to fight, not surrender. "If they wanted to fight open the ball." This was the answer to the flag. The Union command returned to the courthouse and opened fire. A flag again was sent out, this time by the Federals. The carrier was almost taken prisoner. Again they proceeded to do battle. Getting information that reinforcements would be arriving for the Confederates, the courthouse was further fortified. They used everything possible at hand, encircling the whole courthouse square. Men and horses were all moved inside and there they waited while the Confederates slipped quietly away. The chase began the next day with Captain Valentine Preuitt leading the pursuit to Brown's Ferry. He brought in only five ragged, poor men, too poor to live as prisoners. Later, Captain Preuitt was censored by Major Josephus Robbins for the inept way he handled the pursuit. The Captain had taken tired, worn men and jaded horses for this pursuit, leaving the fresh behind. Thus he could not catch up to them.

December 9th-19th...Scouting party again from Houston. The scouting party left Houston in the direction of Mountain Store after marching to Opossum Creek, a distance of 15 miles. There a fresh trail of the Confederates was struck. After doubling back and retracing his trail, a band of rebels was located that had just robbed some Union families. This trail was also lost. After being absent four days on the trip, they came up with a man named Clark, who was supposed to be a notorious rebel. During this scouting mission they camped upon the property of Widow Brown near Big Creek, scouted the headwaters of the North Fork of White River, West Plains, Indian Creek, Howell Valley, Jack's Fork, Johnson's Mill and Piney. Only Mr. Clark was found.

December 23rd-25th...Centerville is attacked and there is pursuit of the Confederates. An entire company of the 3rd Missouri State Militia was captured at Centerville, Reynolds County, by the Confederate troops under Reves on the 23rd, and on Christmas Day Major Wilson of the 3rd Militia overtook them and attacked. Thirty-five Confederates were killed and 150 were taken prisoner, of which 13 were officers. Also taken were equipage, ammunition and 125 horses. All the prisoners taken on the 23rd were recaptured. The Union loss was one killed and eight wounded. There were also skirmishes at Pulliam's. Pulliam's is 17 miles southwest of Doniphan.

December 24th-29th...Two scouting parties left Cassville to obtain information as to the position of Stand Watie (Indian Confederate). Scouting beyond Pineville. The command arrived at Cowskin Prairie and found Stand Watie had already gone. The trail was followed to the line and abandoned. The command then proceeded a short distance into Arkansas. There they destroyed a series of camps within some caves along Butler's Creek.

December 26th-28th...Scouting from Salem on the Current River proceeding down Gladden Valley. Returning by the Current River, a party of about eight Bushwhackers was discovered. Three were killed. They were Eli Louis, Samuel Louis and Bill Boyce. The dead are the same men who killed old Mr. Wasson a few days past.

December 26th-January 2nd...Scouting party from Forsyth to Batesville, Arkansas.

This ended another year of the Civil War. The guerilla bands were getting smaller and farther apart. Missouri was heavily Federally occupied. In the political world concerning the war, a captured woman, Mary Ann Pittman, turned, as we would call it, "state's witness." She admitted and gave information concerning an organization known as the "Order of American Knights." This organization was made up of some men in high places in northern and southern cities and states, working undercover to advance the Southern Cause in secret meetings with secret hand signals and passwords, etc. Many names came to light. Miss Pittman, in her testimony, told the investigators she was a lieutenant in Forrest's Cavalry. She had made at least three trips to St. Louis and had purchased ammunition from Beauvais and Co. for Forrest and had successfully smuggled it through. As her story unfolded others got into the picture and more names came to the surface, even in Missouri's heartland. Investigators also named one Douglas as one of the most active conspirators of the Knights in Missouri and is also a special emissary of Price. He was arrested while in the act of transporting a box of 40 revolvers by railroad to a guerilla camp in the interior of the State. In Jefferson City a government spy reports that Easterbrook's Saloon in the City Hotel is their principal haunt. Men can regularly be seen chatting treason among themselves in the persons of General Reid (uncle), Tom Miller, Captain Rogers, Ransom W.D. Kerr, old Mr. Davis and old Mr. Parsons, father of the rebel general. Another meeting place used in Jefferson City is the Commercial Hotel at the corner of Fifth and Washington Streets. Also used were two saloons on Washington Street (left-hand side as you go from Fifth to Fourth Street). There an acquaintance was made of a man named Kimber, who is a member of the "S.L." (maybe Sons of Liberty?), who states the meetings have ceased being held. Also named in Jefferson City was Mrs. Riggins, whose husband and two sons are in the Confederate Army. She is slated as one of the prating rebels of the town and also said to give aid and comfort whenever required to do so. Another is Miss Merritt, a woman of the same style, and boasts that rebel spies are in Jefferson City everyday. In Renick, Randolph County, it is reported that the Temple of O.A.K. is located within a half mile of the town, of which Dr. Christian was Grand Worthy. His arrest caused great uproar among the citizens. The following are named as being members: Dr. Hamilton; Colin Williams, a farmer who lives a half mile from Renick and is active; Mr. Jacobs, merchant, not very active; John Herrold, tobacconist, active; ____ Douglas, clerk for Jacobs, medium active; Little James Hardin, a farmer who lives four miles from Renick, active; Squire Collins, a farmer who lives one mile from Renick, active; Joseph Blackford, a farmer who lives three miles from Renick; Burrell Hunter (has a son in the bush); ___ Marshal, wagonmaker; ____ Marshal, blacksmith; _____ Wilcoyen, farmer; Dr. Callaway, Fayette, Howard County, very active and Newton Duncan from the same place. The investigator made a trip to Palmyra and stopped at the National Hotel, the proprietor of which is Mr. Overton. His son is a member of the Order. Other members were identified at Palmyra: James Overton, Samuel Anderson and Captain Pratt. The Lodges at Hannibal have stopped meeting.

The year of 1864 would be the breaking point of the Confederacy in Missouri. The big raids of Price, Shelby and Marmaduke will be repeated but to no avail. However, the devastation is still there and the food supply is even shorter. The citizens of the border counties will be planting crops in their new lands. The homeless and burned out will be more than ever before. There will be more localized killings than before. Yes, these things will still be there long after the great Union and Confederate generals are gone.

And so it was with record cold, below zero temperatures, blinding snow and much suffering from the effects of all that went before that we start a new year in the cruel war.

1864

In early January of this third year of the war, an all-out campaign against the Confederate forces in Arkansas was launched. It had been reported the Confederates were gathering in Newton, Searcy, Izard and Carroll Counties in Arkansas, with the object of attack being Springfield, Missouri. It was rumored this force numbered well over 1,000 men. The Federals came out of virtually every post in Missouri and headed south. The Confederates were ready and waiting. "The welcome mat was out!" Although there appears on paper various victories, some for each, the real losers were the people of Arkansas. For almost two years they had fed, helped clothe and supported, and more times than not unwillingly, the armies of various Confederate regiments. They had been left to the hands of the Kansas troops who marauded at will, disguising their deeds as just a part of war. They were left to deal with the guerilla bands that sought safety from the Militia and the homespun "vigilante" of Missouri. Huge armies hid in the hills, stripping the trees of their lush forests for their campfires, canoes and skiffs. They killed all the young breeding stock for food. The crops didn't stand a chance of ripening, especially the corn. It was eaten green and in other various stages of ripeness. The little patches of wheat were trampled by the horses. The granary was burned. It really didn't matter since one or the other of the armies would get it. No laws. No courts. Just military justice meted out by the one in residence that day.

But, back in Missouri...

January 1st...The Department of Kansas and the Department of Missouri will now again become separated.

January 15th-17th...Confederate campfires were still burning in a camp discovered in Jackson County about three miles west of the Lafayette County line, nearly west of Chapel Hill, when discovered by Lieutenant Couch of the 1st Missouri Militia. The Lieutenant reported that Blunt's command numbered about 50. Another detail commanded by Todd was in the vicinity of Round Prairie in Jackson County and that Lieutenant Kessinger found a camp near Pink Hill, also in Jackson County.

January 23rd...Thirty men of the 8th Missouri Militia Cavalry went into the Seneca Nation. It was reported that a squad of Confederates was encamped there. After riding about 18 miles through the woods to avoid detection, a halt was finally called. The march resumed the next morning. About one hour after sunrise the detail of 10 Confederates was discovered in a house. Leaving two killed and several wounded, the balance managed to reach the brush and safety of Cowskin Bottom. One of those killed was a deserter named Hardin Talifaro from the 6th Kansas Regiment, a lieutenant in Stand Watie's command.

112

January 23rd-27th...A scouting party from Patterson chased Reves and his squad of about 20 men for miles. They killed four of Reves' command and finally chased him across the river into Arkansas.

February 1st-March 1st...Leaving their post at Rolla on February 1st, the scouts, C.L. Woods, D. Causort, Aaron S. Vail, B.R. Moore and F.L. Hurd, were ordered to report to Captain Murphy commanding the post at Houston. They finally started on their mission January 5th with about 30 men under the command of Lieutenant Boyd, 6th Regiment of Enrolled Militia. The first day out they marched to Eaton's of Jack's Fork, about 22 miles from Houston; on the 6th they marched to Gilliland's in Peace Valley; the 7th they marched to Widow Thomas' place, or Gunter Valley in Howell County. There it was reported that some guerillas were in the immediate vicinity, and that a small party of them had, on the 6th, hanged a man by the name of Judd, nearly to death. Upon arriving at Mr. Judd's, they learned that the "small band" numbered about 84 men, and they were encamped about 10 miles up the road awaiting their approach. That night the scouts encamped on Judd's farm. On the morning of the 8th they scouted and foraged around the neighborhood and camped at Prock's. By the 9th reinforcements had arrived and they went in pursuit of Mr. Judd's aggressor. The band of guerillas, learning of the increase in numbers, moved on to Perkin's place on Warm Fork of Spring River. The scouts encamped this night at Robert's place. Within the next few days a man named Ben Carter and several others were killed. At Jane's Creek, a house was found in which were stored two barrels of salt, some guns and ammunition. This house was put to the torch. The scouts were only a safe distance away when a loud explosion was heard. Evidently a keg of gunpowder had been stored under the house. Later in the scouting foray William Lamb, who is a brother-in-law to Colonel Freeman, was killed by the scouts and command. The scouting party made its way back to the post, camping at the homes of James Harris on Turkey Oak; back to Eaton's on Jack's Fork; Mr. Coats' on Possum Creek and down the Possum to Joe Harris' place. The party learned that Bill Coats had moved his command down to the Big Piney, crossed the Piney near James Johnston's, camped at Smiley's Mill, camped at Joseph Gladden's place and headed home. Another report concerning this scouting party makes mention of their being in pursuit of Frank Smith, a "notorious outlaw." His camp was discovered near the farm of one Lowe in Texas County on the Roubidoux. The camp was taken with all supplies and destroyed. Another search resulted from the firing into the stage en route between Waynesville and the Gasconade. They encountered and attempted to capture J.E. Tigg, although he made good an escape. Burt Woods was reported about five miles south of Waynesville. Mr. Woods was killed in the ensuing skirmish.

February 2nd...Eight prisoners, one of whom is John Bolin, were taken prisoner by Captain Shibley (Union). Bolin and his men were attacked on Halcolm Island while foraging. Fifteen wagons of corn, the wagons belonging to the local citizens, were also captured. It was reported that 400 men were going to cross at Jones' Ferry. Captain Shibley destroyed the ferry (HQ Bloomfield).

February 5th-17th...A scouting party from Houston in pursuit of Colonel Freeman (CSA) left on the 5th and penetrated into Arkansas.

February 6th-10th...Captain C.F. Coleman scouted around Sni Hills, Jackson County.

February 12th...The westbound stagecoach was attacked four miles west of California House. It was escorted by nine men of the 8th Militia Cavalry, one of whom was killed by the ambush or in the skirmish that followed.

February 15th...Charleston, Missouri was the site of a sharp skirmish today. A scouting party of about 20 men and two guides went in search of a reported band of guerillas. The command split up, each hoping to find the trail. Corporal Philliber with 10 men surrounded the house of one Vernon. The woman of the house told them no one was there. Upon entering the house first, E.C. Edwards and Henry P. Bronson were killed by the guerillas hidden inside. One of the remainder of the detail went for help, but the guerillas made good their escape. The help arrived and by then it was dark. Bronson and Edwards were brought back to town, the remainder of the men left to watch the house. These men were fired upon from ambush, and Corporal Thomas M. Philliber and a citizen named Hughes were seriously wounded, their lives now endangered. The next day the party again proceeded to Vernon's house. Thoroughly searching the brush, etc. they found two horses tied and ready to ride hidden in the brush. The house was burned along with all the buildings. Mrs. Vernon has been ordered to leave the country. It is with much regret, according to the report, that she cannot be shot. The citizens, the guerilla contacts, were forced to haul in all the grain found on Vernon's place. Every house that harbors these "scoundrels" will be burned.

February 18th...A camp of mail robbers was found near the headwaters of the Piney. Several articles were recovered belonging to the stage passengers.

February 22nd-24th...Captain Blunt's Confederates were attacked today by Captain McFerran's command of the 4th Militia Cavalry, being driven out of the brush of the Blackwater about 12 miles from Warrensburg. The command of Captain Blunt moved to safer quarters but were attacked again on the 23rd.

February 23rd-March 9th...Scouting party from Springfield, Missouri into Northern Arkansas. Part of this mission, with about 30 men, was to escort refugees desiring to emigrate to Springfield.

February 27th...A Confederate train was captured and burned below Poplar Bluff. It contained a great many shotguns, rifles and corn. Two Jayhawkers were killed in its taking.

February 29th-March 13th...Expedition from Rolla to Batesville, Arkansas. With squadrons of men from St. Louis and some that had been serving in Southwest Missouri, the heavily-laden train left Rolla on the afternoon of the 29th. It encamped about five miles south of the same on the Little Beaver. On March 1st the train only made 13 miles as the wagons were heavily loaded and the roads bad. The journey was not one of skirmishes. Encampments were made at Thomas Reid's place close to a fine spring, 16 miles; Arthur's Creek, 16 miles; Elk River, 20 miles; Black Pond in Howell County; West Plains, Howell County; and on the 8th arrived in Arkansas at South Fork of Spring River, Fulton County.

March 16th-25th...Scouting party from Pilot Knob to the Arkansas line. This party marched the first day with 100 men and encamped three miles north of Buford's Ford on Black River. The next day it passed through Barnesville and encamped six miles from the Current River on Hen Peck Creek. The next day found them on the main road to Alton, encamped three miles north of Eleven Point River. A scouting party was sent out here. They encountered some desperadoes (?) in an old house. In the skirmish a private was killed and Sergeant Burks of the 3rd Militia was wounded. By the 20th the scouting party was making their way to Pocahontas.

March 17th-April 1st...Scouting party from Lebanon into Northern Arkansas. This scouting party marched through to Thomasville, Oregon County, without incident. It was only after crossing over the line into Arkansas that the party encountered severe skirmishing.

March 19th-22nd...A telegram from General Rosecrans informed Brigadier General Egbert Brown that there were apprehensions of a large outbreak that was to occur about the 20th. Recruits from Platte County will join it. Greenton Valley should be concentrated on with all forces to cooperate in putting this down. A scouting party was sent out and covered the area thoroughly. No one was found. It was reported that Colonel Jeans had been in the area during the winter recruiting for the Confederacy, but now has departed.

March 20th-30th...Captain Burris (same man who made the scout on the 19th to 22nd) and 47 men started on a scouting party on the 20th. They wounded Colonel Jeans, captured his camp, blankets and some horses in Jackson County. Literally hundreds of miles were traversed by this scouting party. Four details were out criss-crossing Jackson County.

March 27th...On the night of the 26th Mr. Short of Deepwater Township, Henry County, came to the post to inform that a party of

Bushwhackers was in his neighborhood menacing the citizens and committing the most outrageous acts of plunder, also threatening those who had enrolled for police duty at Germantown (Henry County). Sergeant John W. Barkley was sent with a detail in pursuit of these lawless ones. One of the Bushwhackers had, in the meantime, been severely wounded by a citizen, Mr. Archibald Colson. The band, taking the wounded man, and having it slow their movements, allowed Sergeant Barkley to catch up to them. They were found strongly entrenched in the house of a citizen, Matthew Dunn. Mr. Dunn has long been expected to help in their cause. Upon ordering a surrender, Sergeant Barkley and his men were fired on and returned the same. Volley after volley. The leader of the band gave his name as Captain A.D. Jones (CSA) and informed Barkley that he could defend himself. After many rounds, Sergeant Barkley sent for help. The other Bushwhackers, who had still been out pillaging the neighboring homes, heard the shots and returned, encouraging their comrades within the house to come out. Captain Jones opened the door and immediately changed his mind. The fight lasted throughout the night. Reinforcements arrived in the morning, but they were not needed. By then Captain Jones had surrendered. When he asked about terms, he was told that if he could prove he was a Confederate soldier, he would be treated as a prisoner of war. If not, he could face the consequences. Upon their surrender, it was found they were dressed in Federal overcoats, used Remington Federally-issued firearms and had a quantity of ammunition. Upon being brought to camp, they were given food. The leader ate voraciously, the other captive, a man named Ratliff, was sullen and refused to eat. Neither would give any truthful answer to any questions asked.

After they had been allowed to rest a few hours and the citizens came and claimed their goods, which were captured with the prisoners, the trial began. The witnesses were duly sworn and identified the men as belonging to the band who had committed numerous outrages during the winter. The leader, Jones, made a shrewd defense until he found himself trapped, when he then became bold and replied that if he had it to do over again, he would have sent some of the squads to the lower region before he went there. If he had to die, he had paid for his life nine times. At 10:00 they were executed. They were allowed to write their friends and send their trinkets thusly. It was only at the last moment they made their true identity known. The leader proved to be one Benton Gann of Lafayette County, who has long commanded a marauding band along the border. The other was George Herold of Cass County, one of Gann's men. They calmly walked to the grave, knelt down and said they were ready. They met death with a dauntless courage worthy "of a better cause." The injured man, Jones, is very much mutilated by buckshot wounds and was sent to Clinton to be operated on by Surgeon Hart. It is doubtful he will survive, but if he should, he can expect the same fate.

March 30th...A detail of the 1st Militia followed a fresh trail of some Bushwhackers about five miles on foot. Near the town of Greenton, Jackson County, they came upon them and attacked. James H. Waller, a member of the band, was killed. Waller was one of Captain Blunt's men (CSA). He participated in the murder of Mockabee and Saunders at the residence of Arthur G. Young on the night of February 22nd.

April 1st...One man from Kitchen's (CSA) command was killed today near Bloomfield. Captain Shibley came upon them in the act of robbing a Union man's house. Two of the men ended up as prisoners. One claims to be from Illinois, the other from Douglas County, Missouri.

April 10th...Mississippi, Dunklin and Pemiscot Counties have been inundated by numerous deeds of depredations committed by the roving bands of guerillas and Confederates during the past three weeks. It has now spilled over into New Madrid County. All the inhabitants of these counties are strong secession sympathizers and do not report until a day or two after they are robbed and, often, not at all. The country is filled up with guerilla bands composed of returned out-of-service Confederate soldiers. A strong force left New Madrid and headed down into the swamp and bayou country of Arkansas to attack the various bands.

April 18th...Three Bushwhackers came into Hunnewell today armed to the teeth to plunder. The citizens resisted. One of the men is now dead and one mortally wounded, and Captain Farnam (Militia) is badly wounded.

April 19th-20th...A detachment of a regiment stationed at Charleston had a fight with guerillas on the 19th, killing four of them. On the 20th they were discovered in a house. A spirited skirmish took place. Eight men were killed and the house burned. This past week Philip Davis, guerilla chief, was also killed.

April 21st...Brookfield in Linn County was robbed this past week. Sergeant Thomas J. Westly in charge of a squad at Laclede is in pursuit. The two forces met in Chariton County. In the clash one horse was killed and two men, swimming for horses, were run into Elk Creek and may have drowned. The prisoners taken were William Hickman, William Hines and Jackson Bazier, all desperate men and well-known Bushwhackers. The first had taken the oath last year in Carroll County. He was a guide for a party of guerillas who robbed every Union man on Perche's Prairie Sunday night last. He shot one man, a German named John Smith.

April 28th-30th...The 1st Missouri Militia of Warrensburg had a merry chase after a band of guerillas. The guerillas crossed the Grand River at Dayton, moving toward Rose Hill, taking with them Sergeant P. Russell who commanded the post at Dayton as prisoner. The pursuit that followed started at daylight the next morning with a detail of about 50 men. Upon reaching the bridge over Big Creek, they found it partially destroyed. They repaired it after a fashion and crossed. The trail was still clear, following it to Holden; now they were only about six hours behind. The trail out of Holden was followed north and west until within about three miles of Chapel Hill. There it was learned of the massacre of First Lieutenant James E. Couch, Bugler Francis N. Kelly and Joseph T. Mason, private of the 1st Militia Cavalry, by Quantrill's men. Quantrill's men, 80 to 100, newly-arrived and fresh from the south, being well armed and mounted, took the command of Lieutenant Couch by surprise. They were all dressed in Federal uniforms. The trail being unreadable now, the command returned after orders from Lieutenant Stanton of the 2nd Colorado to proceed toward Napoleon. The trail of about 10 guerillas appeared and was followed about four miles from Lone Jack. The two forces met under unusual circumstances in pursuit of each other. The Militia detail, thinking the guerillas were Federal troops, rode right into the midst of them. Finally the grevious error was discovered and the pursuit was again taken up by the Militia until the horses gave out. Privates G. Wells and J. Freestone of the Militia lost their lives in the ruse.

April 28th-May 7th...Scouting party (Militia) from Springfield toward Fayetteville, Arkansas. Eighty men and two commissioned officers left Springfield with the intent of establishing telegraphic communications with the Fayetteville post. After arriving, the Militia was advised of the repairs already having been made to the telegraph. The Confederate commands were threatening to move north and attack the station at Neosho. Skirmishing across Cowskin Prairie with stragglers of Colonel Adair's command, it was virtually certain they were headed toward Neosho. Later it was learned that the main body of the Confederates had been ordered to recross the Grand River to the west of Cowskin Prairie, about 30 hours ahead of the Militia. The Militia again turned toward Springfield. Upon arrival back at Springfield, the fort was being made ready for an attack.

May 2nd...A scouting party met up with a camp of guerillas upon Bee Creek. Three of the band started to run and were soon overtaken and killed. The rest made it to safety in the mountains. The scouting party worked over the areas of Bee and Bear Creeks for three days. Those killed were Campbell, Williams and Parkes, all of Missouri. (We take this area to be near Forsyth, Missouri and through Arkansas.)

May 6th...The scouts returned this day. Lieutenant Toney of the 2nd Militia chased them about 25 miles below Bloomfield. Two men were killed, Whitson and Saddler. Saddler carried a parole in his pocket issued by the Provost-Marshal at New Madrid last December.

May 6th-11th...A large detail of Militia left Patterson and proceeded toward Poplar Bluff, 33 miles; then to Cleveland in the swamps, 40 miles; then to the ferry on Current River near Pocahontas, Arkansas. Finding the ferry destroyed, and it being impossible to cross either the Current or the Black, the command proceeded back up the Current about 10 miles. The Confederates were found there lined for battle in the road. After some skirmishing, the Confederates retreated into the thick brush. (Skirmish took place at Cherokee Bay, Arkansas.)

May 10th-25th...Scouting party from Pilot Knob to Gainsville, Arkansas.

May 13th...Sixteen of the 15th Militia and a small party of Enrolled Missouri Militia suddenly called together, fell upon a party of about 30 guerillas going north six miles northeast of Cuba. They are being pursued.

May 16th...Skirmishing at Drywood Creek, about 35 miles southeast of Fort Scott, Kansas. A raid led by Confederate Captain Henry Taylor, formerly the sheriff of Vernon County, was made upon Drywood, south and southeast of Fort Scott, Kansas. Houses were plundered all along the route and all male occupants of the houses were taken prisoner. He leaves behind a trail easily followed from house to house. By the time Captain Taylor had reached the house of one Ury, he held eight prisoners. Ury, the younger, was a special prize for the Captain as he had acted as a guide for the Militia. The scouts, only five in number, were sent in pursuit of Captain Taylor, feeling his party was also small in number, found this not so. Two men were sent back for assistance, leaving three to stop Taylor. These three men came up just as the Captain and his men were leading the prisoners out the gate at Ury's house. Yelling and firing as rapidly as possible, they rode their horses right into the Confederate command. This caused much confusion. The younger Ury, seizing the opportunity, grabbed a stick of wood and dispatched the one next to him and made a getaway amid all the commotion, as did all the other prisoners. The only injury was sustained by the elder Ury, he being injured in the hip but not seriously. Young Ury hurried right for the camp of Company C, got five fresh men and a horse and joined in the pursuit.

May 16th-25th...Expedition from Patterson to Bloomfield and Pilot Knob. This expedition traversed down into Arkansas and recrossed the Black River and came back up the other side into Missouri. Confederate Colonel Kitchen is reported as going down the St. Francis into Arkansas for supplies. The expedition started its return to Bloomfield on Thursday the 18th. The Bushwhackers posted the camp that night. Captain Huiskamp (Militia) was wounded in the arm during a visit to the camp pickets.

May 18th-23rd...Scouting parties out near Neosho and Carthage. It has been reported that about 75-80 Confederates passed between Newtonia and Neosho on the 18th. A scouting party was sent to investigate the robberies of citizens on Spring River about eight miles above Carthage. This scouting party followed the command of Confederates all through the area. They never got close enough for battle and never caught up to them.

May 20th...Lamar was attacked by some 100 Confederates about daylight this day. This is suspected to be the same command that passed through Granby on the 18th. It is later reported by dispatch that Marmaduke, with 500 men, was engaged in fighting at Newtonia all day of the 19th. Answering reports to this news, the commander, Colonel Charles W. Blair, doesn't think that it is Marmaduke who is attacking Newtonia and, if it is, that 500 men would only be his advance. He is known not to travel or attack with less than 5,000 to 6,000 men. The attacking party at Lamar was found to be under Confederate Colonel Adair.

May 21st...Nine men acting as escort of a prisoner named Hopkins, was attacked by some 30 or so Bushwhackers about one-half mile east of the crossing of Blue River. The escort was surrounded and fired on from ambush from all directions, causing a general confusion among the guards. The Bushwhackers, thought to be led by the prisoner's father, were hidden in the brush, firing at no less than 20 yards. The escort, some dismounted and some on horseback, made for the brush. Two of the guards were killed, Corporal John Sowell and Private Anton Voght. Private Austin Means is missing. The Bushwhackers set fire to the wagon, burning the bed, then shooting and wounding all of the mules. In the melee the Corporal succeeded in killing the elder Hopkins, whose family has been run out of the country twice previously for their activities.

May 23rd-25th...A scouting party left Warrensburg in the pursuit and rousting of several parties of guerillas marauding in the area of Warrensburg. Attacking some four miles northeast of Chilhowee were Sergeant Solathel Ston and five men, one of whom was Judge King of Captain W.H. Thompson's Company of Citizen Guards. Judge King was killed. The Sergeant and three of his men were captured. Only one managed to escape. At this same time another party of about 15 was reported as being seen the previous night near the railroad east of Holden. Lieutenant Hardesty reported 100 guerillas crossed the Osage at Taberville coming north. A lady reported that a band of about 30 men had taken her husband's horse the night before about six miles east of Holden and north of the road, and they went north. Messengers finally arrived and reported the sight of Quantrill with about 200 men heading toward Holden. Messages were immediately sent to Kingsville for assistance. A relief party of 27 men left and proceeded to Hopewell by railroad. About eight miles from Holden, the party was joined by the 20 men from Kingsville and 15 Citizen Guards of Captain Jones' Company, all reaching Hopewell at daybreak. Messages were sent to Captain Burriss who came with an additional 65 men, and the party reached Holden about 4:00 in the afternoon, then learning Quantrill had moved north during the night. Captain Burriss, after scouting the area, returned to his camp on Walton's farm in Texas Prairie and the remainder returned to Warrensburg, with one company being left at Kingsville.

May 26th...A search party left the post at Rolla in hopes of locating Sergeant Leland Carter and four men, all belonging to the 2nd Wisconsin, who are thought to have been taken prisoner. Leaving camp on the morning of the 27th and traveling about 20 miles northwesterly, they struck the Waynesville and Vienna Road near the house of Mr. Bull on Maries Creek. They learned then from citizens there assembled that the Sergeant and his men were all lying about a mile from that place in the woods. They had been shot and left there by some party, supposed to be Bushwhackers. The citizens knew but little about the circumstances. A colored lady said finally that she saw the men about sundown in the road near Mr. Bull's and saw a party of men dressed in Federal uniform, numbering about 15, each party telling the other to "halt." She said there was some loud talk and then the whole rode off together into the woods and later shots were heard. A lady afterward told of meeting the men, some 15 or so, on the road, and they asked her about seeing any Bushwhackers in the area passing themselves off as Federal soldiers from Jefferson City. The bodies were recovered and returned to camp. It was evident the Sergeant and his men had put up a valiant struggle. The body of the Sergeant had been stripped and a pair of old worn shoes replaced his boots.

May 27th...The Citizen Guards, or a part of them, some being absent, and a band of guerillas had a skirmish at Shanghi in Johnson County. The town was captured and burned by the guerillas. Militia companies are gathering to retaliate this offense.

May 28th...Confederates under Taylor and Marchbanks entered the town of Lamar at 12:00 this morning and burned nearly every house in the town, together with most household goods. All the books and records of the county again went up in flames. The women and children sat outdoors trying to guard what little they managed to salvage. Assistance was requested from the commander of the Carthage post. He could spare no one. Assistance was sought from Mount Vernon, the colonel in command was absent. "I do not know what the loyal citizens of that place have done that has subjected them to such treatment from the military. We were promised better things; but, alas, again we find ourselves the victims of mistaken confidence, etc." citizen, Nathan Bray.

May 30th-31st...Leaving on May 29th, Captain John Kelso of the 8th Missouri Militia, with a command of about 30 men, marched in the direction of Huff's Mill in Arkansas. As they proceeded down Indian Creek in McDonald County, they learned that two Bushwhackers had passed down a few hours in advance, robbing several poor families as they went by. Following their trail and ambuscading the road, they set out the next morning and proceeded through Rutledge, having learned that the original two, plus now several others, had passed up Mill Creek. Finding the trail, they followed it to a house of a Bushwhacker by the name of Waitman, there discovering a considerable quantity of provisions and some Federal clothing. Believing this was a place of main rendezvous, the area was scouted up the ravines. Sharp firing was soon heard and two Bushwhackers were no longer living. Presenting the horses of the luckless two to the men, the party proceeded over the hills to Butler's Creek. There a hidden tanyard was found and destroyed. The detail then proceeded toward Honey Creek, where they had heard a dancing party was going on. It was attended by, no less, the notorious Lieutenant McGee (CSA) and seven of his men. The detail missed the dancing. Their approach was signaled by guns hidden in the hills. They accomplished nothing, only capturing some quilts and blankets at the campsite. The surrounding houses or "hovels" were burned, where they had supposedly been harbored, and then proceeded to find the party. At a house "consulting," a man thought to be Lieutenant McGee "discovered us and got up and dusted." He was followed on foot by Lieutenant Hunter and several others, all of whom, however, were distanced in the race and came back, except Lieutenant Hunter and three others. The four followed until they were a full mile from the command when they ran right upon McGee and his party of seven men. They charged like madmen, killing two of McGee's men on the spot and wounding another. The remainder of the command was chased for more than a mile. Tiring, they gathered up as many horses as they could and rode back to camp, expressing themselves as highly pleased with their "fun." While the horses grazed, Captain Kelso and one other man removed their coats and made themselves up to appear as Bushwhackers. They set out on a dead run to a rebel house a half-mile away, rushing in, all covered with sweat and dust. Exclaiming to the startled lady that they "had just ran into some 200 Federals, and that Lieutenant McGee had sent them after every valuable horse that would do to ride." She soon furnished three fine horses belonging to McGee's command which the sweaty men very politely received and went upon their way rejoicing. The happy little detail then headed for their home post at Neosho feeling no little pride.

June 1st...A desperate fight occurred this morning between a detachment of Militia and Bushwhackers in the southeastern part of Buchanan County. The Militia being outnumbered and totally surprised, lost three men killed. Two hundred mounted men are now in pursuit of the guerillas. Apprehended by the Militia were two men who confessed to the murders of Wilson and Christian (?), and named their confederates in crime. Later in the day it was reported that this same band of guerillas made a raid on New Market, Platte County, for plunder. They stole horses, guns and money and then headed for Platte City. They are believed to be a portion of Quantrill's band.

June 3rd...A detachment, numbering 40 men of the Militia, scouted the Willow Ford on Lamine Creek in Cooper County. Dividing forces, a portion scouted Mastim's Bridge on Lamine Creek, on the main road from Boonville to Georgetown. Hearing of a band of guerillas in the vicinity of the Pilot Grove post office, the detail started for there but reached their destination too late. The guerillas had moved on. Left behind dead was Captain James Mayo of Cooper County, who just happened to be in the post office at the time. Mr. Brownfield, a local citizen, was also injured being shot in the hand. The guerillas turned down the same road the detachment had traveled upon entering the town. The guerillas went directly to Longwoode and there robbed the citizens. A man named Warren of Knob Knoster area is reported to be with the band. It is thought the plunder stolen was for the relief of their families. The brave, ruthless band numbered only a mere 12 men.

June 5th-9th...A scouting party left on foot for a five-day trek through Johnson County. They reported random minor skirmishes and occasional firing on the journey, marching about 50 miles.

June 5th-12th...Checking considerable signs of guerillas in the vicinity of Beaver and Big Creeks and Little North Fork, a detail left Forsyth on the 5th. At Mountain Home two men were captured and two others escaped to safety. One more man was taken prisoner about seven miles south of Mountain Home. At the home of Mr. Wolf, the remains of a large encampment that had left the previous day for Salem was found. There were no other signs. During a heavy rainstorm on the 10th two of the prisoners attempted to escape, and one made it good and the other was killed. This scouting party traversed through Ozark and Douglas Counties.

June 7th...Colonel J.B. Rogers' command of the 2nd Militia came upon six guerillas at Sikeston, killing one notorious man named Wright. The others escaped, but it is believed from a trail of blood found, that some were wounded. One prisoner was taken, being too drunk to kill. Wright was a man of desperate character. He had just shot a horse because it carried the U.S. brand, and he had shot a negro man only a moment before his capture. The negro was found lying there dead. He also said he was the commander of the party who fired on the soldiers last Saturday, killing eleven of them at New Madrid. He admitted tearing down the telegraph line, and if the commander didn't believe him to look in his saddlebags. A roll of telegraph wire was in them. Wright said he would keep on so long as he could raise an arm. It is reported that Mr. Wright departed this life last evening in his attempt to escape. Also on June 7th, in Saline County, a citizen from New Frankfort brought in news that the place was attacked by a least 20 Bushwhackers. They committed all sorts of depredations and infamies on the citizenry.

June 8th-19th...Another scouting party on the Osage River and vicinity. All was well with this scouting party until they marched from Pleasant Gap about eight miles to a ford on the Osage, two miles east of Papinsville. There some of the men and large wagon were secreted behind some hedges at the Widow Barrow's house, and a lookout was posted atop the house. Later in the day the lookout reported riders approaching, six mounted men coming down the river bottom past Papinsville. They proved to be Bushwhackers and a running fight ensued to the timber of Papinsville. Three made good an escape into the brush. Two were killed and two were wounded. One apparently died in the muddy slough his horse went through. The horse emerged riderless. One horse was captured, along with some $250.00 in Confederate money, some clothing, calico, coffee, etc. that was thrown away in their flight. Four of the loose horses ran up the river bottom. Men on fresh horses were sent to follow them. The trail took them eight miles in the direction of Double Branches. Here 12-14 Bushwhackers rode out of the brush near Miami Missions, gathering the loose horses and all headed off together. They were believed to be part of Potter's gang which had been operating on the Kansas side of the border. All were well armed and splendidly mounted. The pursuit party finally giving it up, returned to camp. Sergeant Hutchins with a portion of the command was left at Barrow's place to guard the ford and bury the dead Bushwhackers. On the 14th this scouting party sent a wagon back to Balltown for corn. The other 15 men were sent to scout and found a deserted campsite at Stumptown. They struck a trail and followed it to Hog Skin Prairie. There it scattered. (The party traveled a total of 30 miles this day. Hog Skin Prairie is evidently 15 miles from the starting place of Double Branches on the Marais-des-Cygne River?) The guerilla camp is thought to be on an island in the Marais-des-Cygne.

June 9th...A detail of the 65th Militia went to the Welden neighborhood bent upon capturing an escaped prisoner. They set up in the bushes around the Widow Welden's house and part of them at the home of E.E. Welden. They arrived at the appointed places about 1:00 in the morning. At about daylight, horsemen were heard approaching. The guards called a halt, which was ignored. The guard fired and it was sharply returned. A general engagement developed. Captain Givens of the Caldwell County Enrolled Militia was killed and two more of the Militia badly wounded. (Welden is in the vicinity of Breckenridge.)

June 9th-14th...Scouting party from Cassville to Cross Hollow, Arkansas. The party of the 2nd Arkansas (Union) proceeded secretly in the direction of Cross Hollow by back roads. About 12 miles from Cassville they made camp. By June 10th, the next day, they are within a few miles of their destination. At Cross Hollow they repaired telegraph wires and arrested Mrs. and Misses Gibson, who were caught in an attempt to cut the wire they had just repaired.

June 10th...Captain Herring and Lieutenant Roberts, 3rd Militia Cavalry, stationed at St. James, rode out of camp and encountered a Confederate detail of about 25 men dressed in Federal uniform, in the act of crossing the railroad. They were fired upon and Captain Herring was seriously wounded. The rebels then scattered. Later in the day, five of them came to Dillon and set fire to two boxcars and were in the act of firing the tank when the returning scouting party fired upon them. Three of their horses were captured. One of the horses that had been captured by them was one belonging to Lieutenant Roberts.

June 10th-15th...A scouting party was detailed to scout from Sedalia with 42 men and proceeded via Georgetown to Longwood. On the morning of the 11th the detail was sent to investigate a raid upon Renick's farm, 12 miles northwest of Marshall. When they arrived at the farm, they found no trace of an enemy. They moved on to Mr. Ney's, a "good Union man," and inquired from him the circumstances of which, he said, nothing happened at Renick's. Further on into the scouting mission a trail of some horses was found and tracked to the house of Mrs. Haney. There two men were seen running out from the back of the house, jumping over the fence and running into the woods. Outside of the house stood two tied horses. In the house was found rebel mail and a quantity of merchandise. At the campsite another U.S. mailbag, horses and goods were recovered. Mrs. Haney, two Misses Haney and a Miss Williams, who proudly stated they fed the Bushwhackers and "would do it again" and "relished the Bushwhackers," were arrested.

June 10th-23rd...Confederate Dick Yeager was killed, the one and same who led the guerillas that killed 12 Militiamen near Kingsville and eight with the train near Lexington. Other incidents today concerned a skirmish at Lexington with about 70 guerillas and 23 Militiamen. There were two minor skirmishes in Jackson County with Captain Burriss and his men and a small band of guerillas. It is reported by Brigadier General E.B. Brown that the scouting parties that have emerged and scouted through Johnson County and vicinity in the past 10 days, from the 10th until the 19th, have been over 3,810 miles, had 23 men killed and wounded, one horse and two revolvers lost, two wagons burned and 12 mules killed. During the dispatch of their duty they have killed 27 men, seven horses and captured six stands of small arms.

June 11th...A detachment of Militia was attacked by Captain Overson, formerly of Kansas, and Lieutenant Oldham, both of Colonel Calhoun Thornton's command (CSA). William Oldham is the son of a planter of Platte County. Captain Overson was killed and the Lieutenant is to be executed within the hour. These men committed the murders at Arnoldsville (?). Eleven of this command appear on the rolls of a Militia company and carried a Federal musket all last winter. In the skirmish they killed one Militiaman and wounded four others. Among the plunder was found some important papers belonging to the Confederate commander and $110.00 in Confederate money. These men were also guilty of killing Thomas H. Bailey of the 16th Kansas Cavalry who was home on furlough, about five miles from Weston. (Report made from Ridgely in Platte County.)

June 12th...The day proved to be very eventful in Missouri history! A Confederate command was spotted going through Montevallo last week.   Today about 30 of them made up a party that attacked Lieutenant C.B. Willsey of the 3rd Wisconsin at Montevallo.   A train is reported just in at Fort Scott, Kansas carrying 1,000 refugees from Fort Smith, Arkansas.   This day also saw a raid on Calhoun, Missouri.   About 20 guerillas made a dash into the town, burned one church, one tavern and two dwelling houses and robbed two stores.   A scouting party working in the area of Kingsville Railroad encamped for the night on the farm of Mrs. Longacre, about one-half mile north of the railroad about three miles west of Kingsville.   The following morning, having only traveled a short distance, they were totally surprised and surrounded by Colonel Yeager, Confederate Commander, and assisted by Bill Anderson who is the captain of a guerilla band.   Twelve of the scouting party were killed outright.   The opinion was that the men were shot after surrendering, and one was scalped (Corporal Ireland).   All were strippped of their outer clothing.   The deceased were sent to Holden for burial.   Another detail was sent out in pursuit, and the trail of Yeager and his men was picked up in the Sni Hills, about three miles west of the Widow Hill's, where Lewis Spainhower had lived since early spring.   A skirmish followed and one of the guerilla command was seriously wounded.   The rest escaped.   Their trail was followed through the thick brush and the dense woods to about five miles south of Lone Jack.

June 13th-16th...Major R.H. Hunt, 15th Kansas Cavalry, proceeded from Fort Leavenworth in Kansas to Weston, Missouri, starting for Platte County via Leavenworth City.   It was then reported the guerillas had already started for Platte City, the scouting party following suit.   About a half mile down the road they were informed that a party of Bushwhackers, about eight men, had returned to Farley.   The scouting party retraced their march and entered Farley.   About this time a group of citizens appeared under Mr. Losee and cut off the retreat of the supposed Bushwhackers.   The Bushwhackers turned out to be returning Militia from Platte City. While at Farley it was learned that the guerillas and the town Militia fought desperately, the citizens having saved their lives and property by the aid of "rifle whiskey."   The energetic guide, David Causort, soon found the trail of where the guerillas had passed.   Following the trail, they soon crossed the Platte, which they had to swim.   Finally night came on and the trail was lost. In the early morning of the next day, they started for Platte City and from there to Ridgely, about six miles, where they found the Captain and the citizens under arms and happy to see the party arrive.   The skirmish involved the commands of Confederate Captain Overson and Lieutenant Oldham (now supposedly deceased!).   Some of the men fought well, but seven ran away.   Three were never to return.   While at Platte City, the report came that troops were approaching.   These also proved to be friends returning.   Staying in town until after dark, the party set out for the Goose Neck country around Weston by a very circuitous route, feeling that perhaps the rebels would be camped there.   Crossing the Platte River again, the journey began about 2:00 in the morning.   Seven miles from Weston, at the house of a man named Fulton, the advance espied a mounted Confederate, but he got away. The old man, Fulton, was ordered to accompany them, and when he refused to do so, was handled "pretty roughly." At that moment a daughter of Fulton made her appearance and aimed a revolver at Sergeant Gill and David Causort, the guide. The latter, however, disarmed the fair damsel. He also took from her a Bowie knife and flask of powder, all of which the scout now has in his possession as a "love token." No more arms were located on the premises, but the opinion was they were concealed. The old man was taken against his will, but the commanding officer promised the family his safe return. Within five miles of Weston a stop was made and the St. Joseph troops, who had accompanied the party thus far, took the old man out and hanged him "a little." The old man just calmly requested that his body should be returned to his wife, but the promise of his safe return saved him. "The whole family is plucky and the guerillas should find them valuable auxiliaries." At Weston the blacksmith shop was visited. This was where Private Bailey was taken by three or four guerillas and killed. The search for his body was in vain. The smithy, Thomas Newnham, was absent. His wife carried on an amiable conversation and informed the party her husband had done no work for weeks, adding that he had no coal. Upon entering the shop, they found the fire laid in the forge and evidence that work had been done there only a few hours before. Mr. Newnham denied shoeing any horses for the guerillas and knew nothing of Private Bailey. He finally did remember shoeing horses and seeing Private Bailey passing. The scouting party in conclusion feels there are about 300 organized Confederates in the counties of Platte, Clay and Buchanan under the command of Colonel Thornton, brother-in-law to Colonel Doniphan of Weston.

June 14th...A memorable day! Around sunrise about 75 Bushwhackers rode into the sleepy little town of Melville in Dade County. They succeeded in burning the town and killing several men, mostly citizens. The Militia of the town under Major Morgan was scouting in the area of Horse Creek and not present. The guerilla/rebels? were commanded by Pete Roberts, leaving town in a northwesterly direction toward White Hare or Sons Point. They burned several houses on Sac River in passing. Captain Higgenbotham's company has just moved into town from Pennsylvania Prairie and has taken up the pursuit with 20 men. Fighting broke out at Lexington. A detachment of 35 men sent to Lexington for rations were returning to their post at Warrensburg. About 12 miles from Lexington they were attacked by about 100 guerillas under the command of William Whitset. Finally after making three attempts to repel the superior force, eight of the escort were killed and two wounded. Two wagons of rations were lost and 15 of the mules killed. Also on the 14th a scouting party left Pleasant Hill for a mission along the Lafayette and Jackson County borders. A command of about 100 men scoured the country around the Sni Hills, Blue and Oak Hollows and traversed to a line about six miles below Lone Jack.

June 15th...Major Mitchell and the command under him came upon the force that burned Melville today at White Hare. Six of the arsonists were killed on the spot and a large number wounded. Eleven horses were captured and the force scattered in all directions. The command was made up from Peter Roberts' and Hinch West's bands. A large amount of the property was returned to the residents of Melville. The rebels were caught in the act of a private auction of the goods from Melville and taken by surprise. They are now thought to have left the country for safer surroundings.

June 16th...Report is made by Colonel C.W. Blair (we get the feeling that all is not contained as far as facts concerning the success of this skirmish...read on). About noon today a party of 30 men of Company C, 3rd Wisconsin Cavalry, was attacked in the brush by Confederates 40 miles south of Fort Scott on the Carthage Road, as they returned from a scout, killing one of the scouting party and two of their own. Sergeant Smith, with his command of Militia, moved onto the open prairie to have a fair chance. The enemy declined to follow. (Now Colonel Ehle tells another grim story.) "The body undoubtedly lies there, and I would like permission to go down with a body of men sufficient to obtain it and to make such endeavor as would be prudent to obtain the cattle. My first duty is to put my company in fighting trim. We need forty carbines, twenty-five pistols, and at least forty saddles. We have the horses, but no saddles." (It appears that a herd of cattle was lost and a body left at the skirmish site. Nothing is referenced by the Colonel.) The skirmish site was Big North Fork Creek, lower ford, near Preston. (In the third report Sergeant Smith tells us still another story.) The command was bringing out cattle for the use of the Government trains. Forty-six rebels came out a short distance from the timber and kept up a continuous firing while the command was so badly scattered there was no possible time for them to form a line. Retreat was ordered, and finally a line was formed almost 100 yards to the rear of the first attack. The retreat continued away from the timber out onto the open prairie. The cattle all running off into the timber. Private Eugene Hunt was killed at the onset of the skirmish.

June 16th-17th...Expedition by boat from Fort Leavenworth to Farley, Missouri, Platte County. Nothing of significance. Dr. Holt's house was searched by Farley in hopes of locating the doctor's son. He was not found, but an older brother from Falls City, Nebraska was present. He was relieved of his pistol.

June 16th-20th...Troops from Kansas into Missouri. This all started with a communication of "enemy 500 strong near Sni Hills. Proceed to Aubrey and there troops will be concentrated, and take command. Have Colonel Snoody call the militia." dated 13th of June, Paola, Kansas. The soldiers in blue coats came from every direction and crossed and recrossed the whole of Jackson and Cass Counties ranging into Johnson. There were sightings only twice of any sort of enemy. Those were small parties of five to 15 men. No one was injured in the random shots fired.

June 17th...Major Evans and an escort of five soldiers left Centralia this morning with 50 shotguns to deliver. About two miles from Columbia, where the arms were to be delivered, the small party was attacked. The first encounter wounded two of the escort, the second encounter some two miles farther down the road. The Major and the two remaining men were overpowered and all arms were lost along with the wagon in which they were being transported. The citizens needed the arms very badly in Columbia in order to defend themselves.

June 18th-19th...Confederate Captain Holtzclaw of Howard County, with 16 men, rode into Laclede (Linn County) and arrested virtually any citizen they could find. They took some reported 50 to 60 prisoners and robbed the stores of money and goods, whatever they could carry. In the ruckus that developed a man named Crowder, from his position in a window, shot one of the Confederates. The man turned, though wounded, and he in turn killed Crowder, firing back through the same window. Also shot was a citizen named Jones who started to run. A town messenger started to Brookfield to get assistance at the first sight of them. The command under Lieutenant Billings mounted up and went in pursuit, along with a group from the town who took up the chase with a train engine. Holtzclaw stopped the mail hack and commandeered it to carry the wounded. One of the men from the train got off a lucky shot and took out one in the hack.

One of Holtzclaw's men is a brother to a man who killed one Brock. The other deceased was named Callahan. The Confederate camp was found in a log house at the forks of Yellow Creek and Grand River, laden with bacon, bread, some corn and meat. This was furnished by someone, but the premises is now ashes. Many were recognized as those who took the oath of allegiance in 1861. Holtzclaw was again within 2 1/2 miles of Laclede by the next night, being well protected by the law-abiding citizens of the area. The amounts of damages and stolen goods will be levied on those of their friends that harbor and protect the men. The Lieutenant in pursuit left behind some incidents. The Lieutenant stopped at one house of a known rebel and demanded breakfast, and after much argument, finally got it. At this house a paper, The New York Day Book, was found. One of the soldiers, upon reading some article that he felt was rather unflattering, destroyed every copy he could find within the house. In the next house, the soldier who tore up the paper spied another copy of the same, and it was destroyed. In the next house they visited in order to procure information as to Holtzclaw's whereabouts, a young man insulted one of the Lieutenant's men, who promptly dismounted and knocked him down, then calmly remounted his horse and followed leisurely after his company. At the next home was a young lady who ran out to meet them. She told them she had just left a house not a quarter of a mile off, where she thought a man named Bolon lived, that there were six strange men there. Upon arriving at the house, it was found to be empty and deserted. A few caps, some lead and powder were left behind. The next was the home of one Wingate. Wingate was reported to have purchased a brand new revolver. Upon seeing them coming, he made for the woods with the prized new revolver in hand. Mrs. Wingate knew nothing about the new gun. Even upon threatening to burn down her house, she remained honestly steadfast that she knew nothing. A man named McDonald was also at this house, a very insolent man who, at first, refused to tell them anything. He was taken outside and with the assistance of a noose in the long rope threatening to hang him, he divulged to where Wingate had disappeared. At this house a search was conducted for arms. Three old rifles and a brand new U.S. musket, complete with cartridges, boxes and belt were found. About $514.80 in cash money was found on one of the Bushwhackers the next day and was divided among the ladies of the town who had lost their husbands in the incident. Poor Mrs. Crowder is left with several children and no means but charity for support. (It is noted that some of the citizens this command visited resided in Livingston County close to the line.) Captain E.J. Crandall has organized the citizens into groups for the protection of themselves. He has supplied guards for Mr. Corman, the sheriff of Chariton County. They dare not go home unguarded. The damages are in, over $1,000.00 for one man alone. At the present time over 40 Union families are in town seeking safety, moving from one place to another, trying to stay away from being molested. These families are destitute. The David M. Crowder that was killed was a discharged soldier from the 1st Missouri State Militia. Mr. Jonathan H. Jones was a well-respected attorney. The man killed belonging to Holtzclaw's command was James Nave. The reported losses were John F. Pershing, $811.00 in money and goods; Praty & Clarkson, $1,277.00 in money and goods; Thomas Spencer, $587.00 mostly money; J.J. Friend, $445.00 watches and jewelry; John A. Riggen, $220.00, a fine mare, revolver, etc.; L. Seymore, $110.00 money and merchandise; J.L. Reynolds, groceries and $24.00; Samuel Moore, groceries and liquors; J.M. Brown, fine silver watch, $40.00; Preston O'Neil, a fine mare, saddle and bridle, $200.00.

June 18th-20th...A scouting party from Kansas City under Colonel Thomas Moonlight, consisting of four companies, and Colonel James H. Ford with a command, arrived at Lone Jack by daylight. The area in all directions was scouted. Only minor skirmishes resulted. Small parties were encountered at the edge of the timber in a few places in Jackson County. Areas in the vicinity of Pleasant Hill were covered also.

June 19th-25th...Scouting party from Mount Vernon. Trying to ascertain the number of Confederates in the area, the scouting party left Marionville on the 19th and scouted the countryside around Newtonia and found no trace of activity. The party the next day moved to Carthage. No sign there. On Jones' Creek a campsite was located, just recently vacated. The morning of the 22nd the party heads for Lamar in Barton County with 75 men determined to find them if they were south of the Osage River. No one was found. The next day a small skirmish ensued. After laying a trap for the small party of about eight, the trap sprung incorrectly and the scouting party was surrounded. The scouting party retreated to avail themselves of a better opportunity. And, on June 20th a scouting party left from Cassville to Cross Hollow, Arkansas. On this mission tragedy befell the Todd family. Lieutenant Colonel Hugh Cameron heard reports that the Todd (guerillas?) family was making demonstrations in the neighborhood below, near the edge of Stone County on Flat Creek. He sent with the citizens four enlisted men of Company I, 2nd Arkansas Cavalry (Benjamin F. Lee, John B. Jones, Alexander L. Harris and Andrew J. Chancellor), with instructions to take the Todds. It was represented that they only numbered two, deserters from the 1st Arkansas Cavalry. The party arrived some time before daylight on June 24th and waited for the Todds to come to breakfast, concealing themselves in the thick brush around the house. The Todds came and gained entrance to the house before the men could manage an arrest. They then divided into squads and moved closer around the house. The soldiers being denied entrance to the house, opened fire upon the house. The occupants returned the fire promptly from the cracks in the logs, resulting in the killing of Alexander L. Harris, a private, and wounding the three Todds. The father and two sons. The case was promptly reported and an ambulance dispatched to bring them in. In the meantime Lieutenant Garner, Company B, 2nd Arkansas Cavalry, returning from Cassville to Forsyth with about 12 or 15 men, and on passing by, entered the house and killed the three wounded Todds. The escort returned, reporting the facts and bringing in the body of Private Harris. The citizens in the vicinity had taken it in hand to bury the Todds. Also today, Captain Powell of the 2nd Arkansas left with another scouting party toward Cross Hollow, Arkansas.

June 26th...Captain Joseph Parke, Company E, 4th Militia Cavalry, found seven Bushwhackers wearing the red badge on their hats in the heavy brush about 1 1/2 miles east of the road leading from Sedalia to Marshall, while he and his command of scouts were scouring the brush north of the Blackwater, killing three and wounding two, capturing six horses and one mule, a Springfield rifle, a musket and revolver.

June 27th-28th...A command of 50 Militiamen proceeded to Kirkpatrick's Mill, near the Lafayette County line. Arriving at Knob Knoster, they learned a squad of Confederates near Dunksburg had been engaged by a group of citizens in a fight which resulted in the death of citizens McGuire and Bales. The Confederates left Dunksburg in a southerly direction. The trail was struck about three miles south of the town, trailing them some 18 miles, an encounter took place at the headwaters of the Big Muddy. Private William H. Crawford, when the order to charge was given, had a much swifter horse and got out ahead of the command, turning in front of the enemy in order to change his position, he then ran head-on into them and lost his life. The Confederates retreated, and as they did, they passed the house of a widow by the name of Cooper. As they ran through the lane, they shot her two sons, killing one and wounding the other. The retreat continued, as well as the pursuit, for over two miles across a prairie until they struck Muddy Creek timber. There the Militia dismounted and pursued them on foot through the brush picking up overcoats, letters and other items which had been dropped to lighten the load. Mention is made of the valuable service tendered by the Militia's scout and guide, William E. Chester, a citizen of Knob Knoster, and also Thomas Foster. Upon returning to the battleground in search of one of the men who had been wounded, it was found he was no longer there and is now thought to have been captured. The trail of the Confederates was finally struck again and followed to the west prong of Post Oak Creek where the trail was lost and the search abandoned.

While on the expedition the Militia visited the house of Mr. and Mrs. Spencer and their four grown daughters. The family was at breakfast when the soldiers entered the house, and some of the soldiers asked for some bread. The woman of the house told them that they couldn't have it. Their dogs needed it.

July 1st...Skirmish at Fayette. Two to one were Holtzclaw's Confederates' odds in their favor when the skirmish occurred six miles from Fayette. Holtzclaw had taken his breakfast at the home of one Henry Miller. Not one loyal citizen reported the presence of the force. Sergeant Koontze happened upon him. Confederate losses were two killed and one wounded. The Militia lost one killed and one wounded. It is reported that 150 Confederates and guerillas are now in the Perche Hills.

July 7th...After reaching his home today, Major John M. Clarke, 82nd Infantry (EMM), received a dispatch from Lieutenant Nash, Company C, that guerillas made an attack upon Parkville and captured the place. One man was killed, two wounded and, also, one woman was slightly wounded. They robbed the stores (including the store of Major Clarke) of their contents, taking all the money they could get, and left in the direction of Platte City.

July 8th...Skirmish near Richmond. Captain D.P. Whitmer makes a report of his command that met up with a detachment of Price's men. Lieutenant Page of this (Union) company fell from wounds, Sergeant Goods rallied the men, even though seriously wounded himself, and scattered the band of Confederates. Papers found in their pockets confirmed their identity as part of Price's men. The first volley killed Lieutenant Page and two others, plus five horses. Lieutenant Page was buried with full military honors at Richmond on the 9th. On the 8th a scouting party left from Patterson to Buffalo Creek in Ripley County. They marched by way of Moss Ferry on Black River and Van Buren on Current River, then in the direction of Pocahontas, Arkansas to the mouth of the Big Baum Creek and down the same to Current River, down the Current to the mouth of Buffalo and up the same about 10 miles to the house of one John Land, a noted guerilla. He was found lurking in the vicinity and was shot. Starting from Land's they made their way through the country traveling by paths to Shelton's Mill on Current River and from there back to Patterson. On Brush Creek in Centre County (?), two guerillas were killed while attempting to escape "and the corn crop looks good."

July 9th...Captain Seymour W. Wagoner, 2nd Colorado, with his scouting party of about 25 men, was proceeding from Raytown, Jackson County, down the Little Blue when he was attacked by a detail of Confederates, numbering about 100 or more, under the command of Todd. The attack took place in a pass two miles south of the Little Blue on the road between Independence and Pleasant Hill. Captain Wagoner and seven of his men departed life this day, as did several of the rebels. Todd then seized the stage to move his wounded to safety.

July 10th...Major S.R. Curtis (Union) reports that a combined force of cavalry belonging to the Departments of Kansas and Missouri made a raid on a Confederate camp in Camden, Platte County. One man was lost. Confederate losses were 15 killed. The pursuit turned southward. Also on this quiet Sunday, religion played no little part in this war. Confederate Captain/Colonel (?) Wilhite was killed today in the yard of Warders Church near Wellington. He was joined by four others. Wilhite had been actively engaged in robbing the mails and people of Lafayette County. He also led the party that attacked Judge Ryland and his son. He is also the man who wounded Captain Ewing of the Citizen Guards. The party of Confederates was attending church and fired upon Captain Henslee's (Militia) advance of his scouting party from the windows of the church. Then a general exchange of shots took place in the midst of citizens, women and children and, yet, while Wilhite had 28 balls through him and another had 18, no one person but the guerillas and Confederates was hit. The Militia had one man wounded and two horses killed. "The guerillas, people, and priest seemed to be worshiping together as innocent lambs." signed by E.B. Brown, Brig-Genl. Another report made of this incident describes it as, "Warder's Church - distant two miles, where a Hardshell was in the habit of preaching to the brushers, the unsearchable riches of good whiskey and guerilla warfare." The church being located on a high eminence, a bluff overlooking the Sni River, the command had to reach this church by a narrow road necessitating it to cross a bridge within 20 paces of the building and then ascend a very abrupt bank. The guerillas were then seven or eight in number, besides some outpost pickets on the Lexington Road. The cry of "Feds, Feds" thundered from the audience and the worthy pastor, who was in the midst of a fervent supplication, found his flock highly demoralized and concluded it wasn't worthwhile to pray any longer under the circumstances. The guerillas were on the alert, some at their horses, some in the church, and one, who was to be married that day to the pastor's daughter, was standing by the window making love to his inamorata. After the fighting moved outside, John T. Anderson, Company L and James D. Barnes, Company D, Anderson, being of the advance, passed the church. He received three shots through his clothes, one knocking the skin off his nose and one striking the pistol in his hand. He rode right through the midst of the scoundrels and with great coolness and great precision, shot right and left emptying 12 barrels and loading four more, all the while directing the soldiers around him. Anderson was badly wounded a year ago in a hand-to-hand fight with Livingston in Southwest Missouri. Barnes, discovering one of the Bushwhackers making his escape, singled him out, charged on him discharging his rifle, flung it aside and with a drawn pistol, spurred forward chasing for a half mile. The rebel fired back at him. Barnes, holding his fire until he was drawn up on his man, was just in the act of shooting at short range when his horse fell headlong, throwing Barnes over his head with a fearful fall. The horse got up and trotted after the fleeing Confederate. All equipment, saddle, bridle and horse, all the property of Barnes, was now lost to him. "Barnes is but a mere boy, very small, but as bold and dashing a trooper as ever looked an enemy in the eye." Reported by Colonel Jonathan Philips.

July 13th...Gregg (Conf/guerilla?) and his band attempted to rob the town of Versailles, Morgan County. They were driven off by the Citizen Guards.

July 14th...Captain George A. Holloway, Assistant Adjutant General, had a fight in Camden Point. The town was burned and he "mustered out a few devils," but the rest were routed. Part of Noland's (?) command has joined them and some of the guns they had are gone also. Nearly all the young men of rebel families from the Camden Point neighborhood have taken to the brush.

July 15th...On this morning of July 15th a party of Bushwhackers, numbering about 27, rode into the little town of Lindley in Grundy County and robbed the citizens of money, horses, guns and pistols. Captain E.L. Winters of Lindley took up the pursuit, overtaking them about eight miles from town. In the fighting that took place, Captain Winters had five of his men wounded. At a later confrontation in the afternoon, the Captain had a man killed and another wounded. The guerillas are very well armed.

July 17th...Two guerillas rode onto the ferryboat opposite Boonville and compelled the master to carry them across the river. On landing at the upper part of town, they passed into the countryside. They robbed one local citizen of a span of horses and killed another for resisting his own robbery. Also on the 17th, Hutchins' and Steward's bands of guerillas were attacked on Clear Fork (near Warrensburg, Johnson County) by Captain Turley of the 7th State Militia, killing five of the lawless band. That makes a total of 81 killed since the 1st of June, that have left this world at the hands of the troops under Brigadier General Egbert Brown. The 17th was not your average quiet Sunday in Missouri. Captain Moses, with 47 men, while scouting 17 miles northeast of Liberty near Fredericksburg, Ray County, came onto a large force of Confederates under Colonel Thornton. After a severe fight Captain Moses had to retreat. He rallied his men. They had fired the last shot remaining in their revolvers when Captain Moses gave the order to disband and do the best they could. Captain Moses lost six killed and four wounded. Colonel Thornton lost 16 men and 21 more wounded. Captain Moses took five bullets through his clothes and his horse was wounded by bullets four times, but managed to carry him off the field. The Captain made it through with only a slight grazing wound on his forehead. The carbines failed again and reliance upon the pistols was the order. Major Pritchard was sent in pursuit of Colonel Thornton, chasing him to Knoxville, where Thornton broke up his command into small groups, scattering in every direction. As Sunday finally wore down, Major Douglas Dale, 4th Militia, had cleared all the skiffs, canoes, flatboats, etc. off the river, and is now on board the steamer Post Boy at Lexington. He reported that a small band had killed from eight to 12 Union citizens and former Union soldiers in Carroll County. Supposedly these are the same ones that robbed Huntsville. (He doesn't identify which Confederate command this is.) The 14th also saw a skirmish near Bloomfield in which one man of the Enrolled Militia was killed and one of the 2nd Cavalry of Militia was wounded. The Confederates/guerillas (?) made off with three splendid horses and all equipment.

July 18th...Franklin was robbed today by a band of guerillas. Reports of about 150 are working now in Howard County. And, a scouting party of 60 men left Salem for a scout through Shannon

County. Bushwhackers were reported to be about 65 miles from Salem at a place called Hay Hollow on Rock Creek in the southeast corner of Shannon County. The scouts traveled all night on Monday and finally arrived on Tuesday about 2:00, only to find the Bushwhackers had left a few days previous with their stock, leaving behind about eight young horses, which they could not make off with. These were brought in by the scouts, as they had been stolen from the local Union men and were now returned to them. On Wednesday the party divided, one squad up Jack's Fork and the Current and Gladden Valley, one squad up the Current to the mouth of Big Sinking then up to its headwaters and the other squad coming up Bushy Creek and the Big Creek. Here the detail heard of the passing of about 15 Confederates the evening before. Camping that night in a meadow, the scouts were fired upon from the brush. The fire was returned into the darkness. Departing, the hidden foe left behind four horses and equipment and their arms, but made good their escape into the night. On Thursday the detail proceeded on the divide in the southeast corner of Dent County about 20 miles from Salem. There they came across 20 of the 3rd Missouri Militia from Centreville. They were dressed in every way, some with citizen hats and in their shirtsleeves. The scouts took them to be the sought-after Bushwhackers but didn't fire upon them. They discovered the scouting party and halted, seeing the all blue uniforms. They were under the command of a lieutenant who had sent 10 men up the creek. It was then ascertained these were the ones the scouting party had fired into the evening before. The captured horses and equipment were turned over to him. The scouting party has learned that Colonel Freeman himself is on the Ash Flat. One hundred of his men were on the Warm Fork of Spring River with the rest of the command on the North Fork of White River. Colonel Shelby is riding with Marmaduke.

A scout started today throughout Southwest Missouri and a skirmish erupted near Maysville, Arkansas and again at Carthage on July 20th. In this campaign Captain Turner's (Union) Company, stationed at Hartsville, attacked 25 Bushwhackers going north last week and killed six of them. Captain Sallee's (Union) Company in Douglass attacked a band of about 30 the first of the week (around the 21st) and killed 14 of them. Captain Roher killed four more on Cane Creek. Colonel Pickler and six of his men were killed last week (around this date, 18th) by a detachment of the 1st Arkansas in Benton County (Arkansas?). Brown's and Pickler's forces then moved north to Baxter Springs and attacked about 19 of the Enrolled Militia while herding their horses in the vicinity of Carthage. The Militia, being surprised, lost six men and 11 were taken prisoner and later released. (This appears possibly to be Confederate forces rather than guerillas?) Those killed around Carthage were Lieutenant Henry (Militia) and eight unnamed men. In Mississippi County James Bayou and two Bushwhackers were killed and a lot of horses were brought in, which they had been quietly tending in a canebreak.

July 19th...Twenty-five Bushwhackers robbed the town of Webster, located about 15 miles southwest of Potosi, today and made off with $1,500.00 worth of goods, killed one man, six horses and took two men with them. The band was last sighted traveling in a westerly direction and passed about three miles west of Potosi headed for Jefferson City.

July 20th...Arrow Rock was burned today. Lieutenant Woodruff was attacked by about 200 men, losing three men and all of his horses in the attack. Lieutenant Woodruff will be sent to Frankfort. The garrisons of Miami and Cambridge are also at Frankfort. Captain Wyckoff with 120 men marched from Miami this morning in pursuit of Todd's Confederates, passing about five miles south of Miami on the gallop going east. Colonel Thornton's men, about 300 strong, were reported at Maudeville yesterday. Also on the 20th Lieutenant Henry F. Goss took a scouting party and proceeded to the neighborhood of Taos and De Kalb in Buchanan County. About 1 1/2 miles from Taos, between that place and De Kalb along the margin of a creek in Murphy's pasture, campfires were discovered. The camp was located about 15 miles from St. Joseph. Information obtained from loyal men reported that no less than 300 men were in the brush. Also captured was a man who recently had been engaged in shooting a German near Sparta. His saddlebags were packed full of clothes and a stud horse belonging to a man named Oats, formerly of Captain Noland's Company of Paw Paws.

July 21st...A report is made of the attack on Lieutenant Henry and his men while grazing their horses near Carthage. It is reported that the Lieutenant and eight of his men were killed on the ground and several others have been reported as missing, no doubt killed. The Confederates were too strong for the company at Carthage, and they didn't come out of the fort. Additional men have now been sent to Carthage.

July 22nd...Colonel J.H. Ford (2nd Colorado Cavalry) left Liberty with 300 of the 2nd Colorado and 190 of the 9th Militia. Learning on the road that a fight had occurred at Plattesburg, the detail concentrated on that area. Two men were lost. It is reported they had started west toward Buchanan County. The detail left the Plattesburg Road and struck west for Gosneyville, passed through Gosneyville and camped at Ross' Mill. They started again at dark and moved out on the prairie to camp, starting again on the track moving northwest to Campden Point. Finally finding a trail, the detail was led around in a circle twice, the ambulances and wagons being very much in the way. Nothing was gained by the expedition as the local citizens are acting as lookouts and pickets and can advise the Confederates of every move. The next trip out will be with a pack-mule train laden with food. They will live in the brush for a couple of weeks.

July 23rd...Todd's Confederates are scattered in the Sni Hills in small bands numbering from 15 to 75. Thornton was above Lexington, within three miles of the Missouri River. It is reported he should cross the river between Sibley and Napoleon. The boat Fanny Ogden is on her way up the river from Glasgow to prevent the crossing and to ferry Colonel James H. Ford's (Militia) command if he arrives at the bank in pursuit. Colonel McFerran is in pursuit. On the 23rd Major S.P. Fox (Union) reports a skirmish four miles north of Campden Point. A portion of the Bushwhackers went back across the Platte River below Union Mills.

July 25th...Colonel J.H. Ford leaves Kansas City today with his pack-mule outfit. Major Samuel P. Cox received orders from General Fisk (Union) while at Breckinridge to "pitch into the rebels." Evidently leaving Breckinridge (?) with his company of Home Guards, they went south about 12 miles where they were joined by Lieutenant Dasha's Company from Chillicothe. After resting and starting again after dark, Colonel Brown came up with two more companies under Captain N.B. Brown and Captain Brunfield. The company commanders at this time were Lieutenant Dasha, Captain N.B. Brown, Captain Woodruff, Captain Leabo and Lieutenant Brown. The party made their way to Kingston, arriving just at sunup, and found the town had been robbed and plundered of at least $10,000.00 in money. The next stop was Mirable where they had taken just about the same amount of money from Dr. Crawford's sale, plus robbing the stores of all they wanted. Then the thieves set out for Plattesburg, the detail was only a few hours behind the band of robbers. The gang had killed one man who was taken from his home and shot about 12 miles east of Plattesburg. Arriving at Plattesburg, the band demanded a surrender. This was refused by Captain B.F. Poe who was in command. Captain Turney had been killed earlier by this same band. The demand was signed by Major John Thrailkill, Confederate forces. Captain Turney and First Lieutenant George W. McCullough had gone out to reconnoiter the position of the enemy and had met them in a fight and were cut off from returning. The place was held. Thrailkill left after some spirited fighting, retreating toward Haynesville. On the morning of the 22nd the detail turned south to Carpenter's store. The Confederates had camped there the previous night. A grave of one man belonging to Thrailkill's command, who had been injured at Plattesburg, was found. The detail then moved in the direction of Union Mills, following the tracks into the worst brush imaginable. There the two forces met, three times they charged, firing, fighting. Each time pulling back to reload. The horses stampeded from the shots and the men yelled. James B. Ayres (Union/Militia?) was killed and the wounded were James Tucker, John Acord, John Carter and several others slightly wounded. The loss to the enemy, as near as could be ascertained, was two men killed and 16 wounded. The scouting party them moved on to Campden Point and camped. Captain Ford took up the pursuit to Staner's Mills. Leaving the trail the next day and passing where the battle had transpired, they arrested H.M. Herman who was acting as the guide for those hunting the Bushwhacker's camp. Herman was a noted guerilla. (This report was made from Gallatin on the 25th.)

July 30th-August 1st...Colonel A. Sigel (Union), commanding the post at Rolla, gave the order for 30 men to work a scouting party through Phelps and Maries Counties. Dividing his command into threes; one detail taking the Vienna Road, one taking Lane's Prairie Road, and Lieutenant Charles Adamson taking the Dillon Road, they scouted the byroads and country thoroughly. The command met and encamped for the night at Dillon. The next day the Vienna Road, Lane's Prairie and Borben's Bottoms were scouted a little farther to the east. The command gathered for the return trip to Dyer's farm, five miles from Rolla. Then they returned to camp. Only one man was arrested on suspicion.

August 1st...Captain Edward P. Elmer, 2nd Colorado, makes his report of the scouting party which left on July 10th. They marched about 495 miles, all around Liberty, Weston, Campden Point, Smithville, Platte City, Union Mills and returned to headquarters at Pleasant Hill. It was out 12 days. (Appears maybe two minor skirmishes.) In the other part of the State a scouting party of Militia, which was Confederate and guerilla hunting, proceeded through the murky swamps and crossed the brush-laden hills of Mississippi, Stoddard, New Madrid, Pemiscot and Dunklin Counties. Independence, Missouri had some spirited action around it today. Sergeant Coy (Union), while scouting the swamp area near Independence, ran into two camps of guerillas. One camp held about 25, the other near 40. (Colonel J.H. Ford describes, "Sent Sergeant Coy and his pet lambs south.") Also today a scouting party left Mount Vernon, Missouri for a trip toward the Baxter Springs area. Today another party of scouts left Pleasant Hill for scouting upon the Independence Road to Gunter's Mill. The guerillas were found encamped in little squads just east of the Independence Road. Confederate Commander Todd and seven men had eaten breakfast at Hackett's but left it unfinished. The band again eluded the pursuers.

August 1st-28th...Operations are picking up a new fervor in Southwest Missouri. The scouting itinerary is given below:

August 2nd...Captain Ruark, 8th Militia, killed Lieutenant Goode of the Confederate Army in the vicinity of Diamond Grove near Carthage.

August 4th...Lieutenant Hunter, 8th Militia, with 60 men, left on a scout in the direction of McDonald County. William Haycock acted as their guide. The Confederates were encountered, about 300 strong, near Rutledge resulting in a sharp skirmish. Three of the Militia were killed and one wounded. The Confederate loss was three killed and several wounded. It is thought the Confederates were led by Pickler with Buck Brown's men, and their leader was Rector Johnson, formerly a resident of the area.

August 7th...Major Burch, 8th Militia, in command of about 175 men, marched on to Neosho, came into combat with the Confederates near Enterprise and killed one of their pickets but was unable to draw fire from the Confederates commanded by Major Piercy. The command was composed of portions of Pickler's and Stand Watie's men.

August 10th...Colonel Gravely, 8th Militia, with 100 men, left Springfield to operate against the Confederates on the western border of the district, but found the Confederates had moved on southward.

August 28th...Lieutenant S.A.M. George, 8th Militia, was killed by guerillas at Osage Springs, Arkansas today.

On the body of Lieutenant Goode were papers identifying his command and contacts in the area. They were J.R. Goode, Richard Hall, Callaway Johnson, J.W. Scaggs, L.H. Scaggs, T.H. Hawkins, T.V. Parnell, E.M. Martin, James Ramsey, W.F. Ray, John Harmon, Taylor Buskirk, Hiram Mayeld and Monroe Hewit. Most lived in the southern part of Jasper and the northern portion of Newton County.

August 1st was also the date used on a report from Brigadier General Clinton B. Fisk (Union) commanding the District of Northern Missouri. It tells of the meaning and the use of the term "Paw Paw Militia." They are described as disloyal citizens and returned soldiers and officers of the Confederate Army who have been enrolled as disloyal under General Order No. 24, series of 1862, from headquarters State of Missouri. These men were organized into companies and regiments under the direction of the Governor of the State of Missouri in the summer of 1863 for some unknown purpose (to Fisk). Of the policy that dictated this organization, or of the effect upon the loyal element that must be guarded and protected and watched by armed rebels, many of them fresh from the Confederate Army, "I have nothing to say" (Fisk). In short, the loyal element has complained to the proper authorities with no results. These men are doing a great amount of harm to the loyal sentiment in Missouri, and it is further shown in many instances that these troops would in no case fight the guerillas and thieves who infested the neighborhoods where they were stationed in the northwestern portion of this State. The officers of the 82nd Regiment Enrolled Missouri Militia let Confederate Colonel Winston remain safely harbored and protected in the county of Clay during the winter of '63 and '64. No exertion was used to arrest him, although his very presence in their midst was a well-established fact. After the capture finally of Colonel Winston by Captain Kemper's 9th Militia, it was reported continually that he had left behind a companion in Clay County. This was Coon Thornton, known otherwise as John C. Calhoun Thornton, who is also reported to be a colonel in the rebel army. This man is a well-known recruiter for the Confederate Army and has several agents working in Clay, Ray and Platte Counties. The 82nd and the 81st Enrolled Militia, it is said, "is in with this man." And, that men of certain companies have joined his organization. Numerous attempts to capture this man have failed. The citizens in the area in which he operates aided him and informed him, and his work went "briskly on." The 81st has been relieved of duty but has been permitted to take their arms to their homes. It is now reported that these men, one by one, are slipping off and going back to their old commands. It was ordered then that all arms be brought into the arsenal at St. Joseph. Upon receiving the arms at Camden Point, preparatory to sending them to the armory, the guns were stored in an old warehouse and a small company left to guard them. The same night a small body of unarmed guerillas rode into town, surprised the guard, and carried off the guns and other accoutrements. Captain Bywater's Company has not been heard of since. They belonged to the 81st. On the morning of July 7th a body of guerilla thieves headed by Coon Thornton, in person, made its appearance at Parkville, Platte County. They entered the town without the least opposition from Captain Wilson's 82nd Enrolled Militia which was stationed at that place. On the 10th Major John M. Clark commanding the post of the 82nd Militia at Platte City, went off to visit his family and left the post command under Captain R.D. Johnston, although it was well known to the Major that his First Lieutenant, William Downing, openly went among the rebels and held open conversation with them. It was also known to Major Clark of the incident at Parkville. Captain Johnston saw the force coming and immediately held counsel with his officers and decided he could do no better than to just surrender them. Downing refused to fight them. When they left, the American flag had been torn to shreds and adorned the horse bridles. The largest portion of the 82nd rode with them. It made the guerilla command a force of 130 men all total who were actually on duty as U.S. soldiers. Major John M. Clark will now stand disciplinary action. (Extracted from Fisk's report to Colonel O.D. Greene, Assistant Adjutant.)

August 3rd...Major Reeves of the 9th Militia Cavalry at Fayette ran into a band of guerillas near Fayette, chasing them about 15 miles until dusk.

August 4th...Returning from a scouting party, Lieutenant Hiller struck a trail and followed. He soon came upon the pickets of Confederate Lieutenant Hedges. The rebels scattered but were pursued by Lieutenant Hiller and his advance guards and Sergeant Wright's party of scouts, following the Confederates into the watery swamps of Dogskin Swamp. Lieutenant Hedges was overtaken and killed here. The command escaped even deeper into the dark swamp. Finally they made a stand in a dense forest two miles south of Elk Chute in Pemiscot County. A running fight was kept over logs, downed trees, through wetlands with the men yelling and in great confusion. The rebels finally, after a hotly-contested fight, gave way and took to the water, some swimming, some swimming their horses and others hiding in the very dense brush. Confederate losses were 30 killed, six mortally wounded and about 40 less seriously wounded. The Militia losses were one man,

Captain Francis, mortally wounded and two enlisted men slightly wounded.

August 6th-9th...Lieutenant Colonel B.F. Lazear scouted Saline County in the direction of Miami and, upon learning that a force of about 400 were in Marshall, the command of Militia changed course. Arriving at Marshall on the 6th, they learned 10 guerillas had visited the place on the 5th burning the courthouse and one other building. Some of the inhabitants were plundered and five negroes were shot in the town and four others a short distance from town. If the citizens would have remained at home, this raid on Marshall would not have been made according to Lazear. On August 7th the scouting party moved on to Arrow Rock. They encountered a couple of minor skirmishes, one with a party of about 15 or 20 men. The other skirmish concerned a detail of about 20 men. One of the band was killed and several wounded. The guerillas had encamped upon the property of Marshall Piper. Mr. Piper gave the Militia no information of the encampment and, being a "notorious rebel" and under bond, for his failure, he was shot. Lieutenant Colonel Lazear makes note of arresting several women and several of the worst of the guerilla families and is holding them hostage for the lives of Union men. He also makes note that Saline County is one of the very worst that he has scouted.

On the morning of the 7th, leaving Huntsville, a small detachment commanded by Sergeant Fisher and Lieutenant Dunn, came upon the trail of Jim Anderson, a most notorious robber and guerilla, about five miles south of Huntsville. After following for about two hours, the trail was lost. The detachment emerged from the heavy underbrush-covered trail at the house of Owen Bagby on the Huntsville and Fayette Road. As they approached the house, Anderson's men opened fire from within the house. Getting the detail under control and ordering a dismount, the house was being surrounded when Anderson and his men left through the backyard of the house and made good their escape through the fields. The scouting party mounted and a most spirited chase took place in which a running battle became the order of the afternoon. Finally running upon the rear of Anderson's men, a horse carrying double and which had fallen behind, was shot from under his load. The two men scaled the fence and took off across a pasture. There it ended for the luckless two guerillas. Of the 10 men still holed up at Bagby's, one man was killed and another mortally wounded. Upon the deceased's body was found about $90.00 in gold, $286.00 in greenbacks, $4.50 in silver and $16.00 W.B.M. for a total of $396.50. It is also reported that Jim Anderson was shot through the nose. It appears now that Bill Anderson's threat of concentrating about 200 men in Randolph County must be true from the evidence of the band hanging around the neighborhood.

August 7th-8th...Leaving Independence this morning about 4:00, about 128 men under Lieutenants Parsons and Ducey scouted south on the Pleasant Hill Road as far as Grenter's farm, then to Round

Prairie where they were joined by a detail under Captain Blair. The combined force then moved to the Jackson and Lafayette County line and encamped upon the farm of Mr. Harp. Reliable neighbors gave information that Thornton, Quantrill, Todd, Yeager, Taylor, Thrailkill and Anderson were encamped upon the farm of John Campbell about four miles from the place with about 300 to 500 men. The next morning the detail set out in search of the camp. It was found that it had been abandoned the previous night. According to Mrs. Campbell, the band of about 150 broke up into small groups and headed in the direction of Blue River and Raytown.

August 11th-19th...Scouting operations are constant now in Johnson County from the vicinity of Holden. On the 11th Lieutenant Marr and 20 men scouted to Walnut Creek. That same day Lieutenant Pharis and 15 men went on a foot scout north on the Blackwater. On the 12th Corporal Adams and 10 men in charge of a forage train ran into Hutchinson's gang, eight in number, at Lotspeich's farm. A lively little skirmish erupted. On the 16th Lieutenant Marr and 30 men went to Norris Creek, then to Honey Creek. There they found three Bushwhackers and ran them from their houses. Also on the 16th Captain Baker and Lieutenant Combs with 30 men rode Panther Creek and Walnut Creek. On the 17th Lieutenant Pharis with 25 men went out again, this time in pursuit of those responsible for burning the stage, but returned empty-handed.

August 12th-16th...Bill Anderson's guerillas, numbering about 100, attacked Captain Colley's Company of 20 men of the Ray County Militia at Fredericksburg in Ray County. A most desperate fight took place in which several of the guerillas and Captain Colley and four of his men were killed. The 6th Missouri Cavalry Veterans left in pursuit of Anderson. Anderson is reported to be very well mounted on some of Missouri's finest horseflesh. Those in pursuit are in a very sad state for horses. The outlaw band was last seen headed toward Richmond. Trying to drive the band toward a trap, Major John Grimes sent Lieutenant Ralston to a point six miles northeast of Richmond, and Lieutenant McKown ordered him to move on the Knoxville Road, thus intersecting. The trap missed by a few miles. Anderson passed about six miles northwest of Richmond and later crossed the Knoxville Road nine miles north of Richmond, going east and proceeding in a southeasterly direction crossing East Fork of Crooked River at Keal's Mills about 2 1/2 miles south of Milville, Ray County. Then they traveled to Shaw's Shop and on in the direction of the Missouri River at the mouth of the Wakanda or Shanghi Town in Carroll County. By that night they had arrived at Moberly's Landing in Carroll County and traveled about 40 miles. The band, in passing through the countryside, murdered three soldiers - one returning from his home to Richmond and two, Samuel Forseen and Daniel Vansant, who were bearing dispatches to Lieutenant Baker. Forseen's throat had been cut from ear to ear and then was scalped. One citizen, James Maupin, while driving his wagon was treated the same. They burned one house, stole a number of horses and committed other depredations.

August 13th-22nd...On the 13th Captain Meredith overtook a band of Bushwhackers in the eastern part of Saline County. One Bushwhacker was killed and seven horses captured. On the 15th a detachment of Militia under the command of Sergeant I.E. Wood surprised a gang encamped in the brush, wounding two of them. This same day Captain E.W. Kingsbury of the 2nd Colorado Cavalry left Independence striking the trail and proceeding northeast of Lexington and then striking the Missouri River four miles south of Richfield. He patroled the river bank and vicinity for a distance of about five miles above Richfield, encamping that night on the Young farm near the mouth of the Blue River. While here he learned that Fletch Taylor, Thrailkill and others had been in the vicinity. Starting the next morning he scouted the area thoroughly in the vicinity of Six-Mile, learning that Taylor, being severely wounded, had procured a buggy and started for Lafayette County. Striking the trail again and being unable to follow it, he finally arrived at the farm of one Ish in Lafayette County. He disguised himself as a guerilla, and by imploring a boy of the family, he learned that a camp of about 100 of them were encamped in Big Bottom about six miles from the farm. He also learned that Drs. Murphy and Regan of Wellington had amputated Taylor's arm the morning before. Dr. Murphy was arrested at Ewing's farm and then released. This party encamped or crossed the farms and lands of Fishback, Gardiners, Bone Hill, Judge Gray and a family named Bord. Mr. Bord suffered a "little hanging" to improve his memory as to the location of the campsites. The trail was lost when crossing Fire Prairie. On the 16th Captain Joseph Parke, commanding at Boonville, crossed the north side of the river and scouted the country for two days, encountering several small bands, wounding some of them and capturing some weapons. On the 20th Lieutenant Colonel Lazear surprised a camp of about 40 to 60 Confederates in the vicinity of Dover, Lafayette County. Killed were three of their men. Captured were four horses and a small rebel flag. This same day Major Henry Suess, chief of cavalry commanding the steamer Fanny Ogden, reports that Thornton, Thrailkill, Yeager, Todd, Campbell and Taylor had a meeting this past week in Greenton Valley, Lafayette County. It was upon returning from this meeting that Taylor was killed. On the 22nd a detachment surprised a small band of Confederates on the Tabo, Lafayette County. Lieutenant Colonel Lazear encountered a small detail of them, also on Davis Creek, Lafayette County.

August 14th...The pursuit of Bill Anderson continued today. It erupted into a frantic skirmish about noon on the east side of the Wakenda Prairie, Carroll County. Anderson took up a position in dense undergrowth. After a desperate 30 minutes he was dislodged and retreated toward Grand River. The Carroll County Militia lost four men killed and six wounded.

August 23rd...This past week has been fruitful in the pursuit of the Confederate bands of Perkins, Holtzclaw, Cyrus Gordon and Taylor. Thirty-five of their number have been killed. Two of the pursuers were killed and eight wounded. The party has reported "taking no prisoners." Captain Taylor is reported as being dead. Thrailkill is dangerously wounded. His injury was dressed by a Union lady a few days back. He is reported now to be in hiding in Platte County.

August 15th...Captain William Hebard with a small detachment from Glasgow was encamped near Dripping Springs in Boone County. The posted sentinels were attacked about 11:00. This resulted in the mortal wounding of Private William Meutling of the 17th Illinois Cavalry and Private J.H. Hall, who was severely wounded. The morning's light brought on another attack, overwhelming odds, but no casualties. On Saturday, August 20th, the command of Captain Hebard encountered the cruel commander, Bill Anderson, and his band. Anderson retreated to safety but not before wounding William Marvin of Captain Hebard's command. By the morning of the 16th Holtzclaw and his men were 10 miles northwest of Columbia. A severe skirmish took place and resulted in the death of four of his men and wounding of several others. The Militia fell back about five miles as Holtzclaw was joined by reinforcments. His large force is now concentrated in Boone County.

August 15th-24th...Commands were sent into Southwestern Missouri and Northwestern Arkansas.

August 22nd-30th...(Holden)   August 22nd Lieutenant Pharis and a detail of 30 men arrested the families of Durrett, Stoner, Cowarden and Scott.   They were charged with feeding the local Bushwhackers. On the 24th the Lieutenant escorted prisoners to Warrensburg.   On the 26th the paymaster required an escort to Chapel Hill.   Also on the 26th a detail was sent to cooperate with Captain Queen at Warrensburg in his guerilla hunt.   On the 27th the detail went to the home of Mr. Tackett in Lafayette County, and there learned that Confederate Commander Palmer, with 140 new recruits, had passed between Harrisonville and Pleasant Hill.   On the 28th the detail surprised a small Confederate camp, and a running battle resulted. The remainder of the scout was rather uneventful with only minor sightings.

August 23rd...Scouts are out constantly in St. Francis and Washington Counties, detailing from Pilot Knob.   It was reported that about 50 Confederates entered the town of Webster and helped themselves to the plunder of the town again.

August 23rd-26th...Scouting party left Ozark, Missouri, ranging as far south as the Dubuque Crossing and Sugar Loaf Prairie in Arkansas.   This same day an expedition started from Cassville to Fayetteville, Arkansas.   They left Big Spring near Cassville on the morning of the 23rd with their trains, following the trail cautiously to Little Sugar Creek.   There they encamped.   The next morning the wire road was followed into Arkansas.

August 25th...Around Independence and on Fire Prairie the search for Bill Anderson continues.   Also today a scouting party left St. Joseph for a scout through Platte County, touching the following places: crossing Agency Ford in a zig-zag course, Arnoldsville, Matney's Mill, Union Mills, Ridgeley, Ringgold, Jordan's Ford on Smith's Fork, Platte River, Medling's Old Mill, Smithville, Second Creek, Union Church, Todd's Creek, Hampton, Parkville, a point opposite Atchison, Kansas, Farly, Bee Creek Bridge, New Market, Taos, Clauser's Old Mill, Sparta, Wright's Ford, The Hackle, Easton and the Platte River Bridge near St. Joseph.   This command was in pursuit of, and trying to ascertain the location of, Cyrus Gordon, Kit Chiles and their commands.   Also on this eventful day another scouting party left Camp Grover for Crisp's Mill on Big Creek with skirmishes near Rose Hill.   Fifty Militiamen, under the command of Lieutenant Samuel W. McGuire, proceeded through Post Oak timber, Bear Creek and Panther Creek.   The most eventful thing was running into the citizen patrols and following their trails, rather than those of importance.   The command of Confederate Captain Palmer and his 140 men left a clear trail, and this proved to be a cold two-day-old trail.   At Crisp's Mill the commander from Holden, Captain Foster, ran into two small skirmishes, capturing a very fine gray horse and full rig with a U.S. mailsack under the saddle.   This fine animal belonged to a Bushwhacker named John Reeves.   Scouting operations continued on the Texas Prairie in Jackson County.

August 27th...One of the horses taken in the Confederate raid on Arrow Rock was found tied to a tree at Pool's Settlement by a Militia foot scout. A guard was posted and the waiting began. At nightfall a man named Rutherford brought feed and water to the horse. He ended up deceased and the horse wounded.

August 28th...Captain Parke, Commander of the 4th Militia Cavalry, after Holtzclaw, crossed the river on the 28th at Boonville with 44 men. Near Rocheport he came upon two of Holtzclaw's men, wounding one and capturing both horses. Advancing only a mile, he was attacked in the rear guard by a band numbering 100 men commanded by Holtzclaw and Anderson. Captain Parke reportedly fought furiously for 15 minutes, and in that 15 minutes left seven of his men dead on the field, two wounded and three missing. The men killed were massacred, four being scalped and one being hanged and scalped. Three had their throats cut. Their bodies were later recovered and buried at Boonville. Major General A. Pleasonton now recommends that Captain Parke be dismissed from service. He evidently was surprised on the march and did no fighting in resistance to the attack.

August 29th...Major General Sterling Price assumes command of the Confederate Expeditionary Forces at Princeton, Arkansas.

August 30th...Mr. Worbridge and five boys arrived at Springfield and brought news of the Confederate commands in Arkansas. They are on the move into Missouri. Confederate Captain Pace of the 10th Missouri was attacked and killed in Polk County.

August 31st...The town of Steelville was robbed at dawn today by the Confederate command of Lennox. Reverend Butler, Baptist minister, was mortally wounded and the town thoroughly plundered. Upon leaving the town Lennox's men encountered five Militiamen who were coming in to join their companies. All five were killed by the Confederates.

September 1st...Tipton was attacked by about 42 Confederates at 6:00 this morning killing two townsmen. They left in the direction of their next suspected target, Boonville. Today in Johnson County brought renewed scouting of the hills and the brush. At Holden Lieutenant Marr reported an encounter with about 15 Bushwhackers about five miles south of Lone Jack or about 12 miles northeast of Holden, at the house of Mrs. Simpson. A "very lively" skirmish developed. One man was killed on each side. The Militiaman has been identified as Jacob F. Rank of the 7th Militia Cavalry. Two men were severely injured by falling horses.

September 2nd...Captain Stotts (Militia) was encamped at Cave Springs with 25 men of his own command and a portion of Captain Stemmon's Company. They discovered a Confederate command and sought assistance, being far outnumbered. The assistance call was answered by Captain Morris with about 60 men detailed by Colonel

John D. Allen. These men were to reinforce Captain Stotts in protecting Mount Vernon, which was under siege and in jeopardy of being taken by about 400 Confederates. Upon going to the rescue, Captain Morris met the Confederates in force five miles west of Mount Vernon, there an engagement took place. Being far outnumbered almost five to one, Captain Morris fell back to safety. Colonel Allen, receiving a message informing him of the skirmish and the numbers involved, rallied all the citizens available and all of the Militia he could muster and set out to join Captain Morris. The joint commands then went back to the scene of the engagement. There it was learned that the Confederates had left and headed southwest. Proceeding in a southwesterly direction, the command saw about 50 men drawn up in line as if to do battle far out on the prairie. The order to "charge" was given and the running battle started. After pursuing these men about three miles, the Colonel and his men finally got close enough to recognize Captain Stotts and his men. The Confederates slipped away safely from all concerned.

September 2nd-4th...A Confederate camp was located on Buffalo Prairie in Cooper County. Its strength was about 150 men. Captain Vansickler, in command of the Militia post at Sedalia with about 47 men, set out after them. The trail was finally picked up on the Lamine at Pond Bottom. Part of the detail wanted to return, part wanted to proceed, and with much difficult persuasion Lieutenant William Argo won out, and they proceeded to follow the Confederates under Todd. Information gathered revealed that Todd had captured about 30 to 40 horses, a large number of arms, merchandise, etc. They killed about eight to 10 citizens, among whom was Captain Davis, formerly of the 4th Militia Cavalry, one soldier who had been discharged at Tipton, a butcher also of Tipton, at or near Pilot Grove a man by the name of Zellers, another old gentleman by the name of Fuller, another named Beel and several Germans whose names were unattainable. The trail of Todd was followed until it crossed the Blackwater of Scott's Ford, having ascertained they had been at Marshall's Ford the previous night. Lieutenant Stephens refused to give permission for the further pursuit of Todd. In Jackson County today a large scouting detail that lasted eight days commenced. It wasn't until the 8th that any sign of a camp was located and this at the home of John Moore in the timber about the Little Blue. Then the pursuit was foiled by a piece of telegraph wire which had been strung between the two trees and across the road. This throwing of horse and rider created enough confusion that enabled the Bushwhackers to escape to safety along the brush-lined banks of the Little Blue. Following fresh trails that went in each direction, the scouting party started their return on the Independence Road. It was here they learned that the Bushwhackers had just preceded them, visiting many houses along this road and taking the Militia uniforms, overcoats and blankets that had been issued by the U.S. Government.

September 3rd...Constantly fighting the Bushwhackers and small Confederate camps has become the order of the day around Glasgow. The latest skirmish took the lives of 12 Militiamen by the hand of Bill Anderson's men. Anderson's men suffered the loss of six men, upon whose bodies were recovered no less than 30 revolvers. The second Militia assault on Anderson cost him four more men and 25 good horses. Reports have it the area of Boone and Howard Counties are virtually swarming with Bushwhackers, rebel Confederate bands and outlaws of all nature.

September 3rd...A detail of Militia, about 30 men, proceeded to the neighborhood of one Stone. This mission was to collect $800.00 in damages from his loyal neighbors for the damages suffered when he burned the stagecoach.

September 6th...Colonel William E. Moberly, 35th Infantry (EMM), reported that Sergeant Henry Shrader and a small squad of men, partially unarmed, were taken prisoner near Brunswick, Chariton County. Sergeant Shrader had been sent out for clean clothing and to notify absent men to report. The business at hand was interrupted by a heavy rainstorm. The Bushwhackers, learning of the details, surrounded the Sergeant. They were stripped of all clothing and four guns. This incident led to many others over the next six days in Boone and Howard Counties through which the rebel commands of Todd and others were moving. Small groups were left to pass by the Militia details in hope of following their trails to bag a much larger number. This attempt only caused Todd's command to be broken up for a day or so. The camp of Bill Anderson, although very much sought after, was not found in the vicinity of Rocheport. Holtzclaw and his Confederates are still operating in Howard County.

September 7th...The band of Bill Anderson stopped a freight train on the North Missouri Railroad near Centralia Station early this fall morning. Four carloads of horses were stolen. It is hoped by Isaac H. Sturgeon that a levy of about $15,000.00 may be made on the sympathizers near Centralia to pay for the horses and be collected at once.

September 7th...A Militia escort was used to protect some Union families who are moving out of the Walnut Creek neighborhood.

September 8th...Confederate Commanders, Colonel Clark and Major Parrott, met up with the forces of Militia sent out from Cape Girardeau in Dunklin County. The Confederates were discovered camped four miles below Hornersville near the Arkansas line. In the two confrontations 20 of the Confederate command were killed and two prisoners taken, along with a number of horses and arms. The Confederates are reported as having left the state now. (A subsequent report states the Confederates were encountered while proceeding toward Gayoso, their being encamped at Pemiscot Bayou? Perhaps two separate commands?)

September 9th...The Warrensburg mail was robbed a few days previous. Scouting parties through Johnson County have been unable to locate the guilty, although one was wounded in the breaking up and pursuit of the mail robbers. The guilty are reported to now be in western Lafayette County.

September 10th...Major Austin A. King, Howard County, had a run-in with 60 of Holtzclaw's command east of Roanoke in Howard County. Captain Turner (Militia) succeeded in a running fight that covered five miles, killing six of them and capturing a quantity of their shotguns. Following this report by Major King, Brigadier General Clinton B. Fisk congratulates him. "I congratulate you on the good beginning of the bushwhacking campaign. Strike with vigor and determination. Take no prisoners. We have enough of that sort on hand now. Pursue and kill. I have two of Holtzclaw's men, just captured. They state that he camps when in Howard County, in the rear of old man Hackley's farm, not far from Fayette. Make a dash in there at night and get him if possible. Let a detachment secretly watch his mother's residence. He is home almost daily, and his sisters are great comforters of the bushwhackers. Old man Hackley has a son in the brush. I shall soon send out of the district the bushwhacking families. Go ahead and give us a good report." Signed by Brigadier General Clinton B. Fisk, St. Joseph Missouri.

September 10th...This day saw a skirmish at Pisgah, Missouri, Cooper County. Confederate Commander Captain Taylor, described as a new man on the south side of the river, encountered Lieutenant Kerr of the Militia about five miles northeast of Pisgah this evening. Kerr managed to kill four and wound several others before his horses gave out in the pursuit.

September 11th-16th...Captain John D. Meredith, 39th Missouri Infantry, upon orders from Hannibal, left on the 11th from Camp Kuntzer at Hannibal with a detail of 25 men in search of a guerilla band that had been molesting and committing depredations in the neighborhood of Sidney, Ralls County. Taking his command down the Centreville Road toward West Ely, he proceeded to comply with his orders of taking fresh mounts from the disloyal owners. It was while attempting to catch one in the pasture of Dr. Hays that a sergeant, who had been detailed to guard the road, was fired upon by two men in hiding. The sergeant was uninjured but had been thrown to the ground by his horse when it reared up and the saddle turned. The two men escaped. In the pasture a party of about eight or so fired upon those attempting to catch the horse. The rest of the mission was rather uneventful, even though they joined other commands to cover the alleged upcoming attack on Florida. This didn't materialize, as the guerilla, Frank Davis, threatened. The detail discovered a small band of eight or so at a known place of rendezvous, the home of a man named Garrett. They were fired upon from the house. The house was then torched. This is not the first time troops had been fired upon from this residence. It was hoped it would prove a warning to other disloyal citizens of the neighborhood. After covering many miles through the counties of Monroe and Ralls, the detail returned to post.

September 11th-18th...Scouting parties struck the trail of guerillas that had been sighted three or four miles from the Militia camp on the Big Piney. The trail was followed to Tuscumbia, the guerillas ahead by a half-day's ride. Captain Brown, commanding a small group of Militia at Tuscumbia, had already encountered the band and had killed two of them and captured some of their horses. The scouting party, learning that at least seven of their command had been killed by this band at Mount Pleasant, set out in pursuit again. Not locating the band, they moved on to Tipton in Moniteau County. When seven miles from High Point, between Tipton and High Point, they suddenly came upon a small party, killing two of them and capturing one horse. Upon arriving back at their post, they reported the countryside full of excitement. Union men dare not stay at home. No men are sleeping at home with the exception of the rebel sympathizers. If something is not done and soon, the Union men will be forced to leave the state or be murdered.

September 18th...A command of 150 attacked a camp of 30 Militiamen in Ray County seven miles from Lexington. The Militia were pretty badly handled.

September 19th...MAJOR GENERAL STERLING PRICE, WITH AN ESTIMATED 10,000, HAS CROSSED THE BORDER INTO SOUTHEASTERN MISSOURI. Aside from this predicted rumor, now fact, life went on as usual in the rest of the state. Scouting in Lafayette County and a skirmish developed on the Arrow Rock and Brownsville Road with Bill Jackson and five of his men. Firing commenced immediately. The guerillas took off up the steep rock banks sending a shower of loose rocks down, dislodged by the frantic horses seeking footing. The scouting party followed after them in the same dashing style of horsemanship. The shots fired by both ringing out in the stillness of the early hour across the hills. Only one of the fleeing guerillas lost his life in this skirmish. The tired scouts returned to their post, having covered the country surrounding Dug Ford on the Lamine, Willow Ford and Buffalo Prairie. (It is noted that Willow Ford is a main crossing between Cooper and Saline Counties on the Lamine River.) Thompson Allison and William Chester are commended for their bravery and ability as guides through this rugged country.

September 22nd...Carthage was burned today. This information was given by some women who had left the town. The guerillas numbered about 100, and a skirmish took place with the troops stationed at Carthage. Meanwhile near Longwood, Major Mullins of the 1st Militia Cavalry, had a skirmish with Bill Jackson and Tom Woodson's band, numbering 123 men, about six miles north of Longwood this evening. Ten guerillas laid down their lives and several more were wounded. Their pack animals, with 15 days' subsistence, were captured.

September 24th...Confederate Commander Joseph Shelby is reported south of Pilot Knob moving toward Farmington with 5,000 men and four pieces of artillery. Federal Commander Thomas Ewing, Jr. is ordered to concentrate the troops in the southern part of his district at Pilot Knob and Cape Girardeau and to verify reports as to the strength and locations of the advancing Confederate armies. Federal soldiers are beginning to arrive in Missouri from surrounding states. Major General William S. Rosecrans describes the home scene. "Women's fingers were busy making clothes for the rebel soldiers out of goods plundered by the guerillas; women's tongues were busy telling Union neighbors 'their time was now coming.' General Fisk, with all his forces had been scouring the brush for weeks in the river counties in pursuit of hostile bands, composed largely of recruits from among that class of inhabitants who claim protection, yet, decline to perform the full duty of citizens on the ground that they, 'never tuck no sides,' etc." Signed William S. Rosecrans, Major General (extracted from his report).

Reports of the guerilla-type warfare are many. Neighbors, living side by side, loyal and disloyal, had remained in relative peace until this last proposed raid was planned. Then the guerilla-style of war gained all prominence in the history of Missouri, such as riding up to a neighbor's house and asking for a drink of water. When offered, the bullet of death accompanied it. Your friend could well turn out to be your foe tomorrow. In the single subdistrict of Mexico, its commanding officer furnished a list of nearly 100 Union men who, in the course of six weeks, had been killed, maimed or run off because they were "radical Union men or damned abolitionists." By the other token, Federal Commander Clinton B. Fisk orders his troops to take no prisoners. This basic order under the wrong commander could vastly enrich the retaliation aspect of the war. There still existed the code of war and the rules by which it should be played. Commanders from both the Union and the Confederacy, with the license of the uniform, abused such privileges. By this stage in Missouri's war no one cared. The innocent of both loyalties died.

September 27th...Centralia mourned this day. Bloody Bill Anderson and his men were joined by George Todd's, and supposedly the James boys, and attacked a train at Centralia. A cold-blooded massacre of the 24 ill soldiers on board was carried out. It is reported that some of the bodies were placed upon the train tracks and the engine moved over them. Some were scalped. It was death in a cruel manner, befitting of the dealer. The train depot and some cars were set ablaze. Pure terror and carnage was all that was left behind when they departed. Later that same evening Major A.V.E. Johnson along with part of the 39th Missouri Infantry, about

120 men, arrived at Centralia. Upon seeing the smoking ruins of the depot and cars and the bloody, ghastly corpses of the slain, unarmed soldiers, the Major and his command went after Bill Anderson with a vengeance. The band of Anderson and Todd, numbering over 300 men, was encountered. After furious fighting and the stampeding of Johnson's horses, his green raw recruits were badly outnumbered. And when it was over, Major A.V.E. Johnson and 115 others lay dead upon the field of their last stand. Anderson and Todd lived to spread terror another day. Venturing into the scene of the bloodshed the next morning were Dr. Snead, Dr. F.G. Burton, W.R. Burton and Jacob Kanatzar. Eighty-three bodies were brought into Centralia. Seventy-nine were buried by the citizens of Centralia in a large grave near the railroad east of town. The remaining bodies were buried at an unknown location. (According to Boone County Missouri History, these bodies were later removed and buried with honors at Jefferson City National Cemetery.)

The attack on Missouri, led by Major General Sterling Price, was fast developing into a full-scale invasion. The commands led by Price had now split into threes. Each approaching from Missouri's borders by a slightly different route. Each leaving death and destruction in its wake. Each stripping the citizens of the hard-earned and preciously-protected corn and hay crops, to feed their half-starved armies. Horses by the hundreds were stolen or traded unwillingly for their worn mounts. Banks, if not boarded and abandoned, became easy prey. The railroads and bridges became mere firewood and scattered rails. The homes of the poorest of her people, in many cases mere hovels, were ransacked and all taken that could be loaded or carried off, leaving families homeless and destitute. Their sympathies mattered little. Peaceable men once more took up arms of any sort. Some to join in the invasion in the name of the spirit of the Confederacy. Others to defend home and hearth. Neutrality was not impossible, so vast and wide-spread were these armies. Honor and duty, for men of the Union and the Confederacy, must now prevail.

Battle of Pilot Knob...This was one of the first major engagements of Price's armies. Twelve hundred Federals held off a full-scale attack on Fort Davidson on September 27th. During the night hours Brigadier General Thomas Ewing, Jr. slipped away unnoticed, leaving behind some men to "blow the magazine." This was a very rude awakening to the Confederates by morning's early light. By then Ewing was nearly safe from further assault.

September 28th...Being harassed and pursued, Ewing is found making his retreat. Being pushed into taking a stand, Ewing used his time well by taking a path through the hills toward the Meremac, hoping to get to the railroad and pull his troops back toward St. Louis. It was very much the target of Price's army. Ewing fought his way along a ridge where the Confederates could not flank him but meeting at Harrison's Station. There using some old breastworks that had been thrown up by the Militia, he held the Confederates at bay for 36 hours. The Confederates finally left him and he made his way, mostly intact, to Rolla. The next order of business was to fortify and man the cities of St. Louis, Jefferson City and Rolla.

About 4,500 infantry and the mounted force they could raise, the 7th Kansas just in from Memphis, part of the 13th Missouri Volunteer Cavalry under Colonel Catherwood, and the recruits of Merrill's Horse, hastily mounted and organized a total of 1,500 men. This was all the force that could be mustered to place between an advancing army of 15,000 and the strategic points of Missouri. Another 4,500 men were raised by the various Militia companies being called in and the cancellation of exemptions. The 100-day men from Illinois started arriving by September 30th. By October 11th all were organized into brigades or just armed and detailed for protection of St. Louis. From here the various commands fanned out to intercept the oncoming fearless Confederate Army. The blue-coated fan covered points to Franklin, Richwoods Road, Kirkwood and Jefferson City. On the 30th the forces met. Moselle Bridge was burned, as was the depot at Franklin. The Confederates seemed to be held at bay with the 1,500 mounted men and the 4,500 mounted. At least the Federals were certainly not going to attempt an offensive action. The Confederates seemed also to delay, but each day of delay brought reinforcements for the Federals from Arkansas. Help was on the way, but that took time.

By the October 2nd the Confederates were reported to be amassing at Union on the road either to Jefferson City or Rolla. General Smith was then ordered with his command to Franklin, but the Confederates slowly swung to the west and on the 3rd General Smith advanced to Gray's Summit and General Pike moved to Franklin. The chess game of lives and the big armies had begun.

On October 4th the Federals pushed toward the Gasconade, advancing the infantry as far as Union. Following were General Pike's Militia. By the 5th Price's command took the beautiful old town of Hermann, burned the Gasconade Bridge and was crossing that river at the Old State Road Ford. General Smith followed him. This day General Mower reported his arrival at Cape Girardeau. He was not in good shape; his teams worn down, some of his horses unshod, part of his cavalry by now dismounted and his men fatigued beyond endurance, but he had arrived and with him came hope.

Boats were dispatched and by the 8th and the 9th his command had reached St. Louis. From there his infantry was pushed by water as far as possible to join General Smith. The cavalry, under Winslow, now reshod, started across the country from St. Louis to Jefferson City, which place they reached by October 16th. That made the garrison strength at Jefferson City to consist of about 4,100 cavalry and 2,000 infantry. It was determined to meet the Confederates at the banks of the Moreau, then fall back to the entrenchments at Jefferson City. The Moreau is, at this stage, just a small stream with muddy banks and a bad bottom four or five miles east of the city. The Confederates burned the Osage Bridge and crossed the river on October 6th. On the 7th they crossed the river after sharp fighting and drew up a battle line four miles long, stretching east, south and west of the city. Evidently upon discovering the earthworks that had been hastily thrown up by sheer physical labor of all concerned, and with his past experience at Pilot Knob of attacking a fort with earthworks, he drew in the long lines and passed around the city leaving it unmolested.

The long gray line of the Confederate Army spread for miles. Its rear guard was well behind the advance. This made harassment easier for the Federals. This constant pushing and skirmishing was kept up until the town of Versailles was reached. Not knowing which way the Confederates were going to turn, they pushed harder and as the long gray line swung in the direction of Boonville, the Federals followed and finally drove the Confederates to form another battle line there. Almost finding himself surrounded, General Sanborn with his Federal command made a hasty retreat and falling back they joined Catherwood's force, and with him, arrived at California, Missouri on the morning of October 14th. The Confederates, taking good advantage of this opportunity, crossed the Lamine River at Scott's Ford and Dug Ford and then moved northerly toward Arrow Rock. Sanborn again immediately followed this movement by the Georgetown Bridge, keeping between the Pacific Railroad and the line of Confederate march. Holding the line of the Blackwater, a tributary of the Lamine, while Price, crossing a party of Shelby's command at Arrow Rock on the Boonville ferryboat to the north side of the river, advanced on Glasgow, which town he captured but not until after a long, hard seven-hour fight.

By the 17th the Federals, out of supplies, reported also that Price was between Waverly and Marshall. Also on the 17th the Federal forces had gathered again. The 18th brought orders to General Smith to move his Federal command to Dunksburg near the cavalry headquarters, taking five days' rations and leaving a minimum garrison to protect and handle the stores at Sedalia and Lamine Bridge. This movement was accomplished by the 18th, the cavalry was strung out, a formidable force, with its center near Cook's Store, its right behind the Blackwater toward Marshall and its left near Kirkpatrick's Mills toward Warrensburg. The Confederates being fully aware of this, seemed to hesitate, perhaps determining the direction in which to advance or whether to retrace their line between Sedalia and Jefferson City. The Federal cavalry was ready in either direction. Price then elected to head toward Lexington. Word was received on the 19th that the advance column had arrived. General Blunt, after a sharp fight, retired toward Independence, burning the bridges behind him as he went, trying to check his advance. Blunt was ordered to check his advance at Wellington, the main body of Price's army was still near Waverly. As soon as it could be ascertained if General Price was moving the main force toward Lexington, then Blunt should check his advance, and those who were waiting would close the rear flank.

The Federals now deployed their various commands around in strategic positions that in any direction that General Price would move, the sides of the large Federal sweep would start to encircle him. Thus it went through Lexington and into Independence. Finally on the 22nd the Federal cavalry reached the Little Blue at 10:00 in the morning. There they found the bridge destroyed. A temporary one was constructed, the Confederate skirmishers drive in and the huge Federal command started across. The Confederates promptly opened a murderous fire with artillery, but was inch-by-inch driven toward Independence. At Independence the Confederates were overtaken by a brilliant cavalry charge in which Colonel Catherwood's Regiment captured two complete death-belching guns. Nearly 100 prisoners were now to be dealt with, along with all the dead and the numerous wounded from both armies that had fallen in the wake of the guns. By 8:00 it was reported that all the brigades had been engaged belonging to the Federal command of General Pleasanton. The other Federal commands held strategic positions but were separated within the area, each having their own force of the Confederates to deal with. It was a bloody battle, bravely fought by Price and his command and that of the Federals.

By the morning of the 23rd the big, blue-coated fan was closing. The Federal commands were converging upon the Confederates from all directions and in vast numbers, ever tightening their large circle. The day opened at 7:00 in the morning at the crossing of the Big Blue. The heavy fighting continued until mid-afternoon when Shelby, who had been engaged with General Curtis' command, found that Generals Marmaduke and Fagan were giving way, then amassed and turned all his strength on General Pleasanton again. For awhile it shook Sanborn's Brigade almost to the breaking point. The skillful use of Thurber's Artillery, double-shotted with deadly grape and canister, finally saved the day. This broke the Confederate stronghold and allowed the advance of the Federal infantry. The Confederates, in a last valiant pitch, pushed past the commands of Generals Pleasanton and Curtis that night and moved southward toward Little Santa Fe.

Late in the afternoon of the 23rd General Smith arrived at Independence and was ordered to move by forced march to Hickman Mills. There it was hoped he would be able to strike the flank of the Confederate line. Had General Smith been ordered and marched for that point rather than Independence the day before, he would have arrived in time to strike the now compact columns and trains with 9,000 infantry and five batteries. But now it was just too late. The opening was created and the Confederates took it.

There was nothing to do now but follow, as all had been called into close the circle around the Confederates, and the circle failed to close. The Confederates were now followed by a huge army of

Federals. Skirmishing took place all along the way. Tired, battle-weary men in gray were found just sitting along the roadsides, too weary to go on. The wagon train was being emptied and a long trail of useless plunder was strewn over the trail. The wagons were heavy, the horses worn down from the hard riding from being in virtual constant motion for days. October 24th found the Confederates within 15 miles of Trading Post, Kansas. The raid in Missouri was in all sense over. The Federals engaged them again at midnight at the Marais-des-Cygnes. We have shortly following the only "official" battle of the Civil War fought in Kansas, the Battle of Mine Creek. It was in this battle that General John S. Marmaduke became a prisoner of war. General Price lost control to a certain degree, and General Joseph Shelby rallied the remnants of the beaten commands and again crossed into Arkansas after one more confrontation at Newtonia, Missouri.

Today as we read the battle reports of this raid, one can almost feel the bone-weary exhaustion of the men. They were pushed over 500 miles, trying to live off the countryside in a state that was stripped of edible matter for man or beast. Crossing back into Arkansas must have been accompanied by many tears of exhaustion and a feeling of defeatism. Many were left behind, not to make the return trip to safety. The valiant, courageous men of Price's army did not make another such raid upon Missouri soil. The next time many of them crossed into Missouri, it was small bands which had formed and came for "evening up old scores." For some, the next time they rested their eyes upon their homeland, the war was over.

At a court of inquiry held concerning the execution by General Price of this raid, there was one point that stood out. That was the lack of organization and discipline. The Confederates were recruiting more soldiers on this raid, and as these hundreds of newly-sought men joined, that is just what they did, join. No set rules of camplife were observed. These men had no training in the skills of warfare. Many had just unhitched the plow, put the mule in the barn and went proudly off. The next thing was to follow the leader. No gun, no uniform, usually no horse, no tent, just follow the man ahead of you.

The discipline of an army of this nature was unenforceable. As reports of molestation and robbery became more numerous, the men caught molesting and robbing were shot by the Confederate commanders without a moment's hesitation.

After the war was over, one of Price's commanders remarked that this raid failed in its objective from the lack of discipline executed and demanded by the commanding officer himself, General Price. While the Federal commanders "traveled light," General Price allowed the heavy, cumbersome wagon train to accompany him. This always ended up full of plunder from homes they passed. No food but plunder. It was to a fault that this went on. It created the scene for defeat on more than one occasion. The average soldier had his worldly goods and his rewards from the spoils of war in those trains. He didn't want them left behind. It was said General Price had over 40 wagons in his train when he started his retreat southward from Westport. It is also reported that a trail of fine silk dresses, women's fancy hats, silverware, candleholders, fine china dishes, jewelry and various other items taken from the pillaged homes was strewn from Westport to Trading Post, Kansas.

September 30th...Bill Anderson and 20 of his followers made good their escape again today. Anderson was attacked by First Lieutenant Thomas B. Wright of the 5th Militia Cavalry, in Waynesville. Mr. Anderson left one behind, whom citizens have said is the famous Bill Anderson. The Lieutenant also found that Anderson had stolen clothing from some citizens, robbed the county clerk of $100.00 in cash and burned the stable of one company. Also, by some miracle, the magazine of the fort didn't burn after being lit by the band. In a later communication it is stated this raid was under the command of a man named Burkhart, formerly of Texas County. Burkhart represented himself as belonging to Shelby's command which was considered to be doubtful.

October 9th...A scouting party in St. Francois County broke up a camp of about 300 guerillas under the command of Dick Berryman and Sam _____ in the vicinity of DeSoto. Twenty-one of their number were killed.

October 10th-12th...Confederate Bulge Powell and six of his men were discovered about four miles below Caruthersville in Pemiscot County today. Bulge was seriously wounded and left two dead. The company rollbook belonging to Powell was recovered. Fifty-five names are represented. A cache of buried salt; five barrels, was found at the foot of Wolf Island by the scouts. It appeared to be ready for shipment to Kentucky.

October 14th...The business section of Danville in Montgomery County went up in flames today. Five citizens were killed and another wounded. With this information relayed by S.A. Thompson, the Postmaster at Danville, went a plea for soldiers to provide protection for the former Union soldiers residing in the area. They are marked men for murder.

October 19th...Thrailkill and a concentrated force of about 150 men are occupying the country in and about Montevallo and Horse Creek. It is reported that nine families of southern sympathies are now living on Little Clear Creek, each having about from 50 to 250 bushels of corn, this being the home of Confederates. Thrailkill's man had a run-in with the Stochler Militia, in which one of Thrailkill's men lost his life.

October 25th...Many parties of Confederates were found today on Muddy, Clear Fork, Fiefbeaux and Honey Creeks. A large command was sighted southwest of Clinton. About 250 attacked the town of Clinton today. Seventy Militimen, citizens and the negroes defended the town splendidly. The are now holding both Clinton and Calhoun in safety.

October 27th...It is reported that "Bloody Bill Anderson" will not be killing or spreading terror. He has been reported as being killed today.

October 29th...After dark tonight a reported force of some guerillas, 900 strong (I would imagine these are not guerillas as noted, but a Confederate command), threw off the track a freight train going north five miles beyond Warrenton. The last accounts given depicted fighting with the 30-man escort. After stopping the train, the oncoming passenger train was flagged to prevent destruction, the objective being to rob the passengers. It is suspected among the train's passengers would be Colonel Holmes (Union) with 400 to 500 of his command. Major Montgomery (Union) who was sent to Cap-au-Gris in Lincoln County about four days ago, is now in Wentzville and is en route to Warrenton with assistance. The telegraph lines have been torn down beyond Warrenton.

October 29th-November 8th...Captain Jacob Cassairt of the 8th Militia Cavalry, started today on a scouting foray to Quincy in Hickory County and vicinity, reaching Quincy on October 30th. By the morning of November 1st the reconnoitering party returned with news. A party of Confederates was directly ahead about two miles. After a double-quick march, the Confederates were sighted. In the ensuing running skirmish, Captain Vansickle (CSA) of Texas was killed. This skirmish brought about the release of Judges Owen and Jackman, a Mr. Brown and two other Union men of Benton County who had been taken prisoner by the Confederates. The morning of the 2nd brought information that the Confederate command was about 600 strong. Their trail was struck, and about 2:00 in the afternoon they appeared in sight. The command of Captain Cassairt attacked a portion of the rear of the long column and succeeded in cutting out about 100 men. It was an all-out charge, revolvers emptied, sabers clanked. Pure confusion. Pushing them hard to keep the element of confusion alive the Confederate commander, frantically attempting to rally his command, was killed. This was Colonel Groomes of Shelby's command. Twenty-five more of the dead from his command fell into the hands of the Captain and his little command. It was later reported that the remainder of the command of Colonel Groomes was surrendering. Nine reportedly surrendered to Colonel Halbert, a man of influence in Hickory County, and one was reported as surrendering to a free negro.

November 1st...Near the mouth of the Big Piney at the home of "old man Black," four Bushwhackers were discovered by a scouting party near Waynesville. Two of these were wounded and one taken as prisoner. The prisoner attempted to escape and was killed. Today, November 1st, also saw a skirmish near Lebanon, Missouri. A post forage train en route to Dallas County was attacked by a portion of a Confederate force said to be about 600 strong. Also on the 1st, Major Samuel Henry, Assistant Surgeon John P. Porter and Lieutenant Harles Ashley, Regimental Quartermaster, all of the 89th Indiana, were taken prisoner today at Greenton, Lafayette County. They were taken supposedly by three guerillas. These men were rapidly taken to the brush and shot. Their bodies were found today. All had been shot through the head. A local resident tells the following story in accounting the events: "While the Eighty-ninth Regiment was marching through Greenton these three officers rode up to a house and called for dinner. The lady told them that she had nothing cooked, but that if they could wait, she would soon have something prepared for them. They consented to wait; their command marched on. They had gotten their dinner, left the house for their horses hitched at the gate, where, upon going into the house had also left their arms. Before they reached their horses, three men in Federal uniform came dashing up and ordered them to surrender. The officers at first regarded it as a joke, but upon cocked revolvers being presented they surrendered almost within sight of the regiment and were taken to the woods. I have buried them today. When brought here they had neither overcoats nor vests on; Major Henry's saber hung in a tree near his body." (Reported by Captain W.N. Norville, Post at Lexington.)

November 3rd...The large exodus of the troops involved countering the raid of Major General Price has started this day. This concerns the transfer of the First and Third Divisions, 16th Army Corps, from Missouri to Tennessee. The 95th Ohio Infantry on November 1st left Warrensburg en route to Jefferson City. By November 4th the weather turned stormy and cold. On the 6th Jefferson City was reached. On the 8th the long, weary column started the march toward St. Louis. It finally reached St. Louis on the 15th. There it rested and refitted for the winter campaign until the 23rd when it embarked on steamers for Nashville. Just seven short days later it arrived in Nashville. Many others made this same trip via various routes. Each one wading the cold, icy Missouri rivers, stopping to construct temporary pontoon bridges, caring for the sick and wounded, their trains and baggage strung out over miles of the countryside. Among those whose records we located are the 35th Iowa Infantry, 21st Missouri Infantry, 119th Illinois Infantry, 27th Iowa Infantry, 52nd Indiana Infantry and 33rd Wisconsin Infantry.

November 5th-6th...Captain Deihl (Union) was surprised at breakfast this morning as about 20 mounted Confederates under Colonel Birthright boldly rode into Charleston. Captain Deihl was wounded seriously and another man slightly. Eight men were captured and marched about seven miles outside of town, robbed of all they had and released. Colonel Birthright made it as far as Sikeston. There he was overtaken by Captain Edwards who had been on his trail from Charleston. In the two raids made by Colonel Birthright, it cost his command 20 lives and five taken prisoner.

November 5th-9th...Today a large expedition left Rolla for Licking in Texas County, the purpose of which was to protect the loyal government citizens through an election. The expedition went off without incident until on the return trip. About nine miles from Licking and close to a residence of a gentleman named Reed, the company was attacked by about 400 Confederates. After a spirited skirmish, the Confederates made good their escape, leaving behind three killed and seven wounded. There were no injuries to the expeditionary command.

November 5th-16th...Expedition left today from Springfield, Missouri to Fort Smith, Arkansas.

November 6th-7th...Major Douglas Dale of the 4th Militia Cavalry struck the trail of the Confederate command of Dorsey from Fulton in Callaway County. This trail was followed until midnight when it was lost. Seeking information from some Union families in the neighborhood, it was learned that Dorsey had crossed the river 2 1/2 miles below Cote Sans Dessein at the farm of Swan Ferguson. Upon discovering the crossing, it was too late. Dorsey made good his escape in a stolen steamboat.

November 11th-21st...Scouting party left Springfield, Missouri en route to Huntsville and Yellville, Arkansas. Another hunting party.

November 12th...Bushwhackers struck again 12 miles northwest of Centreville. Three were killed and three wounded. Eleven horses and two rifles were captured. Lieutenant Storz of the 5th Militia Cavalry had one man wounded in the knee and lost a good horse.

November 13th-16th...Captain James Edwards is still in Pemiscot County on the trail of 150 Confederates he can't find. Scouting parties have covered many areas of the county. Only occasional stragglers have been located. Confederate Captain Kelly, who succeeded Bulge Powell, and one of his lieutenants named Walker were captured. Walker was eventually shot, and Captain Kelly is thought to be wounded. Two deserters belonging to Bill Forrest's command (CSA) came over from the Tennessee side of the river.

November 16th-23rd...Captain Eli Crandall (Militia) and his command made an expedition from Brookfield to Brunswick, Keytesville and Salisbury, Missouri. Captain Crandall reached Brunswick on the 17th. While on duty there, several ladies approached and requested permission to remove themselves and their household goods to St. Louis. Knowing these ladies were loyal to the Southern Cause, but that they and their families had remained at home during the past raid of General Price, the Captain thought it wise to have them remove themselves from the city. He knew no reason why they shouldn't. Word of this quickly spread. That night Captain Crandall was visited by several loyal Union citizens concerned about the taking of what would be considered contraband goods, the possessions of the moving families. By the next morning, the Captain had been informed that a Citizen Guard had been watching the warehouse in which the goods had been stored prior to shipping. The citizens, not soldiers, had been prowling around the building all night in a threatening manner for the purpose, it was thought, of destroying the same. On the evening of the 18th an arrangement was made for Lieutenant Bryan and a detail to guard the place. This was done until the whole of the command was ordered into line on account of firing being heard near the Seminary. This proved to be a decoy to lure the guards away from their duty. Upon investigating the firing around the Seminary, the town fire alarm was heard. The warehouse was on fire. Most of the property was saved and the warehouse sustained but little damage. After conversations with several Union men who lived close by, it appeared they were satisfied it was not the work of the soldiers but of outraged Union men who had been treated badly by the families or their friends. "The feelings this type of action creates does more harm then any type of Rebel Army can inflict," perceived the young Captain.

Leaving Brunswick on the next day en route to Glasgow, word was received that the command of Jackson had been sighted. The route was changed to the direction of Becklehamer's Mill, and there they crossed the Chariton River. The scouting party was then split into three separate commands. Captain Roush made contact with Jackson about three miles from Salisbury City, wounding two of his men, capturing three horses and a fancy cap, beautifully decorated with feathers and plumes, worn by Jackson. One of Roush's men was seriously wounded and a horse was lost in the fight. The command is still trailing Jackson and the remainder of his men.

November 16th-25th...Expedition from Cape Girardeau to Patterson, Wayne County, and skirmishes at Reeves Mill and at Buckskull, Randolph County, Arkansas. This detail of 240, all mounted men, was sent out from Cape Girardeau with instructions to proceed to Patterson in Wayne County and rout a Confederate command and open up communications with Pilot Knob and cooperate with the forces sent there. Leaving Jackson they marched down the old telegraph road and encamped at Kinder's farm. The next afternoon they passed through Dallas, Bollinger County, and struck camp at A.M. Side's farm, a half mile on the other side of the Castor River in Wayne County. The weather was very unpleasant, raining without letup for two days. Traveling was slow and tedious at best. Upon reaching Patterson the next day, it was learned that the Confederates sought were now in Arkansas. On the 19th the expedition was joined and started without delay through the pine forests of Ripley County, camping on the farm of William Arnold. A small scouting party sent out killed a notorious Bushwhacker, Ely Garbert, at Reeves Mill about four miles distant of their camp. The mill, found to be a rendezvous place for various guerilla commands, was reduced to smouldering ruins. The command then made its way into Arkansas, crossing over on the November 20th. After one day's work in Arkansas, the commands started north again. The horses fared badly during the return trip. The ice had frozen to a depth of over one inch, and in crossing the swamps several of the horses had to be left behind with severely cut legs from breaking through the icy covering.

November 21st-30th...Six guerillas moved across the corner of the county. On their route about 10 miles west of Fulton, they hanged two negro men and robbed several citizens around Millersburg. A running fight developed with the detail sent in pursuit. Overtaking these men three times, and each time having a running skirmish, they scattered the little band of marauders only to regroup again.

November 29th-December 3rd...The scouting parties left Warrensburg and crossed in separate directions the areas of Hall's Mill, Big Grove and the Greenton Valley. Another took place through Wellington, Pleasant Hill and Lone Jack. The only persons found were stragglers. Two sightings of small bands of guerillas were made. Nothing of any significance occurred, with the possible exception of leaving Mrs. Welsh a note ordering her out of the county within 10 days. Her home was known to be a place of refuge for the guerillas.

December 1st-3th...Operations continued in the vicinity of Waynesville. This resulted in the death of three deserters by the name of Lewis Williams, I.S. Williams and Levi Clark, all members of Company C, 48th Missouri Volunteer Infantry. These men deserted at about the time of the big raid. They were found secreted in a cave about 30 miles from Waynesville on Big Piney. A pass was found on the body of I.S. Williams identifying him as a member of Campbell's Company. Another scouting party killed a man by the name of Charles Withers who was known as a bad character.

December 3rd...A small band of guerillas passed between New Madrid and Charleston. Captain Edwards (Militia) pursued them and killed and captured only two out of the reported 15.

December 7th...At Franklin, the Moselle Bridge on the Southwest Branch Pacific Railroad was the object of a Confederate arsonist who, when discovered with the firebrand in his hand, was the recipient of six bullets. He was not recognized by anyone within the immediate neighborhood.

December 8th...Confederate Captain W.C. Clark, Missouri Cavalry, dressed himself and his command in blue uniforms belonging to the 2nd Colorado. Even their saddles were marked as such. They rode right into Tuscumbia, passed themselves off as 2nd Colorado men and captured the town, disarmed and then paroled about 25 of Captain Brown's Militia Company. The brilliant little ruse was very well executed.

December 14th...Skirmishes today in Cypress Swamp near Cape Girardeau resulted in the untimely death of three guerillas.

December 18th...A band of guerillas made their appearance near Benton, stealing horses. Captain Tanner of Commerce, with 20 men, went in pursuit to Little River. Only two of the stolen horses were recovered.

December 20th-January 4th...A large expeditionary force was sent from Cape Girardeau and Dallas, Missouri to Cherokee Bay, Arkansas and the St. Francois River.

December 30th...Fifteen miles below Carruthersville a party of guerillas made its appearance. The noise of the horses' hooves on the icy ground gave them ample warning of pursuit and they made good their escape. A man named Potter, belonging to the guerilla band, was killed.

The third year of the war has drawn to a close in Missouri.

1865

By 1865 the war in Missouri was winding down. The last-ditch efforts of Price, Marmaduke and Shelby to resurrect the Confederacy in Missouri failed. It now flamed only in spirit. The tired and worn men of Missouri were returning to their homes again. The Confederacy, to recruit and gather up horses and food. Some who were paroled back to Missouri just never returned to their respective commands. The crippled and wounded Union men from service in other states returned. Some to rebuild their fortunes, others to gather up the scattered families and weep at the sight of the burned homes. A part of their life's labors lay in ashes. Both men, in some cases, just loaded up their belongings, left and started a new somewhere else. It wasn't a joyful homecoming for either side. The only happiness was seeing their loved ones again. Many families had vacant chairs around the table as family members and loved ones succumbed to the hardship of war and the ravages of time.

January 2nd-7th...The rumor that 80 Confederates and guerillas were encamped at Jack's Fork in Shannon County proved to be false. Only small groups of three to 10 were found by the Federal scouting parties. In these several camps, six of them were killed and nine of their horses and a rig were taken. Texas County is reported full of the men of the Confederate Jackman's forces, disbanded for the winter. While searching out the little camps, several houses were burned along with a few cribs of good corn that were found secreted, providing them nourishment and feed for their animals. Citizens are being robbed of their foodstuffs and bedclothing now. It is rampant.

January 4th-16th...An expedition started today from Bloomfield to Poplar Bluff, Missouri. This detail had to swim the frigid waters of the St. Francois River. The command suffered much from the cold. The animals had to be pulled out of the mire. In crossing the swamp between Current and Black Rivers, the ambulance and wagon were lost. Nineteen Confederates were killed on this expedition. They were all taken by complete surprise. Fifty contraband horses and mules were confiscated. Of these, 35 have been turned over to the Provost-Marshal at Cape Girardeau, five drowned in the swamp, four head were claimed by citizens and given up and six head were stolen out of the corral at Bloomfield. In the area of Poplar Bluff, forage was totally unavailable even for a day's stayover in the area. The town is destitute of everything.

January 8th...Miss Mary B. Bedichek of Johnson County took a corn knife to intruders who broke into the home she shared with her elderly father. After her father received blows and ill treatment, she snatched up the corn knife and started to even up the odds. She finally dispatched one. His companion, waiting outside, went to his rescue. He too felt the wrath of the corn knife. Finally, trying to make their escape across the yard, one was found dead near the chicken coop and the other was not found. She later was presented with a handsome Colt revolver with which to protect home and hearth.

January 9th-11th...The Militia details are left to clean out Texas County of the robbing guerillas and idle Confederates. There were several skirmishes with Yeates' band of guerillas on the 9th, 10th and 11th. Nine of them were killed, and a wounded man escaped.

January 10th...Skirmishing with Confederate Commander Jackson's escort with the killing of Gray Brown and John Robinson. Jackson was severely wounded, virtually crippled. There was the killing of Forte Campbell near Fayette and the arrest of Mrs. Fanny Duff, her exposition, and the arrest and rigid examination of other parties more or less in sympathy with Jackson. These took the interest of all concerned. Jackson was seriously wounded, being last seen bootless, hatless and unable to use his foot in the stirrup with blood running down his leg. But, the sly one did it again, he escaped. The killing of his escort created nearly a running sequence of events from one point to another. Lieutenant Gannon and Captain Denny, acting with great precision, being in the right places at the right times, culminated in the chase and the death of the escort and the displacement of Jackson. In the push to escape, Jackson left behind his boots. He is hatless. On the bodies of the deceased escort were found $72.25, two pocket knives, one pocket compass, a gold pen and silver holder and the likenesses of two young ladies, along with a hat and the boots. These articles were divided among the men who took part in this daring chase and capture in the vicinity of Glasgow.

January 11th...Two squads of Bushwhackers were sighted today, one at Lexington and the other reported camped at Waverly. The first squad at Lexington made its unannounced appearance at Lawyer Green's on the south edge of town, fired into the house and left going south on the Greenton Road. A running pursuit of these men was kept up over five miles. Each time an advantageous place appeared, the guerillas would form a line of battle, the Militia charged and the guerillas moved on to the next place. Finally the Militia, running out of ammunition, returned to camp.

January 12th-15th...Scouting party from Camp Grover to Texas Prairie. This party followed several trails of various known men of rather notorious reputation, but succeeded in capturing no one. Those appearing were discovered at the home of one Rider, the others at the residences of wives of the guerillas Watson and Clifton. All trails disappeared into the brush and other secret places.

January 12th-17th...Information was all that was gathered in a scouting party from Warrensburg. The party covered the area of Dover, then to Waverly and to Grand Pass Church. It went as far as Miami and followed another trail back. The news of Captain

Burnsides (CSA) and a band of robbers disguised at night, and committing local incidents, was relayed, but there was no sign of any of them.

January 16th-22nd...Six details of scouts have been sent out in operations about Waynesville. One brought a large train in safely from Rolla. Another made a spirited contact with a guerilla camp on the Big Piney a short distance from McCourtney's Mill. There two of the three guerillas were killed, a McCourtney and a man named Anthony. The third, named Bradford, was left and thought to be mortally wounded. He has since appeared very much alive and a detail has been sent to bring him in. Another party has returned from a scout up the Roubideaux and reports all quiet. The remaining have not yet returned.

January 18th-22nd...Another scouting party patrolled the hills and countryside around the headwaters of Blackwater and in the area of the Sni-Bar Hills. Families along the route had nothing to report. Considerable sign, but no show.

January 24th-February 22nd...Expedition from Cape Girardeau, Missouri to Eleven Points, Arkansas. "While in Northern Arkansas and Southern Missouri large numbers of Union refugees immediately prepared to avail themselves of the opportunity thus presented of escaping from the despotism and dangers oppressing them. They were nearly all of the better class of citizens, many of them wealthy farmers, but they owned that if they remained longer there they would almost certainly be conscripted into the rebel army, and, or resisting that, they would be killed. They stated that to attempt to escape, excepting under protection of our forces, would be certain death - a statement, incredible as it may seem, I found to be only too true. One of them, moving a little too quick, and being in advance only about four miles, was shot. There were about thirty families, and I could not abandon them to their fate. I did move slowly, and so arranged my force as to protect them and their teams and household goods and what little stock they had along with them, occasionally taking teams of oxen, with the owners consent, to rest one of the jaded teams for the day, all of which were returned to the owners. I obtained and gave some of the more destitute meal to subsist upon. Paying for the same with my own money, and at other times, obtaining it from the wealthy rebel families along the road. It was a case of stern necessity. It was starvation or food for women and children. It delayed my return by a few days, but, humanity demanded the delay. I could not abandon them; they had already suffered incredible hardships. They will not become a charge upon the Government, but will be able to earn a livelihood. Although this may have not been strictly military. I confidently rely upon the well known charity and kind feelings of the commanding general toward these unfortunate victims of this accursed rebellion to justify me in thus acting toward them." signed by Colonel J.B. Rogers, commanding expedition.

February 1st-5th...Scouting party from Warrensburg to Wagon Knob, Big Grove and Texas Prairie. Actually, two large scouting parties left Warrensburg today. Johnson County was well covered and then recrossed and recovered. At Wagon Knob, leaving their wagon and horses hidden, the detail fanned out into the brush and surprised a camp of six guerillas. They fired point blank into the close-knit gathering. The home of Rider was visited. His wife, Alice, was at home with six children; a boy age 10 years, a boy age nine years, a boy age seven years, a little girl age six years, a girl age four years and another little girl age two years. Rider is on the guerilla list. The home of Welch was also visited. His wife, Mary, and four children; a boy age 12 years, a girl age 10 years, a boy age seven years and a boy age five years were found there. Starting in the direction of Chapel Hill, a trail of two guerillas was discovered. They were followed to the home of the Widow Cobb. They were just leaving as the detail rode up. One of them was wounded in the resulting chase.

The other detail consisted of 48 men. They were scouting from Warrensburg to Tabo Creek, Dover, Oaklin Church and Davis' Creek. This resulted in the confiscation of a Savage revolver and a little ammunition from the home of Mrs. Jay, a widow lady and a five-mile chase of a handful of guerillas that were scared up from the brush near Tabo Creek.

February 3rd-8th...Heavy scouting through Lafayette County has gone on for five days. N.B. Mitchell was killed (described as a Bushwhacker) and four or five others were wounded. More families harboring bushmen were discovered.

February 6th-8th...The remains of three men who had been taken in November from their homes by guerillas were found. These men, James Martin, Sr., John Allcorn and John Coil, were too old for any type of service. They were all citizens of Ozark County. The scouting party moving through Ozark County spent the first night at the home of James Martin. The next day they fell into it with two of Tracy's men and one of Elliott's. They immediately became "hors de combat." Owing to the heavy concentration of random bands of guerillas and Confederates throughout the county, another scouting party will proceed at once through the area.

February 12th...The determined detail of Militia walked a mile bootless in the cold February night. The camp of Jim Carter was surprised. Three of his men were killed and all the rest were crippled. It is supposed they had 10 Arkansas men in their camp. The first shot fired killed Sergeant Thomas J. Kern, 9th Militia, and later Private Tuder was wounded. The camp was located within six or seven miles due north of Columbia. Killed of Carter's command (it doesn't specify Confererate or guerilla) were Jim Carter, William Cavanaugh and Tompkins Robinson.

February 13th...A solitary detail of eight from Confederate Clarke's command rode into Mississippi County. They left empty handed and hotly pursued.

February 16th-20th...Captain James H. Sallee of the 16th Missouri Cavalry, started on the morning of the 16th with 15 days' rations and proceeded to the Little North Fork in Ozark County (report from Lebanon). There the detachment from Company B met up with four citizens; Isham Lamar, Johnson Lamar, William Lamar and George Lamar, who reported that they had been to White River near the Widow Magness' and had found some Confederates (described as rebels) holed up in a cave and wanted assistance to catch them. They immediately started for the cave accompanied by the Lamars as guides. The cave was located and three were found, a Williams, a Riddle and another unknown. Upon the approach, Williams started to run and was killed. The other two, though wounded, made good their escape in the rocky, hilly countryside. After this little affair the detachment was split, one going downstream and the other working upstream of the Little North Fork. Crossing at the home of Mr. Yochan, they learned of several small camps in each direction. Of these seven men, four were killed. The Lamars were seen the next day driving a nice herd of cattle downstream. This was reported as a matter of record. The Lamars are suspected of obtaining cattle for their own use. Not necessarily their own cattle.

February 23rd-March 2nd...Scouting parties from Salem and Licking, Missouri to Spring River Mills, Arkansas in search of the location and strength of Freeman's Confederate command. (Licking is in Texas County, Missouri.)

February 24th...Jackson, the infamous, is on the road again. At Switzler's Mills he robbed a citizen, hanged two negroes and killed a man named Poe.

February 27th...Jackson was sighted again today. He is headed in the direction of the Perche Hills, minus five horses and carrying at least two wounded.

March 3rd-7th...Captain Campbell of the 50th Missouri Infantry, with 50 men of the 7th Kansas and 2nd Missouri Militia, rode into Dunklin County. They came upon a camp of Confederates some 25 miles below Bloomfield. Six of them were killed, including Captain Howard who led them. Two of Captain Campbell's men were wounded in the shootout.

March 5th-12th...On March 5th the body of Andrew Lawson was discovered by Sergeant S.B. Louis who had been sent to bring in the band of guerillas responsible for this murder. Mr. Lawson was taken from a place eight miles north of Waynesville and then south as far as Houston, where he was murdered. This was where his body was found. The Sergeant and his men returned after pursuit of the band as far as the Hutton Valley. Three more details were sent out to bring these men in and none was successful in locating them. It is also noted that six men are detailed each day from the post at Waynesville to ride as escort for the stagecoach to California House.

March 7th-15th..."Captain John B. Meredith, Company D, 39th Missouri Infantry Volunteers, on this mission became himself the same as the lowest type of guerilla. One of those, who fans the seeds of war." (The author.) Starting on the morning of the 7th, his orders were to capture the guerilla, Jim Jackson, and his band and all other Bushwhackers. His command moved in the direction of what is known as the Perche Hills in Howard and Boone Counties. After scouting for a couple of days and finding nothing, he sent Lieutenant Self of his command to the house of a known Union man for assistance and a guide. The man, Mr. Lewis Barnes, not being well, was unable to accompany them as a guide but gave them a list of those around the neighborhood who might harbor them or feed them or would be most likely to know of their haunts. In order to gain such information, Lieutenant Self and four others disguised themselves as Bushwhackers, visited the houses and gathered what information they could.

The first victim was Anthony Drane. He cooked eggs for them and went so far as to give them a pair of socks. He failed the test. He said he was a Southern man from the ground up. He denied seeing any Federals about or any men passing his house. Upon leaving, he directed Lieutenant Self to the best roads where he was most unlikely to encounter any Federal commands. Captain Meredith ordered the old man's house burned. As he went about the neighborhood, he threatened each inhabitant to suffer the same consequences as Mr. Drane should they harbor any of the guerillas around the area. The next victim of this miscreant was Joseph Graves. He too failed the fatal question of would he report guerillas. Graves was described as a very quiet, determined and dangerous man, a man of some influence. The next victim was the family of Hines. Reliable information had it that a sister of Bill Hines was staying at a house in the neighborhood and that probably Hines and his brother could be found close by there. The house was visited but at first the family denied that Miss Hines had been there. Finally it was admitted she had, and the righteous Captain, knowing that in all probability Hines had been there, ordered this home burned and ordered the owner, a Mrs. _____, to leave the country or move to a military post. Another house was burned. Their son was one of the bushmen around the county and had come home on occasion. The other squad of Captain Meredith's burned the home of Bas Maxwell and ordered him out of the country. Upon filing his report and word getting back to Brigadier General Clinton B. Fisk, he ordered Captain Meredith to be held under arrest until further investigation was held. Fisk uses a man named Truman as an example. It seems that Truman was sent into the district by Rosecrans with virtually the same orders. He was held under arrest, imprisoned, tried by a military commission and found guilty of murder, arson and larceny and sentenced to be hanged. He is still at large.

March 7th-25th...Nine different details, with men totaling 114, marched over 625 miles in operations around Licking, Missouri, Texas County. This netted them five dead Bushwhackers, 12 horses and one mule.

March 9th-15th...Lieutenant Robert Davis, back at camp from a scout from Cape Girardeau into Bollinger, Wayne and Stoddard Counties, reports the death of Confederate Commander Lieutenant Reed of Howard's command and five men who were members of the same.

March 11th...Colonel Chester Harding (Union) placed one of his men upon the Warrensburg stage as a driver and placed three more inside posing as passengers. They hoped to catch the stagerobbers who had been robbing the passengers of the line. The stage was attacked by five men about three miles below the Little Blue. Two of the five were killed and one mortally wounded. The remaining went for reinforcements and again attacked the stage, this time with 15 men. The driver endeavored to escape with the stage but was overtaken and robbed, and one horse was taken from the team. The other men and a passenger made good their escape to Independence. So far they have not been apprehended.

March 12th...A foot scout surrounded a house two miles east of Lone Jack this evening and just waited. Finally two Bushwhackers they had been hunting came up. Firing opened and the Bushwhackers made off through the darkness, one of them being wounded.

March 19th-23rd...Scouting parties hunting guerillas, Confederates and Bushwhackers, are operating in Johnson County again. The area from Warrensburg to Columbus was covered. A little side trip was made to the home of Mr. Hamlet whose son is reported in the bush. At the residence a loaded double-barreled shotgun was found. Mr. Hamlet said he kept it loaded for geese and that his son has been forbidden his home. He had not seen him now for weeks. A horse was taken from Mr. Hamlet's to replace a U.S. one that had become very lame. A small band of Bushwhackers was discovered near Greenton and shots were exchanged, but their horses being fresh, pursuit and a chase through the dense brush was fruitless.

March 20th-22nd...Lieutenant Daniel Shumate (Militia) took the Georgetown Road as far as Tabo Creek, 12 miles east of Lexington. A trail of six men was followed as far as the home of Joel Ewing. Night came on and so did a heavy rainstorm. The next day the trail had washed away. Getting back on the road they ventured to the house of Widow Demastus and there found that five guerillas had just left there going west. A very pretty young woman at the house, thought to be the young widow of the Confederate Wilhite, who was killed last year, tried every way to convince them the five had headed east. Outdoors the tracks told the story of westward movement. Upon coming to within 300 yards of them, the race was on. They headed for the fence and the brush beyond. The scouting party managed to get off some shots and wounded perhaps one, but the escape was effected. It is recommended that the Widow Demastus and the Widow Wilhite and their families be banished from the county. She resides half a mile west of the Columbus Road, four miles north of Chatam Ewing's, near Mr. Powell who lives on the Columbus Road.

March 22nd-23rd...The stockade at Stephenson's Mill on the Current River, 16 miles southwest of Salem, was tormented by three Bushwhackers who rode around the area threatening anyone who reported them.] Riding back to the mill, they ordered the miller to have a quantity of meal ground for 250 Confederates by noon. They haven't been heard of since.

March 24th...Sergeant John Y. Baldwin makes a report of his capture while returning from an escort detail to Rolla. Upon returning, the six enlisted men and the Sergeant stopped at the house of Widow Yowell, about seven miles west of Rolla on the Springfield road. The Sergent with two of the escort went into the house for a drink of water. The others sat down by the side of the road to rest. Immediately an officer and a sergeant and three privates dressed in Federal uniform made their appearance with cocked revolvers and demanded the surrender of the men by the roadside. The men, taken by surprise, surrendered. When an inquiry was made as to the number, the leader was told that three were in the house. Three of them then charged upon the house and asked for the surrender. Leveling his gun at the disguised officer was the Sergeant's answer. The Sergeant, firing his rifle, shot the man off his horse. The balance of the men, seeing him fall, started firing at the house and through the windows of the house. The men outside started off on the run taking the detail of prisoners with them. Taking careful aim, the Sergeant put another one down. The balance of the Bushwhackers then commenced shooting at the two prisoners now running back toward the Sergeant. The other prisoner was running in the direction of Rolla. He has not been heard of since. The two wounded men, George Hoffman and John C. Odle, were taken to Rolla for treatment of their wounds.

March 29th-April 22nd...The scouting party from Waynesville left Rolla with 60 men. Finding that crossing the creeks would be impossible, the way around the areas was long and muddy. Nothing was seen or heard of in this area by the scouts.

April 1st-30th...Scouting parties go in search of Bushwhackers in the vicinity of Licking, Missouri. Again, spring rains made the rivers impossible to cross due to the high waters. Finally locating a crossing at the Widow Self's, a trail was struck and this led to the demise of Thompson Tucker. Another trail of six more was found and followed. It led into the band grazing their horses.   A.W. Howell, the supposed leader, was killed and another now thought to be dead named Mose Shumake; pursued another causing him to dismount and jump into the high water.   He probably has drowned.   It was later reported that he is very well and sports the blue Federal uniform that helped him escape through the lines. Other details sent out have marched over 600 miles and killed eight of the outlaws.

April 3rd...Learning that Hilderbrand (CSA) and his men, numbering eight, had breakfasted at Hered's near Big River Mills, a detail was sent in pursuit.   They chased him down the Potosi Road.   The trail then crossed through the hills over unmarked pathways off the Iron Road.   They were evidently making their way to Dent's Station on the Iron Mountain Railroad.   Finding the Federals in pursuit, they changed their course and struck south.   They had about 14 led horses according to locals that saw them pass.   They stopped at the home of an old negro man and killed him.   This was about seven miles from town.   They finally crossed the Pilot Knob plank road about five miles from Farmington and there took six horses from teams on the road.   The detail tracked and chased Hilderbrand as far as Burnham's Mills.   Their horses finally played out, the chase was left.

April 8th-10th...Captain Bob Rucker, Captain Jim Matlock and James Rucker (CSA) were captured today.   These were three noted men from Howard County.   They were apprehended crossing the Mississippi at Alexandria in the northeastern corner of Missouri. A steamboat with her steam up, was pressed into service and reached the Illinois shore before the fleeing men.   They were brought back to Macon City where they were turned over to the Provost-Marshal.   Monies totaling some $236.00 were found upon them.   Of this amount, $117.00 was spent in transportation back.

April 15th...A camp of guerillas was surprised by 20 men belonging to the Kansas Cavalry on McKenzie's Creek near Patterson.   Four of the guerillas were killed.

April 18th-May 27th...Negotiations for the surrender of the Confederate forces belonging to the Trans-Mississippi Department started today.

The Civil War in Missouri was virtually over.   More minor skirmishes from some of the more outlying forces took place, but most were just happy to lay down the guns and go home, or back to what was left of home.

HOME SWEET HOME

The Confederate sympathizer or the worn, tired Confederate soldier upon returning to Missouri found a whole new set of problems. He must apply for amnesty for his so-called treasonous activities. Missouri politicians were not quite ready to forgive and forget. The court systems confiscated their homes, their lands. All they had. Neither age nor not having carried a gun made any difference. In one case, the courts took the lands of an aged blind man. He was guilty of removing his slaves and what little plunder he had to a more southern-located state. He was not guilty of shooting in combat, only of taking his slaves south. He was adjudged guilty of abetting the Confederate Cause by supposedly contributing to their Cause by the removal of his slaves from Missouri to a Southern state, giving them the advantage of his little wealth and slave labor of the farm produce, etc.

It took at least one more generation to leave this earth before things began to shape up to anything like a normal existence again. Teachers began to teach again. Lawyers began to practice law again. Doctors were again allowed to heal the sick. The men of God allowed to preach the Gospel. Yes, even these men were not immune from the treason label. Some of the high-ranking Confederate officers, ones with brilliant minds, ended up again as senators and state representatives, using their West Point and university educations to further develop the state back into a sense of equality to man. Their military career records were now just a matter of conversation.

Some of the men of the Confederacy left their homeland and went into Mexico and there offered their services to the Emperor. This generous offer was declined. It was feared this would strain relations between Mexico and the Unites States Government.

On the night of June 2, 1865 Sterling Price and his son, Captain Heber Price, and some members of his personal escort, set out for Mexico. He made plans for the accommodations for his family. He set out for San Antonio. San Antonio was the planned rendezvous point of all those leaving Missouri behind. Several of these men would rather give up all rather than surrender to a peace and the humility of the politics of the state. The party included some of the most prominent names in the military history of Missouri; Thomas C. Reynolds, former governor after Claiborne Jackson; General E. Kirby Smith; General John B. Macgruder; Governor Allen and General Joseph Shelby. Shelby had with him literally hundreds of his old command, the Iron Brigade. Ironically, crossing the Rio Grande at Eagle Pass on July 4th, the birthday of the United States independence, they laid another government to rest. It was in this stream that divides two great countries that they halted so Shelby's men could sink their honored regimental flag into the muddy waters of the river. The journey was not without incident. The fighting wasn't over. Guerilla bands of a new character attacked them. They finally reached their destination and settled in, forging ahead in their new venture of another life. They built small communities, relying on the labor of their hands to carve a home from the tropical lands. General Price named his new home Carlotta. The little venture started to fail, the outlaws burning and robbing, there was no peace. Finally with General Price's health failing, his wife took matters into her own hands and they returned to Missouri. There, never quite becoming his old self, his illness caused his death in 1867. He was mourned by thousands. Shelby seemed to fare better. He entered the freighting business, but eventually he returned to Missouri and there regained his former stature with much effort. Former Governor Reynolds, who had joined in the venture, remained and there became a successful railroad commissioner. Of the others who accompanied Price and Shelby, Governor Allen established a newspaper with John Edwards. John Edwards was writing as fast as possible on the biography of Shelby. Major Edwards became sole owner of the paper at the death of Allen. General Kirby Smith finally returned to the United States and became a college professor.

Also known to be present at Carlotta was General Price's wife, a daughter and a son, Celsus. They endured a shipwreck in making the journey to Mexico. Most of their belongings were lost. It must have been a drastic culture shock to the family of this famous man. The area they moved to was constantly being raided by the Mexican outlaws, kidnapings for ransom and pillaging in general. It was probably with a great sigh of relief when she envisioned St. Louis again.

Sterling Price attempted to get his law practice running again. Many of his friends pooled money and purchased him a home and backed his business. The proud old general would never request amnesty personally, but it is recorded where many of his friends petitioned in his stead.

Sterling Price who rode proudly over the lands leading his beloved men, a grand old warrior, died in September of 1867. "Old Pap" was gone, but his spirit is still with us today.

And, yes, "mine eyes have seen the glory."

Index Of Recorded Events

Index Of Recorded Events

Index Of Recorded Events

Index Of Recorded Events

Index Of Recorded Events

Index Of Recorded Events

Index Of Recorded Events

Index Of Recorded Events

Index Of Recorded Events

Index Of Recorded Events

Index Of Recorded Events

Index Of Recorded Events

Index Of Recorded Events

Index Of Recorded Events

Index Of Recorded Events

Index Of Recorded Events

Index Of Recorded Events

Index Of Recorded Events

Index Of Recorded Events

Index Of Recorded Events

Index Of Recorded Events

Index Of Recorded Events

Index Of Recorded Events

Index Of Recorded Events

Index Of Recorded Events

Index Of Recorded Events

Index Of Recorded Events

Index Of Recorded Events

Index Of Recorded Events

Index Of Recorded Events

Index Of Recorded Events

Index Of Recorded Events

LOCATIONS

Agency Ford.. Agency located in Buchanan county/Ford?

Albany .. Gentry county

Alton .. Military Pirson in Illinois/ Alton also found in
the vicninty of Eleven Points River

Alton.. Oregon county

Anderson .. Jim and Bill/ brothers

Atlanta .. Macon county

Arnoldsville .. near St. Joseph

Arrow Rock .. on river in Saline county

Arthur's Creek .. unlocated/ probably named for property owner

Ash Hills .. on road toward Pochontas Ark/ east of Poplar
Bluff

Athens .. Gentry county

Aubrey .. Kansas town/ southern Johnson Co Ks

Austin .. Cass county

Auxvasse .. waterway in Callaway county

Bailey's Station .. found on scouting between Otter Creek &
Pilot Knob

Ball's Mill .. unlocated/ property owner

Balltown .. unlocated

Barlin's Mill .. probably in vicinity of Neosho

Barnesville .. near Van Buren probably in Carter county

Barren Fork .. Sinking Creek 20 miles from Salem

Barry .. Platte county

Bay Creek .. on passage to Jack's Fork

Bear Creek .. vicinity of Bee creek?

Beaver Creek .. vicinity of Forsyth

Beaver Station .. also called Fort Lawrence on same creek near
Lawrence's Mill, Taney county

Beckelheimer's Mill .. probably in Chariton county/ Chariton
river

Bee Branch .. 8 miles north of Kirksville

Bee Creek .. also located near Weston/ one located near Forsyth

Bee Creek Bridge.. on scout near St Joseph & Weston

Bellville Valley .. northwest of Ironton

Belwood's Farm .. Saline scouting mission/ farm crossed

Belmont .. on Ky side of Mississippi river

Bennett's Bayou .. unlocated/ probably named for property owner

Benton .. Scott county

Bennight's Mill .. unlocated

Bertrand .. Mississippi county

Bethlehem .. Boo county

Big Baum Creek .. unlocated

Big Berger Creek .. vicinity of Washington, Franklin county

Big Berger Bridge .. probably in vicinity of Washington

Big Creek .. numerous/ Shannon county/ 8 mi from Patterson/
Wright county/ also found near Pleasant Hill, Cass Co./
and one near Forsyth

Big Creek Bluffs .. near Pleasant Hill, Cass county

Big Creek Bottoms .. east of Rose Hill

Big Grive .. found on scouting/ probably Jackson or Lafayette Co.

Big Hill.. near Sibley

Big Hurricane Creek .. unlocated

Big Muddy .. south of Dunksborg

Big Creek North Fork .. unlocated

Big North Fork .. vicinity of Bennett's Bayou
Big Osage .. another name for Marais De Cygne river
Big Piney .. a stream 20 miles from Spring Creek/ Waynesville on
    western edge of Pulaski county
Big River Mills .. near Iron Mtn Railroad
Big River Bridge .. 6 miles above Mineral Point
Big Sni-(river or large stream) in jackson county east of Welling-
ton
Big Springs.. Carter county/ also near Cassville
Birch Prairie .. near Jack's Fork/ BIRCH in Shannon county also
Bird's Point .. Mississippi county
Black Fork .. Boon county waterway
Black Pond .. Howell county
Black Walnut River Bridge .. Sedalia, Pettis county
Blackwater Bridge.. listed as east of Polpar Bluff/ also in Pettis
    or Saline county?
Blackwater Grove .. near Hopewell, Jefferson county
Blackwater River.. several across the State, one near Warrensburg
    in Johnson county/ another listed as being in Wayne county
Blackwell Station .. probably near Blackwell in Jefferson county?
Bloomfield .. Stoddard county
Bloomington .. unlocated on modern maps
Blue Mills .. Jackson county
Blue Mills Landing .. Jackson county
Blue Springs .. Jackson county
Blue Timber .. 15 miles from Hickman Mills
Bolivar .. Polk county
Bollinger's Mills.. owned by Daniel?/ downstream on Castor river
    perhaps in the area of Jackson
Bone Hill .. believed to be in Jackson or Cass county?
Boonville .. Cooper county
Bourbese River .. on line Franklin & Gasconade counties
Bower's Mill .. Taney county also called oregon
Boyce's Mill .. Eleven Points river
Boyce's Ford.. thought to be in vicinity of mill on Boyce property
Bragg's Farm .. unlocated
Breckenridge .. Caldwell county
Brookfield .. Linn county
Brown's Ferry .. in Arkansas
Brownsville road.. leads from Arrow Rock into Lafayette county
Brunswick .. Chariton county
Buck Skull .. Randolph county Ark
Buffalo .. Dallas county
Buffalo Prairie .. Cooper county
Buford's Farm .. on Little Black river
Burnhan/m? Mill.. Burnham in Howell county Eleven Points river
Bushy Creek .. vicinity of Big Creek/ Patterson perhaps Shannon
    county
Butler .. Cass county
Butler's Creek .. near Neosho/ another vicinity of Clinton or
    perhaps named for property owner?
Cain Creek ..we take this to be named for property owner
Caledonia .. northwest of Pilot Knob
Calhoun .. Henry county
California..Moniteau county. HOUSE @ 7 miles fomr Military Post at
    Waynesville/ also located on old stage route.

Locations

Centre Creek.. near Carthage/ runs into Spring river
                another located near Sherwood
Chapel Hill.. west @ 3 miles of Lafayette county /Jackson county?
Chariton.. Chariton county
Chariton River.. crossing probably Adair county
Charleston.. Mississippi county
Cherokee Bay.. Arkansas
Cherry Grove.. Schuyler county
Chillicothe.. Livingston county
Chilowee.. Johnson county
Chilton's Mill.. close on Current River
Cincinnatti.. vicinity of New London & Sidney
Clapp's Ford.. on Faubius probably in Scotland county
Clarence.. 12 miles east of Macon
Clark's Mill.. 15 miles up the Chariton river
Clarkston.. 34 miles southwest of New Madrid
Clarkton.. Dunklin county
Claysville.. in Boone county
Clauser's.. family
Clear Creek.. several locations../ just south of Milford/ near
             Taberville/ in corner of St. Clair county/ 12 miles
             southeast of Warrensburg
Cleveland.. Shelby county
Clinton.. Henry county
Clintonville.. Cedar county
Cogswell Landing.. near Sibley on river
Cold Water Grove.. vicinity of Pleasant Hill
Cole Camp.. Benton county
Columbia.. Boone county
Columbus.. Johnson county
Commerce.. on Mississippi river Scott county
Commercial Hotel.. Cole county in Jefferson City
Conestoga.. a gunboat
Conf.. Confederate
CSA .. also is listed as Confederate State Army
Cooke, Philip St. George.. mentioned in introduction
Cook's Farm...
Cook's Store...
Coon Creek.. near Lamar
Cote Sans Dessein.. Callaway county
Cow Creek.. Military HQ
Cravensville.. Davies county
Crawford.. Indian Territory
Crisp's Mill.. on Big Creek vicinity of Rose Hill
Crooked Creek.. Bollinger county
Crossville.. unlocated
Crow's Station.. probably on Spring River or Creek?
Cuba.. Crawford county
Current Hills.. we take this to be in vicinity of the river?
Current River.. runs through Dent, Shannon & Texas counties
Cypress Swamp.. near Cape Girardeau

Locations

Dallas.. Bollinger county
Danville.. Montgomery county
Davis Creek.. on Sni in Greenton Valley/ near Hopewell
Daylight.. 3 miles south of Carthage
Dayton.. Cass county
De Kalb.. Buchanan county
De Soto.. Jefferson county
Deep Water.. Henry county
Dent's Station.. Iron Mtn Railroad
Dewitt.. Carroll county
Diamond Grove.. 5 miles from Savilla/ vicinity of Carthage and the
          town of Diamond located in Newton county
Dillon.. probably in Maries county
Dog Skin Swamp.. near Elk Chute/ probably Pemiscot county
Doniphan.. Ripley county
Double branch.. Bates county
Dover.. mentioned in scout from Warrensburg to Lafayette county
          probably located in Lafayette county
Dripping Springs.. Boone county
Dry Fork.. a few miles from Carthage.. stream?
Dry Wood Creek.. 35 miles southeast of Fort Scott
Dry Woods.. Nevada/ Vernon county
Dubuque Crossing.. Arkansas
Dug Ford.. crossing on the Lamine River
Dug Springs.. near Springfield
Dunksborg.. vicinity of Knob Knoster
Duroc.. crossing on the Osage river
Eagin's Point.. probably named for property owner/ unlocated
Easterbrook's Saloon .. Jefferson City
Edina.. Knox county
Eleven Points River.. runs through Oregon county into Arkansas
Elk Chute.. Pemiscot county
Elk Creek.. several/ 55 miles from Camp Totten/ Chariton county
Elk Mills.. 30 miles southwest of Neosho
Elliott's Mills.. in the vicinity of Columbus, Johnson county
Elliott's Mrs. home.. evidently located near Linn creek/Platte Co.
Elm Springs.. 5 miles south of Neosho
Eminence.. Shannon county
Enterprise.. 4 miles beyond Elk Mills/ also located in Shelby Co.
Etna.. unlocated on modern maps
Eureka.. Boone county
Ewing's Farm
Farley.. Platte county
Farmington.. Saint Francois county
Faubius Bottoms.. Scotland county
Fayette.. Howard county
Felb's Bridge.. southwest corner Knox Co. Salt River
Fidelity.. Jasper county
Fiebaux? Creek.. possibly Henry county?
Fire Prairie.. in the direction of Sibley from Blue Springs Jackson
          county

Locations

Fishback residence
Fishing River.. near Richfield in Clay county
Flat Creek.. perhaps Saint Francois county/ also listed in Stone
      county
Florence.. Morgan county
Florida.. Monroe county
Forsyth.. Taney county
Fort Davidson.. Pilot Knob
Fort Gamble..
Fort Lawrence.. see Beaver Creek Station
Fort Leavenworth.. Kansas military post/ Leavenworth Kansas
Foster, Thomas.. citizen guide
Four Mile.. a village on road, Saint Luke toward West Prairie in
     Dunklin county
Franklin.. Howard county
Fredericksburg.. Ray county @ 17 miles NE of Liberty
Fredericktown.. Madison county
French Point.. mentioned on scout from Newtonia and Centre Creek
      probably in vicinity of Sherwood
Fulton.. Callaway county
Fulton Landing.. Callaway county/ Auxvasse river?
Gadfly.. unlocated on modern maps
Garden Hollow.. near Pineville in Mc Donald county
Gasconade River.. runs through Gasconade county to La Clede line
Gayoso Bay.. Pemiscot county
Georgetown.. Pettis county
Glass Settlement.. close to Doniphan/ perhaps named for owners?
Glover.. Iron county
Germantown.. Henry county
Golden Grove.. unlocated on map/ mentioned in scout mission
Gosneyville.. probably Clinton or Buchanan county?
Goose Neck Country.. vicinity of Weston
Gouge's Mill.. Cooper county
Granby.. Newton county
Grand Pass Church.. probably Grand Pass in Saline county?
Grand River.. Cass county
Gray's Creek.. on Pacific Railroad
Gray's Summit.. Franklin county
Greenfield.. Dade county
Greenton.. vicinity of Chapel Hill & Hopewell 12 mi from Lexington
Greenville.. 20 miles from Ironton
Greenville Campsite.. near Fredericktown road
Grenter's Farm.. Pleasant Hill road
Gunter Valley.. Howell county
Halcom/Halcomb? Island.. perhaps Dunklin county?
Hall's Mill.. mentioned on scout from Warrensburg
Hallsville.. Boone county
Hambright's Station.. near Independence
Hamburg.. 5 mi NW of Benton/ also in St. Charles county
Hampton.. vicinity of St. Joseph
Hannibal.. Marion county
Harrison Station.. Vicinity of Pilot Knob on road to Rolla

Locations

Harrisonville.. Cass county

Hartville/Hartsville.. Wright county and possibly another near
        Carthage
Hawkins Mill.. south of Waverly
Haynesville.. unlocated
Hay Hollow.. on Rock Creek 65 miles from Salem
Hen Peck.. vicinity of Carter county and Van Buren
Henrytown.. unlocated on modern map
Hered Place.. Potosi road vicinity of Iron Mtn Railroad
Hermann.. Gasconade county
Herold, George.. outlaw? citizen of Cass county
Hibernia.. unlocated on modern map
Hickman Mills.. Jackson county
Hickory Grove.. perhaps same as Hickory Hill in Cole county?
Hickory Place.. Carroll county
High Hill.. Montgomery county
Highland neighborhood.. on the Pomme de Terre
Hog Eye.. Bollinger county
Hog Island.. southern part of Bates county
Hog Skin Prairie.. unlocated
Holcumbs Island.. near Kennett/ Dunklin county
Holden.. Johnson county
Honey Creek neighborhood.. near Clinton
Hopewell.. Lafayette county?
Hornersville.. near Arkansas line/Dunklin county
Horse Creek.. crossing to Golden Grove vicinity of Montevallo
Houston.. Texas county
Hoyle's Run.. near Quincy
Hudson.. unable to locate on modern map
Humansville.. Polk county
Hunnewell.. Shelby county
Hunter's Farm.. near Belmont
Huntsville.. Randolph county
Hutton Valley.. north of West Plains
Iberia.. Miller county
Independence.. Jackson county
Indian Creek.. Newton county also one in Mc Donald county
Indian Ford.. Saint Francois county
Inman Hollow.. downstream from Salem
Iron Mtn Railroad
Ironton.. Iron county
Jack's Fork.. probably fork that flows into Current river.. see
        Chilton Shannon county
Jackson.. Cape Girardeau county
Jacksonport.. on Castor river
Jane's Creek.. possibly located at or near Jane in Mc Donald county
Jefferson Barracks.. St. Louis
Jefferson City.. Cole county
Jefferson City National Cemetery
Johnstown.. near Warrensburg

Locations

Johnson Mill.. 30 miles from Waynesville
Jone's Creek.. near Sarcoxie
Jones, John L. Farm.. 3 miles northeast of Rocheport
Jonesborough.. crossing of Blackwater vicinity of Marshall
Kansas City.. town in Missouri adjoining town in Kansas
        Basic Civil War actions in Kansas City Missouri
Keat's Mill.. Ray county/ appears also as KEAL'S mill
Keytesville.. Chariton county
Kinder's Farm..
Kingsville.. Johnson county
Kirkpatrick's Mill.. near Lafayette county line
Kirksville.. Adair county
Kirkwood.. St. Louis
Klepsford.. near St. Charles
Knob Knoster.. near and south/east of Kansas City
Knoxville.. Ray county
Land Mark.. probably @ Boone county/ flows through that area
La Clede.. also spelled LACLEDE in Linn county
La Mine River.. Cooper county/ runs somewhat through Saline also
        near Otterville/ bridge in Cooper county
Lakeland.. this probably between Greenville & Bloomfield
Lamar.. Barton county
Lancaster.. Schuyler county
Lane's Prairie.. near Rolla
Lawrence's Mill.. Taney county on head of Little Fork creek/river?
Le Grange.. lewis county
Leashure.. on Wood creek
leatherwood.. unlocated
Lebanon.. La Clede county
Lebanon road.. probably enroute to Lebanon/directions unknown
Lexington.. Lafayette county
Liberty.. Clay county
Liberty Arsenal.. Liberty
Licking.. Texas county
Lick Skillet.. 3 miles northeast of Eagin's Point
Lincoln Ford.. vicinity of Warrensburg & Butler/north of Warsaw
Lindley.. Grundy county
Lindsey's Mill.. Boone county
Linden.. Atchison county/ also located Christian county
Linn Creek road.. route to Linn Creek believed to be Camden Co?
Little Berger Bridge.. vicinity of Washington/ Franklin county
Little Blue Branch.. Jackson county 12 miles from Independence
Little Blue.. Jackson county
Little Compton.. unable to locate
Little Fork.. Taney county
Little River.. unable to locate
Little River Bridge.. unable to locate
Little Niangua.. Hickory county/ flows through Ozarks
Little Santa Fe.. Jackson county
Little Sni.. river /creek in Jackson county
Little Sugar Creek.. near Cassville, Arkansas line and one Jackson
        county

Locations

Lone Jack.. south of Independence Jackson county
Long Branch Bridge.. Northern Missouri Railroad bridge
Long Creek.. runs into White river vicinity of Forsyth
Longwood.. Pettis county
Lookout Station.. on train run from California Missouri
Luca's Bend.. opposite side of bend lower from New Madrid/ bend
      in the river
M.S.G... Missouri State Guard
M.S.M... Missouri State Militia
Mc Afee.. Missouri Speaker of the House/ politician
Mc Carty.. editor of Border Star newspaper of Jackson county area
Mc Courtney's Mill.. area of Big Piney
Mc Cubbin's Mill.. unable to locate
Mc Culla's Store.. the farm is located 24 mi Springfield on Fay-
    ettville road
Mc Dowell's College.. later military prison depot St. Louis
Mc Kerk's Crossing.. we feel this should be Mc Girk's crossing
      and landing.
Mc Reynolds.. farm located 2 miles from Waverly
Macon.. Macon county
Macon City.. Macon county/military post
Mahan Creek.. probably named for land owner perhaps Cooper county?
Man's Creek.. on Jack's fork of Current River
Mapa Settlement.. 12 miles from Pink Hill
Marais de Cygne.. large river sometimes called Big Osage.. runs
      across Kansas from or into Cass county
Marchfield.. Webster county??
Marie's Creek.. @ 20 miles northwest of Rolla
Marionville.. vicinity of Newtonia
Marmaton River.. southwest branch of Osage River
Marshall.. Saline county
Marshall Bridge.. evidently on Blackwater vicinity of Marshall?
Marshall' Ford.. unlocated/ perhaps property owner of crossing at
    Marshall?
Marshfield.. Webster county
Martinsburg.. probably Ripley or Butler county/ near Arkansas line/
      SE of Doniphan also Martinsburg in Audrain county
Mastin's Briage.. property owner perhaps on La Mine River
Matney's Mill.. noted on scout vicinity of St. Joseph
Maudeville.. unlocated on modern maps
Mayfield neighborhood.. vicinity of Pomme de Terre
Maysville.. listed as Arkansas
Medicine Creek.. near Chillicothe
Medling's Old Mill.. noted on scout vicinity of St. Joseph
Medoc.. Jasper county
Medora.. unable to locate on modern map
Mellville.. Dade county
Memphis.. Scotland county
Mexico.. military HQ in Audrain county
Miami.. Saline county

Locations

Miami Missions.. Indian Territory? or perhaps in Saline county?
Middle Faubius River.. 10 miles south of Memphis, runs thru Schu-
          yler and Knox county
Milford.. Barton county
Mill or Middle Creek Bridge.. on Iron Mtn Railroad
Miller's Landing.. vicinity of Washington in Franklin county
Miller's Place.. head of Spring river
Millersburg.. Callaway county
Millsville.. Ray county
Mineral Point.. Washington county
Mingo Creek.. 22 miles southwest of Greenville (Mingo Swamp also)
Moberly's Landing.. Carroll county
Monday Hollow.. also known as Dutch Hollow or Wet Glaze near Henry-
          town
Montevallo.. Vernon county
Monticello Briage.. lewis county
Montgomery City.. Callaway county
Moore's Mill.. Auxvasse river in Callaway county
                    one also in White river country
Moreau River.. Jefferson City
Moreau Bridge.. over Moreau river, Pacific Railroad bridge
Moselle Bridge.. at Franklin
Mountain Grove Seminary.. Wright county
Mountain Store.. vicinity of Houston Missouri Texas county
Mount Pleasant.. within riding distance of Tipton
Mount Vernon.. many towns in Missouri named this/Lawrence county
Mount Zion Church.. Boone county
Morristown.. Cass county
Morse's Mill.. north of De Soto in Jefferson county
Murphy's Pasture.. property owner
Murray's Ford.. on Blackwater near Warrensburg Johnson county
Muscle Fork.. branch of Chariton river
Napoleon.. Lafayette or Jackson county
Napoleon Bottoms.. 14 miles from Independence
Neosho.. Newton county
Newark.. Knox county
New Cairo.. on Mississippi river near Belmont and Bird's Point
New Frankfort.. Saline county
New London.. Ralls county
New Market.. Platte county
New Madrid.. New Madrid county
Newtonia.. Newton county
Nevada.. Vernon county
Niagua Creek.. this point located 8 mi east of post at Marshfield
Nigger Woods Swamp.. crosscut to Bloomfield
Norris Creek.. vicinity of Lotspeich farm
North Branch Grand River.. Cass county
Oak Hollows.. probably in Jackson county?
Oaklin Church.. probably in Lafayette county
Old Mill.. mentioned on scout/ vicinity of St. Joseph

Locations

Ogle's Mill.. vicinity of Salt River Bottoms
Old Randolph.. Randolph county?
Opossum Creek.. near Mountain Store, Houston
Order of American Knights
Oregon... town and sometimes called Bower's Mill
Osage Island.. near Butler/ Bates county on Osage river
Osceola.. St. Clair county (then described)
Otter Creek.. area of Little Black/ noted on scout from Doniphan
Otterville.. Cooper county
Ozark.. Christian county
Palmyra.. Marion county
Panther Creek.. Hannibal & St. Joe RR crossing of Chariton river
Paola.. Kansas town Miami county
Papinsville.. Bates county
Paris.. Monroe county
Parkersville.. unlocated on modern map
Parkville.. Platte county
Patterson.. Wayne county
Peace Valley.. Howell county
Pemiscot Bayou.. Pemiscot county?
Pennsylvania Prairie.. unlocated on modern map
Perche's Prairie.. Boone county
Peruque River Bridge.. Perque Creek in Warren county
Philadelphia.. Lewis county
Pierce's Mill.. probably in Scotland county near Memphis
Pike Creek.. near Eleven Points river
Pink Hill.. 19 miles southeast of Independence
Pisgah.. Cooper county
Pittman's Ferry.. also one in Arkansas/ unlocated in Missouri
Platte City.. Platte county
Plattesburg.. Clinton county
Pleasant Gap.. Bates county
Pleasant Hill.. Cass county
Pleasant Hope.. Polk county
Point Pleasant.. New Madrid county

Pomme de Terre.. 17 miles north of Springfield
Pond Bottom.. probably in Cooper county?
Ponder's Mill.. near Doniphan
Pools Prairie.. Jasper county
Poplar Bluff.. Butler county
Pools Settlement.. probably in Jasper county?
Portland.. Callaway county
Possum Creek.. see Opossum Creek
Post Oak Creek.. probably Lafayette county
Potosi.. Washington county
Prairie Chapel.. Callaway county
Preston.. vicinity of Big North Fork Creek
Price's Landing.. 25 miles from Cape Girardeau
Punche's Crossing.. Saint Francis river
Quincy.. Hickory county

Locations

Quinine Brigade.. took part in Battle of Springfield
Raytown.. south & east of Independence
Reeve's Station Road.. probably vicinity of Pilot Knob and on
        Arkansas road?
Renick.. Randolph county
Renick's Farm.. located 12 miles northwest of Marshall
Richfield.. Clay county
Richmond.. Ray county
Richwoods Road.. Richwoods in Washington county?
Riddell's Point.. unlocated on modern map
Ridgley.. Platte county
Ringgold.. Platte county area noted on scout
Ritchie's Mill.. on the Pomme de Terre 9 miles from Cedar Creek
Roanoke.. Randolph county
Roan's Tanyard.. on Silver creek 7 mi south of Huntsville
Robideaux.. a river close to Gasconade.. mentioned in scouting
Robion Springs.. close to Marshall, CSA camp site
Rocheport.. Boone county
Rocky Bluff.. Platte county/ south side of river
Rolla.. Phelps county
Roper's Mill.. opposite Glasgow
Rose Hill.. Johnson county
Round Pond.. Castor river area
Round Prairie.. probably in Cass or Jackson county
Rushe's Ridge.. near Bird's Point, vicinity Beckwith farm
Rutledge.. Mc Donald county
St. Aubert.. Callaway county
St. Francois River.. runs through Wayne & Madison county
St. Francisville.. Clark county
St. James.. Phelps county
St. Joseph.. Buchanan county
Saint Bouef Creek.. we take this to be vicinity of Washington
Saint/St. Clair's.. we take this to be a citizen's home
Saint Luke.. Webster county
Salem.. Dent county
Saline City.. north of Arrow Rock
Salisbury.. Chariton county
Salt River Bridge.. on North Pacific Railroad
Sandtown.. passage from Crow Indian Agency into Missouri
Sarcoxie.. Newton county
Savilla.. outside of Neosho a small village
Scatterville.. noted on scout from Bloomfield
Scoot's Ford.. noted as on La Mine & Blackwater rivers
Scott's Mill.. enroute to Seneca Mills/ unlocated
Sear's Farm.. near Pleasant Hill (Sear's Ford same area?)
Sedalia.. Pettis county
Sedalia Road.. direct route passage 12 mi east of Lexington
Selvidge.. Mrs.. resided Ironton area
Seneca Mills.. Newton county
Shanghi.. Johnson county
Seneca Nation.. located in Indian Territory of Oklahoma

Locations

Shanghi Town.. Carroll county
Shelbina.. Shelby county
Shelbyville.. Shelby county
Shelton's Mill.. on Current river
Sherwood.. Jasper county
Shiloh Camp.. located on Hoyle's Run near Quincy
Shoal Creek.. scout from Fidelity to/ Jasper or Barton county?
Shoal Creek.. also located 12 miles east of Carthage
Shirleys Ford.. on Spring river/ Shirley in Washinton county
Shoal Creek.. located 1 1/4 miles from Granby, Newton county
Shrinkietown.. near Monroe Station area
Sibley.. Jackson county
Sidney.. Ralls county
Sikeston.. Stoddard county
Simpkin's Mill.. vicinity of Alton & area of Eleven Points river
Sim's Cove.. Cedar creek on line Boone & Callaway county
Sinking Creek.. probably in Bates county/ another 20 mi from
      Salem branch of Barren Fork
Sister Creek.. 25 miles from Little Fork
Six- Mile.. area & creek in Jackson county
Smiley's Mill
Smith's Farm.. 5 miles from Clintonville
Smithfield.. 5 miles north of Pleasant Hill
Smithville.. Platte county
Sni-Bar.. Jackson county/ neighborhood and waterway
Sons Point.. unlocated on modern map
Sparta.. Buchanan county
Springfield.. Green county
Springfield Road.. passes thru several counties/ direct route/ one
      passage is 3 miles east of Keytesville
Spring Creek.. runs into Current river
Spring Hill.. Davies county
Spring River.. outside of Carthage
Spring River Mills.. noted on scout from Houston/ unknown location
Spring Valley.. 25 miles southeast of Houston Texas county
Stevenson's Mill.. on Current river 16 mi southwest of Salem
Stockton.. Cedar county
Stringer's Ferry.. on Little River vicinity of Bloomfield
Strother's Fork of Black River.. Iron county
Stumptown.. unlocated
Sturgeon Bridge.. North Missouri Railroad/ town also of Sturgeon
Sugar Creek.. near Wadesburg/ neighborhood in Jackson county
Sugar Creek Hills
Sugar Loaf Prairie.. in Arkansas
Sullivan.. a guide
Sulpher Springs.. unlocated
Syracuse.. Morgan county
Swan Creek.. on road between Ozark & Forsyth
Switzler's Mill.. Chariton county
Sykestown.. Scott county

Locations

Taberville.. St. Clair county area
Tabo.. stream in Lafayette county
Tabo Church.. settlement church 12 miles east of Lexington
Taos.. Buchanan county/ also one in Cole county
Tavern Creek.. near Camp Conant/ unlocated
Texas Prairie.. Jackson or Lafayette county
The Hackle.. noted on scout Buchannan county
Thomasville.. Oregon county
Thomasville Road.. probably vicinity of town vicinity Eleven
        Points river?/ perhaps two towns?
Tipton.. Morgan county/ Or listed as Moniteau county
Todd's Creek.. St. Joseph area?
Totetes.. above Wellington?
Trading Post.. Kansas town on road to Pleasanton & Ft. Scott
Turkey Creek.. runs to/through? Jasper county/ 18 mi Savilla
Turkey Creek.. southeast of Neosho
Turkey Oak.. creek? unlocated
Tuscumbia.. Miller county
Twin Groves.. @ 13 miles from Carthage
Union.. town unlocated
Union Mills.. probably on Platte river?
Union Saline Salt Works
Uniontown.. east line of Schuyler county
Van Buren.. Carter county
Verdigris River.. crossing at Sandtown/passage from Crow Nation
Versailles.. Morgan county
Vienna Road.. between Rolla & Waynesville
Wadesburg.. probably in Cass county
Wagner's Crossing.. on White or Little river?
Wagon Knob.. possibly Jackson county
Wakanda.. stream in Carroll county/ also neighborhood same
Walnut Creek & Grand River Junctions
Walnut Creek.. (many in Missouri)
Warder Church.. near Wellington
Warm Fork.. Spring river
Warrensburg.. Johnson county
Warrenton.. Warren county military HQ
Warsaw.. Benton county
Waverly.. Saline county
Wayman's Mill.. on Spring creek 23 mi SW of Rolla/ WYMAN?
Waynesville.. located in Pulaski county
Webster.. 15 miles southwest of Potosi
Wellington.. Lafayette county
Wellsville.. several small town in Missouri
Wentzville.. St. Charles county
West Plains.. Howell county
West Point.. Bates county
Westport.. Jackson county
Weston.. Platte county
West Ely.. down Centerville road from Sidney

Locations

Wet Glaze.. see Monday Hollow or Dutch Monday
Whaley's Mill.. unlocated
Whitewater.. vicinity of Jackson
White Hare.. unlocated
White River.. 5 miles below Forsyth
White River Country.. described as @ 18 miles from Cassville
White Spring.. close to Missouri & Arkansas line
White Water Bridge.. perhaps close to Jakcson?
Williams's Crossing.. Saint Francis river
Williams's Ferry..
Willow Ford.. on the La Mine river
Wilson's Creek.. Greene county
Wolf Island.. Pemiscot county
Wood's Creek.. Wood's Fork.. unlocated/ probably land owner named
Wright's Ford.. probably land owner named
Wyman's Mill.. see WAYMAN mill
Yellow Creek.. flows into Grand river a fork of same
Young Farm.. residence on Blue river, Jackson county

We sincerely suggest one who is researching these old towns con-
sult as many of the old report maps as possible. Each army used
a different method of naming locations. Thus another may be more
appropriate for your research of an area.

The author..

Carolyn was born into a family of story-tellers. Her interest in history was sparked early in life as she listened to the tales of her Swiss ancestors, who fled out of their homeland in the dark of the night, and sailed for America in the early 1700's. The stories of the hungry wolf that attacked the little cabin in Pennsylvania.. The lonely homestead in the New Mexico Territory and that of the little baby boy buried beneath the cedar tree at the first homestead in Kansas.

In tracing these old ancestors lives, the Civil War came to life again. Carolyn's maternal ancestors gave her a Missouri heritage,

the family making the trip in the early 1800's from Kentucky. Finally putting down roots near Brumley, Missouri. Born and raised in Franklin county, Kansas, Carolyn resides now in western Johnson county, Kansas.

Other titles available..

Civil War Stories of Missouri
Claybrook; A House Of Dreams
Pea Ridge; The Sacrifice
Stand Watie And The First Cherokee Regiment 1861 - 1865

Sources

This compilation has relied upon the Official Records Of The War Of The Rebellion, for sources of reports of the official engagements within Missouri.
As the author, we assumed the privilege, of changing the word, "Guerilla" when we felt it didn't apply to the subject; or if a military rank was denoted for this person.

Excerpts from the Boone County History.. This wonderful old book was used for added detail and confirmation of details concerning the Centralia massacre.

Excerpts taken from The Saline County History.. Detail used in the actions of the scouting party through the county; The execution of Asa Huff and other victims of this county.

Excerpts taken from The Johnson County History; The story of Mary Bedichek and consulted for other details concerning this county.

Missouri Amnesty.. Our own publication compiled from the actual files of those seeking Presidential pardons & amnesty in 1865 and 1866. Story extracted from these files as eye witness account of the Camp Jackson affair.

Excerpts taken from The Jasper County History.. This was used for added detail of citizens accounts of Union retreat through Carthage. This gave physical description of damages, actions, etc.

Our Storehouse of Missouri Places.. A must for locating the old towns, streams, etc.. excellent reference book.

Collier World Atlas & Gazateer, 1941 edition.. locations

Publications of National Archives; Maps, etc. Locations

The Introduction of the war events was extracted from written reports, contained in Battlefields & Leaders.. 1881 publication

Maps; The official records was again consulted for old locations

Although 1162 recorded official engagements took place within the State, we have condensed such numerical reports, as in Price and Shelby's raids. They are given as a whole, rather than each individual engagement.
Others are condensed within a days actions.

Jeff Thompson's departing speech to his men; Confederate Archives